An Introduction to

EARLY JUDAISM

An Introduction to
EARLY JUDAISM

James C. VanderKam

WILLIAM B. EERDMANS PUBLISHING COMPANY
GRAND RAPIDS, MICHIGAN / CAMBRIDGE, U.K.

© 2001 Wm. B. Eerdmans Publishing Co.
All rights reserved

Wm. B. Eerdmans Publishing Co.
255 Jefferson Ave. S.E., Grand Rapids, Michigan 49503 /
P.O. Box 163, Cambridge CB3 9PU U.K.

Printed in the United States of America

06 05 04 03 02 01   7 6 5 4 3 2

Library of Congress Cataloging-in-Publication Data

VanderKam, James C.
An introduction to early Judaism / James C. VanderKam.
p.   cm.
Includes bibliographical references and index.
ISBN 0-8028-4641-6 (alk. paper)
1. Jews — History — 586 B.C.–70 A.D.
2. Judaism — History — Post-exilic period, 586 B.C.–210 A.D.
3. Bible. O.T. Apocrypha — Criticism, interpretation, etc.
4. Apocryphal books (Old Testament) — Criticism, interpretation, etc.
I. Title.

DS121.65.V36 2000
296'.09'014 — dc 21

00-063605

www.eerdmans.com

Contents

Preface

It has been my experience in teaching university classes and speaking to other groups that there is wide interest in knowing more about the part of Jewish history and literature covered by this book. Jewish people want more information about a formative stage in the long history of Judaism, and Christians wish to have a better understanding of what happened "between the testaments." A problem has been that the would-be student does not know where to turn in order to receive guidance into this vast field. Specialists will be familiar with the many excellent resources that are available to scholars today, but to the nonspecialist, for whom such weighty tomes may be too detailed and technical to be of practical value, the period of Early Judaism remains unfamiliar territory.

When Jon Pott and Dan Harlow of the William B. Eerdmans Publishing Company invited me to prepare an introduction to Early Judaism along the same lines as my *The Dead Sea Scrolls Today*, it seemed a good opportunity to fill a need for an introduction that could be used in the classroom and could also serve as a point of entry into the field for any interested reader. I have attempted to prepare a book that provides a significant amount of information about the history, literature, and major archeological sites of the period but that presents it in a form clear and succinct enough so that it is accessible to readers with different levels of interest and varied goals.

In the course of preparing the book, a number of decisions about inclusion and exclusion had to be made. It has become customary in recent decades to call the period in question *Early Judaism,* but the term is not exactly defined in a chronological sense. It is here used to refer to the centuries when the second temple stood in Jerusalem, that is, from 516/15 BCE to 70 CE. Although we know very precisely when that building was erected and when it was destroyed, our evidence is often much less satisfactory regarding when some Jewish texts were written. The texts that are most likely to have been composed during the period of Early Judaism are included here, but a case could be made that others should also have received treatment. For example, one could argue that compositions such as the *Biblical Antiquities* of Pseudo-Philo and *Joseph and Aseneth* should have been covered and that a text such as the *Similitudes* or *Parables of Enoch (1 Enoch 37–71)* should have been excluded as being later in date. Yet, despite some debatable instances, the reader may be sure that decisions about what to cover have been made with care and that the material included gives a good idea of what happened during this period and about the types of texts that were written and the sorts of ideas that were promulgated by Jewish thinkers.

I have received assistance from a number of people as the book was taking shape. The University of Notre Dame and the Department of Theology have provided a wonderful context in which to teach and do research. My colleagues have produced a great quantity of research that has proved valuable in my work, and the program in Christianity and Judaism in Antiquity has attracted a steady stream of talented doctoral students who have helped me think about the period treated in the book. For special contributions to this book, I wish particularly to thank Angela Kim for her care in proofreading and preparing the index.

I dedicate this book with love to my talented and learned wife Mary, who has her own jokes about my interest in subjects like the pseudepigrapha. She is a "capable wife" indeed, one who, like her predecessor in Proverbs 31, "opens her mouth with wisdom, and the teaching of kindness is on her tongue."

CHAPTER 1

The Time of the Second Temple

The second temple period (516/15 BCE–70 CE) was an age in which the Jewish people, wherever they lived, were under the political and military control of other nations. Only for a brief time in the late second and early first centuries BCE did they have their own independent state, which continued to exist under the shadow of far greater powers.

It is useful to begin this introduction to the second temple period with a rapid sketch of historical developments that affected the different Jewish communities during the nearly six centuries involved. The time of the second temple begins in the later Hebrew Bible period and continues well into the first century of the common era. Knowing the principal historical events and characters will make it much easier to use the section about second temple literature in that it will allow the reader to place the texts within their proper historical contexts.

THE PERSIAN PERIOD (538-332 BCE)

The beginnings of the second temple period lie in the time when Persia ruled the ancient Near East.

Beginnings

The biblical histories report that work on the second temple in Jerusalem began after King Cyrus in the first year of his rule over Babylon issued a decree ordering that it be constructed (539-38 BCE; see 2 Chron. 36:22; Ezra 1:1-2; 5:13; cf. 6:3). Even before that year the prophet known as Second Isaiah had quoted the word of the Lord "who says of Cyrus, 'He is my shepherd, and he shall carry out all my purpose'; saying of Jerusalem, 'It shall be rebuilt,' and of the temple, 'Your foundation shall be laid'" (Isa. 44:28). According to the biblical sources, King Cyrus "sent a herald throughout all his kingdom and also declared in a written edict" (2 Chron. 36:22; Ezra 1:1):

> Thus says King Cyrus of Persia: The LORD, the God of heaven, has given me all the kingdoms of the earth, and he has charged me to build him a house at Jerusalem in Judah. Any of those among you who are of his people — may [+ the LORD (2 Chron. 36:23)] their God be with them — are now permitted go up [2 Chron. 36:23 ends] to Jerusalem in Judah, and rebuild the house of the LORD, the God of Israel — he is the God who is in Jerusalem; and let all survivors, in whatever place they reside, be assisted by the people of their place with silver and gold, with goods and with animals, besides freewill offerings for the house of God in Jerusalem. (Ezra 1:2-4)

Cyrus centered his attention, not on the city of Jerusalem, but on the temple where the God who, he professed, had given him his possessions chose to have his residence. The great king, true to his policy, returned the cultic items that King Nebuchadnezzar of Babylon had removed from the Jerusalem temple before destroying it in 587/86 BCE; Cyrus gave them to someone named Sheshbazzar who may have been a descendant of David (see 1 Chron. 3:18 where "Shenazzar" may be another spelling of his name). Whoever he was, Sheshbazzar and many others with him brought the vessels to the site of the former temple in Jerusalem and seem to have begun constructing a temple. They laid the sub-foundations of the future temple (see Ezra 5:16) but seem not to have made much progress, although the reason for their limited success is not known.

It was not until some eighteen years later, in 520, the second year of Darius (522-486 BCE), that the effort to build a new temple resumed in earnest (Ezra 5:1–6:15). The leaders of the rebuilding effort are named in

Ezra. The civil leader was Zerubbabel, who was certainly a descendant of David (1 Chron. 3:19); the high priest was Jeshua (Joshua), who was a descendant of the last high priest in the first temple; and the two prophets Haggai and Zechariah encouraged Zerubbabel, Joshua, and the people to get on with the task. The book of Ezra relates that the temple was completed, with royal permission and support, on the third of the month Adar (the twelfth month) in the sixth year of King Darius (516/15 BCE; Ezra 6:15), thus inaugurating the era known as the second temple period.

Events in Yehud (Judah)

After completion of the second temple the sources in the Hebrew Bible become very spotty in their reporting of events in Judah. For the next century or so the work of just two eminent leaders is recorded, with other events meriting only brief allusions.

The Work of Ezra and Nehemiah

In the year 458 BCE (the seventh year of Artaxerxes I [465-24 BCE]), a priestly scribe named Ezra, "a scholar of the text of the commandments of the LORD and his statutes for Israel" (Ezra 7:11), left Babylon and journeyed to Judah leading a sizable group of other returnees, priestly, levitical, and lay. Ezra came with an extraordinary commission from the king; it specified that he was to put a certain law into effect in the Persian province called Beyond the River, of which Judah was a small part.

> And you, Ezra, according to the God-given wisdom you possess, appoint magistrates and judges who may judge all the people in the province Beyond the River who know the laws of your God; and you shall teach those who do not know them. All who will not obey the law of your God and the law of the king, let judgment be strictly executed on them, whether for death or for banishment or for confiscation of their goods or for imprisonment. (Ezra 7:25-26)

The king and his advisors also continued the policy of Darius's predecessors by contributing lavishly to the running and maintenance of the temple in Jerusalem (Ezra 7:14-24; 8:36).

Shortly after arriving in Jerusalem Ezra learned that a number of Judeans had married outside the group of returned exiles. Ezra, after fasting and tearing his hair and clothing, offered a great prayer of confession (chap. 9) and then demanded that those guilty of such intermarriages send their foreign wives and children away (chap. 10). Their crime — "the holy seed has mixed itself with the peoples of the lands" (9:2) — seems mild enough, but it violated divine law, and such violations, according to Ezra, had led to destruction and captivity at the hands of the Babylonians more than 125 years earlier. His radical solution underscores the fact that a pure genealogy and family were considered essential parts of fidelity to the divine law at the time, at least according to those of Ezra's persuasion.

To this point in the story, Ezra seems not to have done what the king had commissioned him to do; that was not to happen until some fourteen years had elapsed. The Book of Nehemiah tells us that Nehemiah, who was serving as butler to the same Persian king Artaxerxes I, received a disturbing report about conditions in Jerusalem. His brother Hanani came to him with "certain men from Judah" (1:2; the passage shows that there was travel back and forth between Judah and Susa) who told Nehemiah: "The survivors there in the province who escaped captivity are in great trouble and shame; the wall of Jerusalem is broken down, and its gates have been destroyed by fire" (1:3). Whether they meant that the wall had remained in ruins since the Babylonians razed it in 587/586 BCE or that a new set of walls had been demolished, we do not know. But, moved by this information, Nehemiah summoned the courage to ask the king for permission to put aside his official duties for a time and to rebuild the city of Jerusalem. Nehemiah tells us that this occurred in the twentieth year of Artaxerxes (1:1; 2:1) which would be the year 445/444 BCE.

Nehemiah journeyed to Jerusalem with an armed escort and royal letters authorizing him to procure the necessary timber from the king's forests. Once in Jerusalem he organized the effort to rebuild Jerusalem's devastated walls (Neh. 3) and succeeded in carrying out the large undertaking in fifty-two days, but he encountered strong opposition from leaders who lived near Jerusalem and who suspected him of entertaining royal ambitions. Prominent among them were Tobiah the Ammonite and Sanballat the Horonite. Nehemiah effected a number of social reforms in Jerusalem, but the book named after him suddenly deflects attention from the protagonist and places it on Ezra in chapters 8–10. There Ezra finally (fourteen years after his arrival in Jerusalem) did what Artaxerxes had ordered him to do: he read and explained the law to a public assembly consisting of "both men and women and all who could hear with understanding" (8:2). As he read from "the book of the law of Moses, which the LORD had given to Israel" (8:1), the scribe was supported by Levites "who helped the people to understand the law, while the people remained in their places. So they read from the book, from the law of God, with interpretation. They gave the sense, so that the people understood the reading" (8:7-8). The reading led to a proper observance of the festival of booths and also to a confession of sins by the Israelites who had already separated themselves from foreign peoples (chap. 9). In his confession Ezra acknowledged that failure to keep the law had eventuated in exile and the current circumstances of subjugation; hence the people present made "a firm agreement in writing" and sealed it with their names (as is typical in Ezra and Nehemiah, all the names are listed). Their firm agreement involved an oath to obey God's law, not to intermarry with other peoples, not to engage in commerce on the sabbath, to observe the sabbatical year including its remission of debts, to pay one-third of a shekel annually for the costs of the temple service, to bring wood periodically for burning sacrifices, to transport the first fruits annually to the sanctuary, and to pay the tithes (chap. 10). Later Nehemiah effected a number of these items by force (chap. 13).

The book reports that in the king's thirty-second year (433-432 BCE) Nehemiah returned to the monarch (13:6) but after an unspecified time he again traveled to Jerusalem for his second stint as governor. The thirty-second year of Artaxerxes is the last secure date mentioned in the Hebrew Bible, although some of the lists of priestly names in Nehemiah 12 may reach to a much later point in history. For example, the list of high priests extends as far as Jaddua who is supposed to have been the man serving as supreme pontiff when Alexander the Great visited Jerusalem (12:11, 22). Some scholars think, however, he must have been an earlier Jaddua whose name was somehow omitted from other lists of the high priests in this period. "Darius the Persian" who is mentioned in 12:22 is probably Darius II who reigned from 423-404 BCE.

The books of Ezra and Nehemiah show that a group of Judeans, returnees from the eastern diaspora, at times made strong efforts to keep themselves apart from neighboring peoples who may also have worshiped the Lord though in a different way. Sanballat the Horonite was the ancestor of a series of rulers in the area of Samaria, and the people there seem to have had antagonistic relations with the Judeans. The same may be said about the people associated with Tobiah the Ammonite and with Geshem the Arabian (see Neh. 6:1 for example). It appears that a certain Jewish group, centered around the Jerusalem temple, saw in the practice of mingling with other peoples a dangerous way of life that threatened to lead to more trouble in the future. They pledged instead to keep the covenantal law that had been revealed to Moses, including its separatist demands, and thus to insure the deity's good will toward them.

With Nehemiah the curtain closes on the historical stage in Judah, at least for all practical purposes. Very little information has come down to us regarding events between his time and the rise of the Maccabees in the 160s BCE. About the only data that have survived come from the pen of the Jewish historian Josephus in his work *Antiquities of the Jews* (see the section on Josephus in Chapter 2). Josephus wote the *Antiquities* in the 90s CE and apparently had only a few sources of information available about events between Nehemiah's governorship and the Maccabean revolt. One incident that he does narrate in some detail involved the high priest Jaddua, the last high priest mentioned in Nehemiah 12 (vv. 11, 22).

Jaddua and Alexander the Great

According to Josephus this Jaddua was in office when Alexander the Great campaigned through the Levant in 332 BCE. Some scholars have thought that this could hardly be the Jaddua in the book of Nehemiah because of the lengthy high priestly reigns we would have to assume for the last two men in Nehemiah's list. However, reigns of plausible length for them would still allow Jaddua to be the reigning high priest in Alexander's time.

According to Josephus's story, Jaddua was an ally of the last Persian king Darius III and refused to renege on his pledge to the king when Alexander demanded the loyalty of leaders in the area. When the Macedonian monarch marched on Jerusalem to punish him, the high priest led his people, all clothed in white, to meet the conqueror. Alexander then did something highly unexpected: he dismounted, walked toward the high priest, and bowed before him. He claimed that he had seen the high priest in a dream some time before, and Jaddua assured him that his arrival had been predicted in the book of Daniel. Alexander bestowed a number of benefits on the Jews at this time before he resumed his march toward Egypt.

The story has a number of implausible elements in it, and no non-Jewish Greek source mentions a meeting between Alexander and the Jewish high priest. Yet, whatever one thinks of the account, it does reveal a picture of the Judean community under the leadership of the high priest and enjoying good relations with the great powers.

This same story includes a subplot that involves the people who lived directly to the north of Jerusalem, the people of Samaria. The books of Ezra and Nehemiah show in several cases that relations with these neighbors were strained already in the early days of the return from exile. Ezra 4:1 mentioned "the adversaries of Judah and Benjamin" without more closely identifying them, although they claimed that they worshiped the same God as the returned exiles and wished to help rebuild the temple (4:2). Their offer was rejected (4:3). Later, in the time of Artaxerxes, officials from the same area had written to the king warning that the Jews were rebuilding the city of Jerusalem; in his reply Artaxerxes had ordered a stop to the work (4:7-23). One of Nehemiah's group of enemies was Sanballat the Horonite (first mentioned in Neh 2:10); Horon is in the same northern area, and we now have evidence that Sanballat established a dynasty of governors there that may well have lasted until Alexander the Great arrived more than a century later.

Evidence for this claim comes from a set of papryri that were found in the Wadi ed-Daliyeh in the early 1960s. They were written in Aramaic and date from the mid-300s BCE; most of the texts are contracts. In some of them the name Sanballat is preserved, and from those references a family line can be reconstructed. Nehemiah's foe Sanballat seems now to have been the first of three Sanballats to hold the gubernatorial position in Samaria. His son Delaiah is mentioned in one of the Elephantine papyri (see below). A second Sanballat figures in the Samaria Papyri, and the Sanballat that Josephus presents as a contemporary of the high priest Jaddua would be the third. According to Josephus, this Sanballat threw his support to Alexander, and Alexander gave him permission to build a temple in his territory. Sanballat invited the brother of Jaddua to marry his daughter and become the high priest of his new temple. This is supposed to be the origin of a temple in the area of Samaria.

Events in Egypt

Judea was hardly the only area of Jewish population during the time when Persia ruled the Near East. Jews could be found in a number of countries. They were there for a variety of reasons; the best known and documented cause for their dispersion is the process of exile that took place in the early sixth century, an exile that saw the relocation of a considerable number of Judeans into Mesopotamia. The sources for the Persian period and later indicate that Egypt too was a place with a significant Jewish population, which was to grow over the years and become very large indeed.

The book of Jeremiah tells about a migration of Jews to Egypt in the aftermath of Nebuchadnezzar's conquest of Jerusalem in 587/586 BCE. The conquerors appointed a Judean named Gedaliah to be the governor in Judah (Jer. 39:14; 40:5-12), but he was assassinated in 582 BCE (40:13–41:10). The assassins were subsequently defeated by another Judean group and driven out of the country, but the group that had avenged the death of Gedaliah and his men became afraid that the Babylonians would punish them for the death of the governor. As a result they escaped to Egypt and forced the prophet Jeremiah to accompany them (Jer. 43:1-7). Jeremiah, who had earlier declined an invitation to accompany the exiles to Babylon (Jer. 40:1-6) and had urged the fearful Judeans to remain in the land (42:7-22), continued his negative prophetic career among the Jews in Egypt and apparently ended his days there (43:8–44:30). The book of Jeremiah says that there were Judeans "at Migdol, at Tahpanhes, at Memphis, and in the land of Pathros" (44:1) and indicates that they continued their idolatrous practices in those places. The last we hear of Jeremiah is his prophecy that Pharaoh Hophra (588-569 BCE) would be handed over to his enemies (44:30). Therefore, he was still alive and in office at this time.

A series of texts known as the Elephantine Papyri provide evidence for Jewish residence in Egypt at later times. The island of Elephantine lies opposite the city of Assuan, sight of the great modern dam. There several groups of papyri were discovered in the late nineteenth and early twentieth centuries. These texts, which were written in the Aramaic language and date from the late 400s and early 300s BCE, came from a Jewish military colony stationed on the island which is called Yeb in the texts. The Elephantine Papyri will be treated in Chapter 2; here the historical information from them will be sketched.

The Jews of Yeb had a temple where they worshiped the God whom they called Yahu, a form of the biblical name Yahweh (usually translated as "the LORD"). They claimed that their temple had stood on its site even before the Persian king Cambyses invaded Egypt in 525 BCE. However, the sanctuary was destroyed in the year 410, an act incited by the priests who served the Egyptian god Khnum and with permission of Persian authorities. The highest ranking Persian official, the satrap Arsames, happened to be away from Egypt when the attack occurred. The Jews of Elephantine attempted to muster support for the rebuilding of their temple. They wrote to Johanan the high priest in Jerusalem (he is mentioned in Neh. 12:22) but seem to have received no reply from him (no reason for this is known). They also wrote to Bagoas, the governor in Jerusalem, and to Delaiah, a son of Nehemiah's opponent Sanballat; he was at that time the governor in Samaria. These officials advocated the rebuilding program, but, although the temple seems to have been rebuilt, animal sacrifice was no longer permitted there.

There are a number of references in the Elephantine texts to other gods, thus showing that these Jews tended to be syncretistic religiously, just as were the Jews in Egypt whom Jeremiah had criticized so strongly about 170 years earlier.

Events in Babylon and Persia

Second Kings 25 nearly ends with the fall of Jerusalem to the Babylonians and the deportation of many Judeans to areas farther east (no places are specified apart from Babylon). The very last paragraph in the chapter relates that King Evil-merodach of Babylon released the Judean king Jehoiachin in the thirty-seventh year of the latter's imprisonment (598-561 BCE); he also provided well for Jehoiachin: "Every day of his life he dined regularly in the king's presence. For his allowance, a regular allowance was given him by the king, a portion every day, as long as he lived" (25:29-30). This brief notice has received support from Babylonian documents that mention supplies given to Jehoiachin and his sons.

The prophet Ezekiel adds a few pieces of information about the exiles in Babylon. He himself received his famous vision of the divine chariot at the River Chebar where there were other exiles (Ezek. 1:1). Later he mentions exiles at Tel-abib (3:15) located near the same river. His vision regarding the restored land of Judah and the temple that is found at the end of the book (chaps. 40–48) is dated to the year 573 BCE (40:1).

The information about Jews in Mesopotamian lands becomes very sparse after this. Ezra 1, as we have seen, speaks of a return by some from exile, while others remained where they were, supporting the returnees financially. Ezra himself came from Babylon (Ezra 7:9; 8:1). He gathered those who wanted to journey to Jerusalem with him "by the river that runs to Ahava" (8:15; cf. vv. 21, 31), and mentions contacting an exilic leader in Casiphia where there were also temple servants (8:17). Nehemiah was an official in the royal capital of Susa (Neh. 1:1). These few notices, along with passages such as Psalm 137, indicate that there were Jews, perhaps significant in number, at several places in Mesopotamia and Persia, yet the sources do not allow us to write much of a history of them. A few biblical and apocryphal works relate to the eastern diaspora, but it is difficult to situate them historically.

For example, the book of Tobit, which will be treated more fully in Chapter 2, is set in the *Israelite* diaspora that followed the destruction of Samaria in 722 BCE during the time of the Assyrians, long before the Babylonians destroyed Jerusalem and the Persians defeated the Babylonians. Tobit himself, we are told, was in the service of King Shalmaneser (Tob. 1:13-15). His nephew Ahiqar was a high official of kings Sennacherib and Esarhaddon (1:21-22). The book is the first example of a literary setting that will become familiar: Israelites/Jews occupying very high positions in the service of foreign kings.

Biblical examples of such literature are Daniel and Esther, both of which have proved problematic for those who believe they recount historical events. Daniel, we are told, was one of the royal Israelite youths deported by Nebuchadnezzar to serve in his court (Dan. 1:1-7), and there he and his friends distinguished themselves in various ways. Daniel in particular had some spectacular successes interpreting dreams (chaps. 2 and 4) and decoding an inscription (chap. 5). In the second half of the book (chaps. 7–12) he himself became the recipient of dream visions that required interpretation from others. His remarkable career in the courts of foreign kings took place during the times of Nebuchadnezzar (chaps. 1–4) and Belshazzar (chaps. 5, 7, 8) of Babylon, Darius the Mede (chaps. 6, 9; cf. 11:1), and Cyrus of Persia (chaps. 10–12). Nebuchadnezzar and Belshazzar (called a king although he apparently never did become one) are known from other sources, and Cyrus, too, is familiar. However, in Daniel he is not the conqueror of Babylon, and no one knows who is meant by Darius the Mede, pictured in Daniel as the immediate successor of Belshazzar and thus as the conqueror of Babylon. The Persian king Darius was not of Median extraction, while Daniel's Darius is said to be the "son of Ahasuerus, by birth a Mede, who became king over the realm of the Chaldeans" (9:1). These are only a few of the reasons that have led many scholars to conclude that the stories in Daniel are not historical literature.

A second biblical story about Judeans in high positions in foreign courts is Esther. It is set in the days of Ahasuerus who is usually understood to be the Persian monarch Xerxes I (486-465 BCE), famous especially for his invasion of Greek territories. Esther 1:3 mentions the third year of his reign as the time when Queen Vashti fell out of favor and the process that led to Esther the Jewess becoming queen began. The dramatic events that lie at the heart of the story are placed in the king's twelfth year (3:7). Both Esther and her cousin Mordecai who had raised her were able to convince the king to issue a counter-edict to offset the order of the king's evil officer Haman to kill all Jews in the Persian empire; the Jews successfully defended themselves from attack and decided to commemorate the occasion through the festival of Purim. Neither Esther nor Mordecai appears in extra-biblical historical sources about King Xerxes (in them Xerxes has a wife with a different name), and the book has other improbable claims such as the existence of 127 provinces in the empire. So it too does not appear to be a historical account, but like the other texts mentioned above, it pictures capable Jewish people entrusted with high positions in the great foreign empire.

THE HELLENISTIC AGE (332-63 BCE)

After defeating the Persian king Darius III at Issus in 333 BCE, Alexander took almost all of Syria and areas to the south, including Judah, virtually without a fight. He was forced to do battle only at Tyre and Gaza. He then continued into Egypt, where, in addition to being proclaimed a new pharaoh, he was designated son of the god Amon and founded the city of Alexandria, named after himself. From Egypt he continued his campaigns of conquest to the east. He defeated King Darius for a final time at Gaugamela in 330 BCE and took over the vast empire. Not content even with this, he marched as far as India and eventually returned to Babylon where he died at the age of thirty-three in the year 323 BCE. He left a very young son who did succeed him for a short time, but Alexander's great holdings soon were disputed among powerful rivals, important officers in his army. The wars between Alexander's successors were to last more than a generation before some form of stability prevailed in his far-flung empire. The age after Alexander is known as the Hellenistic period, a time when aspects of Greek culture and knowledge of the Greek language became widespread and dominant. The new cultural and political reality left a heavy imprint on Jewish history for the next several centuries.

11

Ptolemaic Control of Egypt and Judea (ca. 305-198 BCE)

Only two of the successors to Alexander are immediately relevant to our topic: Ptolemy in Egypt and surrounding areas, and Seleucus in Syria, Mesopotamia, and neighboring lands (for him see the next section). Ptolemy went to Egypt and claimed it and much additional territory for himself. Among those neighboring regions was the small stretch of land occupied by the ethnic enclave of Jews in Jerusalem and its environs. As a result, Ptolemy became master of the large Jewish population in Egypt and also of the Jewish people in the Holy Land. He struggled for a long time to gain these lands, and he campaigned in Judea a number of times. Judea and southern Syria would be contested between the Ptolemies and the Seleucids for decades to come.

Ptolemy I and Judea

Josephus reports (*Ant.* 12.3-10) that Ptolemy took Jerusalem in a deceptive way. He entered the city on the sabbath and pretended that he had come to offer a sacrifice at the temple. The unsuspecting Jews, who would not fight on the seventh day, thus fell under his control. Once he had taken the city, Ptolemy ruled it cruelly. He took numerous captives from Jerusalem and surrounding areas; these he brought to Egypt and settled there. Because Jewish people were noted for their fidelity in observing the terms of agreements, Ptolemy put them in his garrisons and in Alexandria gave them the very privileges of citizenship enjoyed by his fellow Macedonians. Josephus adds that other Jews went willingly to Egypt because of its good soil and the king's liberality.

Having written this somewhat contradictory description of Ptolemy's treatment of the Jews, Josephus has relatively little to say about the next hundred years that Ptolemy and his descendants ruled over the Jews of Egypt and Judea. For most of his account he relies on two sources — the story about the translation of the Torah into Greek, and the Tobiad Romance — both of which presuppose that there were regular communications between Egypt and Judea.

Ptolemy II and the Greek Translation of the Torah

Josephus's source for the story about the translation is the *Letter of Aristeas,* which will be described more fully in Chapter 2. As the *Letter* tells it, the work of translating the Mosaic law was proposed by the head of the new royal library in Alexandria, approved and supported by the king, and carried out by seventy-two scholars from Israel acting on orders from the high priest. The king in question is Ptolemy II Philadelphus (283-246 BCE), the greatest of the Ptolemaic kings. The story, as it appears in the *Letter of Aristeas,* is generously furnished with the marks of legend, but the under lying claim that the Pentateuch was translated from Hebrew into Greek early in the Hellenistic period is supported by the existence of very early quotations from it (in ca. 200 BCE) and by pre-Christian copies that have survived. The author of the *Letter of Aristeas* burnishes and molds the bare facts into a story that becomes a splendid tribute to the Torah, to the God who had revealed it, to the lawgiver Moses, and to the wisdom of the men who rendered the astonishing text from Hebrew into Greek.

Demetrius of Phaleron, the librarian, informed the bookish monarch that he had learned the Jews had laws that should be included in the king's rapidly growing collection "but which, being written in characters and in a dialect of their own, will cause no small pains in getting them translated into the Greek tongue" (12.14). The king eagerly agreed that the work of translation should be done and ordered that the necessary preparations be made. Aristeas tells us that he himself, who was present in the royal court, took this opportunity to ask the king to free the more than 100,000 Jews who remained enslaved as a result of Ptolemy I's capture of Jerusalem and Judea. The king consented to this as well and ordered a payment of twenty drachmas to each of the enslaved Jews. He also, as other kings did in the second temple period, sent sumptuous gifts for the temple in Jerusalem, gifts described in painful detail by Aristeas (12.17-84).

The arrangements for the translation were made through the high priest (the men who held this office are consistently pictured as the representatives of the Jewish people to foreign rulers in this period). The high priest selected seventy-two Jewish men who were fluent in both Hebrew and Greek to travel to Alexandria to carry out the translation. The number seventy-two resulted from the high priest's selection of six from each of the twelve tribes — one of the legendary features in the story, since most of the tribes were no longer represented in Judea. The translators brought a copy of the Torah with them; it is described as being written on skins in

13

golden letters (12.89). It so happened that the work of translating took seventy-two days (12.107), at which point the resulting rendering of the text was approved by the Jewish community. There was an understanding that if anyone observed something in the translation that required change, the matter could be addressed.

However the translation may have come about, the Torah appears to be the first scriptural text of any religion to be translated into another language. The work of the translators not only gave to the Jews of the Hellenistic world who lived outside of Judea access to their scriptures (something that they no longer had because Hebrew was not their native language), but also made those scriptures available to a wider audience. The translation begun in the early Hellenistic period became known as the *Septuagint* which means "seventy," after the seventy(-two) translators who are supposed to have done the work. This Greek Bible, in various forms, became the scriptures of Hellenistic Judaism and later of the early Christian church.

The Tobiad Romance

The second story told by Josephus as he recounts what happened to the Jews when they were under the control of the Ptolemies concerns the Tobiads, a remarkable family of Jews, several of whose members rose to prominent positions in the Ptolemaic empire. It should be recalled that one of Nehemiah's antagonists was named Tobias and that he was connected with the territory of Ammon on the east side of the Jordan River. It is likely that the Tobiad Romance concerns later members of this Tobias's family. The father of the family in Josephus's story is also named Tobias, and he is known from Ptolemaic records (the Zenon Papyri) to have been a wealthy chieftain in the Transjordan. The Romance is principally about the rise of Joseph, son of Tobias, to great wealth and power in the Ptolemaic empire through his tax-farming work; his great good fortune serves as the background for the adventures of his eighth and most successful son Hyrcanus, who assumed his father's lucrative role. The Tobiads were not only prominent in their own right but were also related by marriage to the high-priestly family. Members of both families appear in the intriguing tale which relates events that occurred in the late third and early second centuries BCE.

As Josephus tells it, the high priest Onias (Onias II) was a miserly

14

man whose refusal to pay tribute to the Ptolemaic treasury placed the Jewish nation in great danger. In this critical situation, the Tobiad Joseph saved the day by offering to visit the king and attempt to rectify the situation. While in Alexandria, Joseph managed, using clever tactics and vast bribes, to purchase the lucrative right to collect taxes in a large area of the empire. He held this position for twenty-two years, during which time he became a very wealthy man. Joseph also became the father of seven sons by his wife and of an eighth, named Hyrcanus, by his niece, whom his brother (her father) had substituted for the foreign dancing girl with whom Joseph had fallen in love. The brother acted in this fashion to protect Joseph from violating the law prohibiting a Jew from having sexual relations with a foreign woman (*Ant.* 12.186-89). Joseph's son Hyrcanus later becomes the protagonist in the story. He, like his father, was exceptionally bold and proved far more adept than his brothers in carrying on their father's legacy (12.190-95).

The rivalry between Hyrcanus and his brothers became a central feature of the political climate in Judea in the following decades. These brothers, we learn, had written "to all the friends of the king that they should make an end of him" (12.202; cf. 12.218). He, of course, outsmarted them and even persuaded the king, who had offered him any gift he desired, to intervene:

> But he asked that the king do no more for him than to write to his father and brothers about him. And so the king, after showing him the highest honour and giving him splendid presents, wrote to his father and brothers and to all his governors and administrators, and sent him away. But when Hyrcanus' brothers heard that he had obtained these favours from the king and was returning with great honour, they went out to meet him and do away with him. . . . (12.219-21)

Even Joseph was angry with Hyrcanus for having spent so much of his money on a royal present. A fratricidal war resulted:

> And when Hyrcanus' brothers encountered him in battle, he killed many of the men with them and also two of the brothers themselves, while the rest escaped to their father in Jerusalem. Hyrcanus therefore went to that city, but as no one admitted him, he withdrew in fear to the country across the river Jordan, and there made his home, levying tribute on the barbarians. (12.222)

After the death of their father Joseph, the conflict between Hyrcanus and his half-brothers continued (see *Ant.* 12.228). "Now on the death of Joseph there arose factional strife among the people on account of his sons. For the elder brothers made war on Hyrcanus, who was the youngest of Joseph's children, and the population was divided into two camps. And the majority fought on the side of the elder brothers, as did the high priest Simon because of his kinship with them" (12.228-29). Josephus credits Hyrcanus with a seven-year rule in parts of the Transjordan and with constructing magnificent quarters there. His end, however, was tragic: "As for Hyrcanus, seeing how great was the power which Antiochus [= Antiochus IV, the Seleucid king] had, and fearing that he might be captured by him and punished for what he had done to the Arabs, he ended his life by his own hand. And all his property was seized by Antiochus" (12.236). With this reminder that Hyrcanus was an enemy of the Seleucid monarch (and presumably a friend of the Egyptian king), the Tobiad Romance ends.

With the Romance Josephus's coverage of the Jews in the Ptolemaic age also comes to a close.

Seleucid Control/Influence in Judea (198-63 BCE)

The second of Alexander the Great's successors who are of special interest in Jewish history was Seleucus, who seized Mesopotamia and territory farther east as well as Syria and parts of Asia Minor. From the beginning of their rule, Seleucid monarchs coveted control of southern Syria and Judea, both of which belonged to the Ptolemies. There was a series of wars (called the Syrian Wars) during the third century for possession of these territories, with the Ptolemies always retaining control of them; the last of these ended in 217 BCE at the battle of Raphia, where the Ptolemaic forces won a surprising victory over the ambitious new king of the Seleucid realm, Antiochus III.

Antiochus III (223-187 BCE)

After spending some years dealing with problems farther east, Antiochus III once again turned his attention toward the south in 201 BCE. At first his forces moved easily through southern Syria and Judea, but the Ptolemaic general Scopas counterattacked and, in the process, took Judea and stationed troops in Jerusalem. The fortunes of the two sides reversed themselves once more in the year 200 BCE when the army of Antiochus III defeated the Ptolemaic forces at the battle of Panion (a place located near the sources of the Jordan River; *Ant.* 12.132). He took Jerusalem in 198 BCE, and for the next century and more the Seleucid government either ruled or had considerable influence in Judea.

Antiochus III, again according to Josephus, made special provisions for the Jewish people in reparation for the area's sufferings during the recent battles between Ptolemaic and Seleucid rulers, and also for the assistance that the residents of Jerusalem had given him when they welcomed him into the city, provided for his troops and elephants, and helped him in his efforts to oust the Ptolemaic garrison from the citadel of Jerusalem. In particular he set up a fund to pay for animals and other supplies needed for sacrifice at the temple; he provided for repairs on the temple and furnished materials to make it more splendid; the nation was to be permitted to live according to its ancestral laws; members of the senate, the priests, temple scribes, and levitical singers were to be exempt from paying taxes; exemption from taxes was also given to residents of Jerusalem and others who would move to it during a prescribed amount of time; he also reduced future taxes by one third and granted freedom and restoration of property for those Jews who had been enslaved (*Ant.* 12.138-46). In another action, the king ordered that two thousand families of Jews be moved from Mesopotamia to Lydia and Phrygia in Asia Minor so that they could assist in putting down a rebellion there. This documents the presence of Jews in yet another area of the Hellenistic world. He granted to them as well the right to live according to their laws and gave them favorable financial considerations (12.147-53). In providing for the Jerusalem cult, Antiochus III was merely following the policy of his predecessors, beginning with Cyrus. Elsewhere we learn that his successor, Seleucus IV (187-175 BCE), did the same (2 Macc. 3:3).

Near the end of his long reign, Antiochus's forces were defeated by the Romans at the battle of Magnesia. The year of the battle, 190 BCE, marked a major turning point in the power politics of the Near East, as Rome's star rose and would continue to do so until she controlled the entire area. The political settlement imposed by Rome in the Peace of Apamea (188 BCE) after its victory over the Seleucids included heavy war indemnities that were to put a strain on the Seleucid treasury for a long time to come.

Antiochus IV, High Priests, and Hellenism

The third of the Seleucid monarchs to control Judea, Antiochus IV (175-164 BCE), is closely associated with one of the most famous periods in Jewish history. Apparently not long before the enlightened young man ascended the throne, trouble developed in connection with Onias III, the high priest in Jerusalem. Second Maccabees describes Onias as a saintly man who was opposed by someone named Simon, the captain of the temple (2 Macc. 3). Their dispute had to do with "the administration of the city market" (2 Macc. 3:4). Simon informed the Seleucid governor of the area that the Jerusalem temple housed incredible sums of money that could become part of the king's coffers, since they were not needed for sacrifices (3:5-6). This led to a visit by Heliodorus, the top official in the kingdom; he was sent to confiscate the money for the king, Seleucus IV. He was apparently unsuccessful, but it is difficult to understand exactly what prevented him from taking the money. According to 2 Maccabees, a spectacular rider on a horse, assisted by two amazingly strong men, pummeled him until he was senseless. Only the intervention and piety of Onias III saved him (3:22-40).

Once Antiochus became king in 175 BCE, a momentous change took place respecting the high-priestly office.

> Jason the brother of Onias obtained the high priesthood by corruption, promising the king at an interview three hundred sixty talents of silver, and from another source of revenue eighty talents. In addition to this he promised to pay one hundred fifty more if permission were given to establish by his authority a gymnasium and a body of youth for it, and to enroll the people of Jerusalem as citizens of Antioch. When the king assented and Jason came to office, he at once shifted his compatriots over to the Greek way of life. (2 Macc. 4:7b-10)

Having had his office snatched from him, Onias III took refuge in Daphne which was near Antioch (2 Macc. 4:33). The promise of larger payments would have appealed to the financially strapped monarch, who at this time broke with precedent and intervened in the centuries long, unbroken line of hereditary high priests. The highest ranking official in Judaism thus became a direct appointee of the foreign overlord. Moreover, Jason (note the Greek name) received permission to introduce into Jerusalem several of the more characteristic Greek institutions, including a gymnasium. The writer of 2 Maccabees indicates that priests were particularly zealous in pursuing the new ways at the expense of traditional Jewish practices (4:14-15). Jason is also credited with welcoming Antiochus enthusiastically when the king visited Jerusalem (4:21-22).

Jason's high priesthood lasted from 175-172 BCE. In 172 BCE he sent a certain Menelaus (brother of the Simon who had caused trouble for Onias III) to the king to make a payment. "But he, when presented to the king, extolled him with an air of authority, and secured the high priesthood for himself, outbidding Jason by three hundred talents of silver. After receiving the king's orders he returned, possessing no qualification for the high priesthood, but having the hot temper of a cruel tyrant and the rage of a savage wild beast" (2 Macc. 4:24-25). Once he had taken over the high-priestly office, Menelaus had trouble meeting his payments; to cover the shortfall he stole and sold temple utensils. His high-handed ways were exposed by Onias III who remained exiled in Daphne. Menelaus then made arrangements to have Onias killed. Onias's son Onias IV subsequently fled to Egypt where he was given royal permission to construct a temple in the city of Leontopolis. There he carried on the Oniad high-priestly tradition, while the Jerusalem temple fell into the hands of others who introduced major changes into the routines of the temple and eventually presided over a change of the religion conducted there.

While Menelaus was high priest (172-162 BCE), Antiochus IV invaded Egypt in 170 BCE and defeated Ptolemy VI Philometor (1 Macc. 1:16-19). However, as he was again moving toward Egypt the next year, he was ordered not to go there by the Roman envoy Popilius Laenas. He turned toward home in a foul mood, and on the way he and his army entered Jerusalem. "He arrogantly entered the sanctuary and took the golden altar, the lampstand for the light, and all its utensils. He took also the table for the bread of the Presence, the cups for drink offerings, the bowls, the golden censers, the curtains, the crowns, and the gold decoration on the front of the temple; he stripped it all off. He took the silver and the gold, and the costly vessels; he took also the hidden treasures that he found. Taking them all, he went into his own land" (1 Macc. 1:21-24a).

More trouble followed for Jerusalem. First Maccabees 1:29-40 describes a time two years later when the king sent a representative to Jerusalem; he came accompanied by a military force which, for unstated reasons, attacked the city and its inhabitants. He tore down the city walls, and he and his men "fortified the city of David with a great strong wall and strong towers, and it became their citadel" (1:33). This citadel, where foreign troops were stationed, became the military center of Seleucid control in Jerusalem and Judea for the next generation.

Apparently in the same year, the year 167 BCE (1 Macc. 1:54), Antiochus IV

> wrote to his whole kingdom that all should be one people, and that all should give up their particular customs. All the Gentiles accepted the command of the king. Many even from Israel gladly adopted his religion; they sacrificed to idols and profaned the sabbath. And the king sent letters by messengers to Jerusalem and the towns of Judah; he directed them to follow customs strange to the land, to forbid burnt offerings and sacrifices and drink offerings in the sanctuary, to profane sabbaths and festivals, to defile the sanctuary and the priests, to build altars and sacred precincts and shrines for idols, to sacrifice swine and other unclean animals, and to leave their sons uncircumcised. They were to make themselves abominable by everything unclean and profane, so that they would forget the law and change all the ordinances. He added, "And whoever does not obey the command of the king shall die." (1 Macc. 1:41-50)

The sanctuary was renamed the temple of Olympian Zeus (2 Macc. 6:2), prostitution was practiced there, animals unfit for sacrifice were offered, and the Jews, during the monthly celebration of the king's birthday, were forced to eat the impure sacrifices. They were also made to participate in a festival of the Greek god Dionysus (2 Macc. 6:3-7). An especially noteworthy event, according to the sources, occurred on Chislev (the ninth month) 15, 167 BCE, when "they erected a desolating sacrilege on the altar of burnt offering" (1 Macc. 1:54). Moreover, books of the law were destroyed (v. 56). This act of the king, which seems to have been contrary to his normal policy in dealing with subject peoples, amounted to a prohibition of the Jewish religion on pain of death. Why did a seemingly enlightened monarch take so radical a step?

The reasons that motivated Antiochus have been debated at length, but it is at least clear that Jerusalem had been a trouble spot for some time and that he regarded the unusual religion of the Jews as the heart of the problem. Second Maccabees 3 describes an incident which is now enveloped in a miraculous tale but in which a Seleucid official had a very difficult time in Jerusalem when he attempted to remove monetary treasures from the temple (see above). Later charges were brought against Menelaus when his brother Lysimachus, whom he had left as his representative in Jerusalem while the high priest traveled to Antioch, had been at the center of a bloody confrontation with Jerusalemites (2 Macc. 4:39-50). Before the incident in which Antiochus, with Menelaus's approval, had plundered the temple of its treasures, there had been a revolt in Jerusalem. Jason, the deposed high priest, had heard a false rumor that Antiochus, campaigning in Egypt, had lost his life. Jason seized the opportunity to oust the king's man Menelaus and regain his former position. His troops caused much damage and killed many people before withdrawing (2 Macc. 5:5-10). Second Maccabees relates that Antiochus, upon hearing of Jason's attack, believed the city was revolting. His experience of being rebuffed in Egypt just when he was on the verge of taking Alexandria had not improved his mood. Hence he took out his anger and frustration in Jerusalem (2 Macc. 5:11-16).

Whatever the causes of Antiochus's decrees may have been, it became nearly impossible to carry out the rites and practices associated with the traditional Jewish way of life. At some point around the time when these orders were issued and enforced, members of the Hasmonean family, a priestly clan from the town of Modein, took the initial steps to oppose the new reality. Second Maccabees 5:27 says that "Judas Maccabeus, with about nine others, got away to the wilderness, and kept himself and his companions alive in the mountains as wild animals do; they continued to live on what grew wild, so that they might not share in the defilement." First Maccabees 2 instead tells a story about Mattathias, the patriarch of the Hasmonean clan, who, when invited to follow the king's new policy and participate in a royally mandated sacrifice, firmly rejected the invitation and the bribe that accompanied it. He also killed a Jew who stepped forward to offer a sacrifice "on the altar in Modein, according to the king's command" (v. 23), executed the king's officer who was enforcing the edict, and tore down the offending altar (vv. 24-25). He then issued a call to arms: "'Let everyone who is zealous for the law and supports the covenant come out with me!' Then he and his sons fled to the hills and left all that they had in the town" (2:27-28). Others fled to the wilderness to escape the new policy (v. 29).

The opposition that began on a small scale was soon large enough that the rebels were able to defeat the Seleucid forces sent to crush them. Mattathias died soon after rallying the traditionalists, and his son Judas became commander of their forces. He was given the nickname *Maccabee* which may mean "hammerer"; the movement he led and the family of which he was a member also became known by this name. Judas and his troops were victorious in a series of battles against Seleucid commanders

(1 Macc. 3:10–4:35) and were eventually able to take Jerusalem. There they set in motion a process of purifying the temple from the various kinds of defilement it had recently suffered. They not only repaired the damage and cleaned the complex of the abominations found in it, but they also constructed a new altar and rededicated the sanctuary to the service of Israel's God. They celebrated the rededication of the temple on Chislev 25, exactly two or three years (depending on whether one follows 2 Maccabees or 1 Maccabees) since pagan sacrifice had begun there. They then decreed that forever after Jews were to celebrate this festival of Hanukkah (= dedication) for eight days, beginning on Chislev 25, just as they had (1 Macc. 4:36-59).

The next several years saw other important events take place. Conflict with the Seleucid regime continued after the dedication of the temple. It was not until the year 162 BCE that the decrees of Antiochus were officially repealed. Judas Maccabeus continued to be a major political and military force in Judea; in fact, he led his troops on several successful forays into neighboring territory, often to protect the Jewish populations in those areas (1 Macc. 5). The high priest Menelaus died in 162 BCE and was succeeded by Alcimus, another royal appointee. Alcimus, too, it seems, was not of the traditional high-priestly line, but he was appointed to the office nevertheless and sent to Judea with a military force. It is interesting that Alcimus went to the king, now Demetrius I (162-150 BCE), with charges against Judas; the royal response was to send troops into Judea, only to have another army defeated by Maccabeus (7:20-50).

First Maccabees 8 adds a significant note to the biography of Judas. He "heard of the fame of the Romans, that they were very strong and were well-disposed toward all who made an alliance with them, that they pledged friendship to those who came to them, and that they were very strong" (8:1-2a). Judas dispatched a delegation to Rome "to establish friendship and alliance, and to free themselves from the yoke; for they saw that the kingdom of the Greeks was enslaving Israel completely" (8:17b-18). This short notice indicates that the Maccabees had hardly succeeded in wresting control of Judea from Seleucid hands. The Roman senate agreed to a treaty with the Maccabean party; this meant that if one nation was attacked the other was obliged to support it (8:22-28). Roman might, which had already played an indirect part in Jewish history when Antiochus IV was ordered out of Egypt, was to prove valuable at different times. Favorable relations with Rome long preceded the hatred that was to arise after Rome became master of Judea about a century later (in 63 BCE).

Judas, who seems never to have held an official post, eventually died in battle in 160 BCE with yet another Seleucid contingent (9:1-18). He was succeeded in the leadership of his forces by his brother Jonathan (the youngest of Mattathias's sons), but the Seleucids had by this time clearly regained the upper hand over the Maccabean party. A year later the high priest Alcimus died (9:54-57). First Maccabees fails to mention the name of his successor, and Josephus, too, does not refer to one. Rather, according to Josephus, the high priesthood remained vacant for seven years after the death of Alcimus. This highly irregular situation, unparalleled in the more than 350-year history of the second temple, has opened the door to speculation about who might have held office then, whether a high priest whose name has been lost (for whatever reason) or a lower priest who served as a substitute in the absence of an official successor to Alcimus (see the section on the Dead Sea Scrolls for the possible relevance of this situation to the origins of the scrolls community).

The last eighty years or so of the Seleucid empire were a time of turmoil, with frequent wars between incumbents and pretenders to the throne. At times the Maccabean leaders were able to turn Seleucid weakness and insecurity to their own advantage, whether personally or for their country. One such moment came in 152 BCE. As we have seen, the sources do not divulge who was high priest from 159 (when Alcimus died) to 152 BCE. In that year Demetrius I, who now held the Seleucid throne, was under intense pressure from a certain Alexander Balas (who claimed to be a son of Antiochus IV) and in need of all the military backing he could muster. Under these circumstances he recognized the strength that Jonathan possessed and offered him the right to recruit troops in exchange for his support. Jonathan exploited the invitation and used his new authority to take Jerusalem and fortify it (2 Macc. 10:1-11). Alexander, not to be outdone, raised the stakes in the dispute over the throne: he wrote to Jonathan: ". . . we have appointed you today to be the high priest of your nation; you are to be called the king's Friend, and you are to take our side and keep friendship with us" (10:20). Jonathan accepted Alexander Balas's offer and, as 1 Maccabees 10:21 phrases it, he "put on the sacred vestments in the seventh month of the one hundred sixtieth year [i.e., of the Seleucid empire, = 152 BCE], at the festival of booths, and he recruited troops and equipped them with arms in abundance." It could hardly be said more clearly that Jonathan became high priest because he commanded an army. He was, of course, from a priestly family, but that quality was not what won the post for him; his military clout did. King Demetrius made a counteroffer that included extravagant tax concessions

(10:22-45), but Jonathan and his forces did not trust him and remained on Alexander Balas's side (10:46-47). The wisdom of their decision soon became apparent when Alexander defeated and killed Demetrius and became king in his place (10:48-50).

Jonathan, the general and ally of the Seleucid king, held the high-priestly office for ten years, although the sources never report a single cultic act that he performed. Diplomacy had become a complicated game at the time as new kings arose in Antioch, but Jonathan proved remarkably successful in battle and in acquiring honors for himself (1 Macc. 10–11). He also was perceptive enough to renew the ties his brother had established with Rome. Rome was eager to hedge in the Seleucid monarchs and was happy to have allies in the immediate vicinity of Syria (1 Macc. 12:1-4).

Josephus, as he rewrote the history of this period in his *Antiquities of the Jews,* chose to add an interesting section to 1 Maccabees (his principal source) at some point during Jonathan's years in office. In *Antiquities* 13.171 he wrote: "Now at this time there were three schools of thought among the Jews, which held different opinions concerning human affairs; the first being that of the Pharisees, the second that of the Sadducees, and the third that of the Essenes." He does not say that the groups originated at that time; he merely notes that they existed and differed about important matters which he then summarizes briefly (13.172-73).

In the end, however, Jonathan allowed himself to be duped by a man named Trypho who was attempting to gain the Seleucid kingdom for himself. He persuaded Jonathan to meet him in the city of Ptolemais and to dismiss almost all of his troops before entering the city. Jonathan's remaining soldiers were then massacred by the residents of the city, and Trypho took Jonathan prisoner (1 Macc. 12:46-53). His misfortune inspired his brother Simon (the second oldest of Mattathias's sons) to assume leadership of the Jewish nation as high priest and commander of the army (chap. 13; for his high priesthood, see v. 36). Simon tried to win the release of his brother but failed; eventually Trypho executed Jonathan near the city of Baskama (13:23).

The Hasmonean State (ca. 140-63 BCE)

Beginning with Simon, a line of Hasmonean rulers was able to win a varying measure of independence for the Jewish state, although the shadow of the Seleucid regime was always present.

The Maccabean/Hasmonean Family

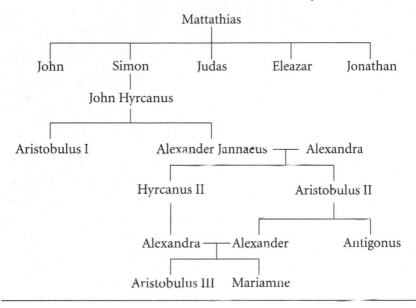

Simon (142-134 BCE)

In some ways Simon seems to have been the greatest of the Maccabees, or perhaps it was the circumstances of his time that allowed him to achieve great success. Among his early accomplishments were:

- strengthening and provisioning national fortresses
- successful negotiations with Demetrius II who was fighting with Trypho for the Seleucid throne. The king granted Simon and the Judeans the gift of peace, the right to keep their strongholds, and exemption from imperial taxes (1 Macc. 13:36-40).

As a result of his achievements, says 1 Maccabees 13:41-42, in the year 142 BCE "the yoke of the Gentiles was removed from Israel, and the people began to write in their documents and contracts, 'In the first year of Simon the great high priest and commander and leader of the Jews.'" In the next year he managed to expel the foreign troops from the citadel in Jerusalem, thus removing the heart of the Seleucid presence from the capital. Simon decreed that the event was to be celebrated annually (13:49-52). The author of 1 Maccabees includes in his account a poem lauding what Simon had done and the peace he had accomplished in his time (14:4-15); he even uses the ancient biblical image that "[a]ll the people sat under their own vines and fig trees" (v. 12).

Simon's deeds and honors continued to grow. The Romans (this time the initiative is attributed to them) renewed their friendship and alliance with him (14:16-19). First Maccabees reserves a larger amount of space, however, for a decree made by a "great assembly of the priests and the people and the rulers of the nation and the elders of the country" (v. 28) that recognized the enormous contributions of Simon and his brothers (only Jonathan is named) because they had "exposed themselves to danger and resisted the enemies of their nation, in order that their sanctuary and the law might be preserved; and they brought great glory to their nation" (v. 29). Simon is credited with spending his own money to arm and pay his soldiers and with the various conquests that had been mentioned in chap. 13 (vv. 32-34). Great power was then officially confirmed for and entrusted to Simon:

- "The Jews and their priests have resolved that Simon should be their leader and high priest forever, until a trustworthy prophet should arise" (v. 41), apparently meaning that these arrangements should last until divine instructions contravened them.
- "that he should be obeyed by all, and that all contracts in the country should be written in his name, and that he should be clothed in purple and wear gold" (v. 43).
- No one could oppose what had been decided or what Simon said, and no one was "to convene an assembly in the country without his permission, or to be clothed in purple or put on a gold buckle" (v. 44). It is possible that these words reflect some opposition to Simon and his rule; the decree was meant to outlaw it.

Having attained such prominence at home, Simon continued to be a desirable ally of Seleucid kings and claimants to the throne. When Demetrius II's brother Antiochus VII was planning an invasion to gain the kingdom for himself, he reaffirmed previous tax concessions to Simon and added a new provision: "I permit you to mint your own coinage as money for your country" (15:6). The experts have debated whether Simon actually minted coins (it seems unlikely), but at least permission to do so was granted to him by a man who became king in Antioch. Soon, however, the agreement between Antiochus VII and Simon collapsed; in fact, Simon's sons Judas and John won a victory over forces that Antiochus sent into Judea (1 Macc. 16:1-10).

First Maccabees ends with the story of Simon's death and the accession of his son John to his various offices. Ptolemy, Simon's son-in-law who was governor in the area of Jericho, entertained Simon and two of his sons at a banquet. When the guests were drunk, he signaled for his men to kill all of them or at least Simon. The high priest died there, and his heir John, who was not present at the banquet, also became the object of an assassination attempt (which failed; 16.11-22).

Simon's death in 134 BCE signaled the end of a remarkable set of brothers who had led their own troops and eventually the nation for more than thirty years. They transformed Judea from a temple state to a semi-independent nation and greatly expanded its holdings and military power. Jonathan and Simon managed to acquire the high priesthood, the highest position in the country, and Simon held all of the other high posts as well. The high-priestly line of Onias that had occupied the office for about 150 years only to be ousted in 175 BCE stood even less chance to retrieve their position, now that it was in the hands of a priestly family that also commanded the army and ruled the nation.

The remainder of the story about the Maccabean or Hasmonean family comes from Josephus, primarily from his *Antiquities of the Jews*, although there is a shorter form of the history in his work *The Jewish War*.

John Hyrcanus (134-104 BCE)

John Hyrcanus began his reign by attempting to punish the Ptolemy who had killed his father and imprisoned his mother and brothers. When John attacked his fortress, Ptolemy had John's mother tortured on top of the wall. He later killed her and her two sons (*Ant.* 13.230-35). Adding to John's problems, Antiochus VII invaded, besieged Jerusalem, tore down its walls, and forced a large payment from the Judeans (13.245-48). Later it seems that John and Antiochus became allies (13.249-53). After Antiochus VII died in 129, John was able to conquer territory in ancient Moab and Samaria where he destroyed the Samaritan temple and forced those who worshiped there to follow Jewish laws such as circumcision (13.254-58).

Following tradition, John renewed the friendship and alliance between the Jews and Romans (13.259-66). In a surprising turn of affairs, John managed to spend most of his years in peace with the Seleucids, in large part because interminable disputes for the throne weakened the once great empire. John, far from being frightened by the various claimants to the throne, is even said to have held them in contempt (13.273-74). Late in his reign he defeated Samaria after a lengthy siege. During that siege the Samaritans twice received assistance from the Seleucid king Antiochus IX Cyzicenus who was defeated on both occasions.

Josephus tells a story that involved John and the Pharisees and Sadducees, a story that shows how the parties were involved in politics at the highest level and were forces that had to be acknowledged by rulers such as Hyrcanus. Josephus says that the Pharisees were especially hostile to Hyrcanus. John had been a "disciple of theirs, and was greatly loved by them" (13.288-92) until a falling out occurred. At a feast to which he invited them he made the mistake of asking whether they had noticed his doing anything wrong and if so to correct him. All praised him except a certain Eleazar, who, says Josephus, enjoyed dissension. He asked Hyrcanus to give up the high priesthood and simply be the civilian leader of the nation. The reason for the request was that "we have heard from our elders that your mother was a captive in the days of Antiochus Epiphanes." Although the story was false (there is no record of this for Antiochus Epiphanes's reign), Eleazar repeated it and infuriated Hyrcanus and his fellow Pharisees as well. Through the machinations of one of his friends who was a Sadducee, John became convinced that Eleazar spoke not just for himself but for the entire Pharisaic party. He then joined the Sadducees and removed the regulations that the Pharisees had put in place. Josephus saw in this incident a reason why the masses, who followed the Pharisees, came to hate John Hyrcanus (13.293-98).

Aristobulus I (104-103 BCE) and Kingship

After John died in 104 BCE, his oldest son Aristobulus succeeded him in his various offices. According to Josephus, he changed the form of the national government to that of a kingdom and took the title of king, the first of the Hasmoneans to do so (13.301). Aristobulus is credited with imprisoning most of his brothers and starving his mother to death. Suspicions about his favorite brother Antigonus eventually led, although apparently not by Aristobulus's orders, to that brother's death (13.307-9). Aristobulus died after reigning just one year (13.318). Josephus, despite what he writes about Aristobulus's relations with his family members, does praise the king (who had the title Philhellene) for his services to the nation, such as conquering Iturea and forcing its inhabitants to be circumcised and live in harmony with Jewish law (13.318-19).

Alexander Jannaeus (103-76 BCE)

Aristobulus's wife Alexandra appointed his brother Alexander Jannaeus as her husband's successor. Early in his reign, his armies suffered a major defeat at the hands of Ptolemy Lathyrus, most recently from Cyprus. Alexander escaped the grave danger to himself and the country only through the military intervention of Ptolemy's mother Cleopatra III. Once he was delivered from Ptolemy, Alexander resumed attacking various places, including Gaza, whose inhabitants he wiped out (13.320-64).

Alexander's military actions took a terrible toll on the population. One year at the festival of tabernacles, as Alexander, who was of course the high priest, stood beside the altar preparing to sacrifice, the people pelted him with fruit (citrons, wands that celebrants carried were made from the branches of citron trees). Furthermore, "they added insult to injury by saying that he was descended from captives and was unfit to hold office and to sacrifice" (13.372). Jannaeus killed thousands more of his fellow citizens in retaliation for this and other acts of opposition to his rule. At one point he is said to have asked what he ought to do: "they all cried out, 'to die'; and they sent to Demetrius Akairos, asking him to come to their assistance" (13.376). That is, his subjects requested help from the Seleucid king against Jannaeus.

Demetrius did in fact invade Judea, fought with Jannaeus, and defeated him (13.377-78). Demetrius eventually withdrew, but Jannaeus, while rid of the foreign menace, continued to have domestic problems. In response he got revenge on some of his staunchest Jewish foes. He captured six thousand of them, brought them to Jerusalem, and punished them in gruesome fashion: "while he feasted with his concubines in a conspicuous place, he ordered some eight hundred of the Jews to be crucified, and slaughtered their children and wives before the eyes of the still living wretches" (13.380). About eight thousand other opponents fled in terror, and Jannaeus, now spared his most vociferous and active critics, was able to live out the remaining years of his kingship in domestic peace. Freedom from troubles at home released the militant prince to pursue his seemingly endless wars against surrounding cities and nations. He proved quite successful in his endeavors (13.393-97). Indeed, he died on a military campaign, one he conducted despite the fact that he had been ill for three years (13.398-404).

On his deathbed Jannaeus is said to have given important and effective instructions to his wife Alexandra (who had been married to Aristobulus). He urged her to "yield a certain amount of power to the Pharisees, for if they praised her in return for this sign of regard, they would dispose the nation favorably toward her" (13.400). With the wisdom of hindsight, he blamed his lack of popularity with the nation on his mistreatment of them (13.401) — a hint that the individuals he had executed so cruelly were Pharisees. Moreover, he is supposed to have told her to inform the Pharisees that she, once she became ruler, would take no official action without their consent (13.403). It is interesting that Josephus does not bother to explain why Jannaeus assumed his wife, rather than one of his sons, would be his successor. At any rate, Alexandra carried out his dying wishes and in so doing gained him a finer burial than he would otherwise have had (13.406).

Salome Alexandra (76-67 BCE)

In a departure from tradition, Queen Alexandra succeeded her husband on the throne of Judea, although she was, of course, ineligible to become high priest. Josephus allows the reader to anticipate some of the problems that would soon beset the nation as he describes the two sons of Jannaeus who were passed over for the throne: "Now although Alexander had left two sons, Hyrcanus and Aristobulus, he had bequeathed the royal power to Alexandra. Of these sons the one, Hyrcanus, was incompetent to govern and in addition much preferred a quiet life, while the younger, Aristobulus, was a man of action and high spirit. As for the queen [literally "woman"] herself, she was loved by the masses because she was thought to disapprove of the crimes committed by her husband" (13.407). Alexandra named the unimpressive Hyrcanus high priest and allowed the Pharisees "to do as they liked in all matters, and also commanded the people to obey them" (13.408).

The Pharisees did take control and also executed many of those responsible for the deaths of the eight hundred in Jannaeus's time (13.408-

15). This caused a deep rift in society and created a forum for the active Aristobulus to speak against his mother publicly (13.416-18). When she became seriously ill, he openly revolted against her by taking all the fortresses in the country. While he was holding them she died, ending a reign of nine years (13.422-30); after the biblical Athaliah, she was the second queen to occupy the throne in Jerusalem. Josephus adds a highly critical postscript to his account of her reign. In it he accuses her of desiring absolute power and leaving the kingdom to regrettable heirs (13.430-32).

Hyrcanus II and Aristobulus II (67-63 BCE)

Once Alexandra was dead, her aggressive son Aristobulus fought against and defeated Hyrcanus II, the queen's heir. They signed an agreement giving Aristobulus the kingship and possibly also the high priesthood, while Hyrcanus apparently agreed to stay out of public affairs and enjoy his wealth (14.4-7). Aristobulus II might have continued as unrivaled ruler, were it not for a friend of Hyrcanus, a man named Antipater, a prominent, wealthy Idumean and father of the one who would become the notorious king Herod the Great. Antipater, who saw that it would be to his advantage to weaken Aristobulus, urged Hyrcanus and others to oppose him and eventually succeeded in his effort. Antipater persuaded Hyrcanus to escape from Jerusalem and go to Aretas, an Arab king who reigned in Petra. Aretas agreed to support Hyrcanus in return for the twelve cities Alexander Jannaeus had taken from him. As a result, Aretas moved against Aristobulus and defeated him in battle, forcing him to flee to Jerusalem. Aretas, Hyrcanus, and their supporters attacked him in the temple and subjected him and the priests there to a siege (14.8-21).

Perhaps affairs would have continued in this unedifying way, with princes of small nations battling each other endlessly for modest gains, but at this juncture a new and greater power moved into the area and changed Jewish history forever. Josephus relates that the Roman general Pompey, as he was moving through Armenia, sent his agent Scaurus ahead of his armies to Damascus. Scaurus soon advanced from there toward Judea. "On his arrival envoys came to him from both Aristobulus and Hyrcanus, each of whom asked him to come to his aid. Aristobulus offered to give him four hundred talents; and though Hyrcanus promised him no less a sum, he accepted the offer of Aristobulus, for he was both wealthy and generous and asked for more moderate terms, whereas Hyrcanus was poor and nig-

31

gardly and held out untrustworthy promises for greater concessions" (14.30-31). Scaurus then ordered Aretas to end his siege or be considered an enemy of Rome. He lifted the siege and departed for his home, but Aristobulus exploited the opportunity to attack him and Hyrcanus and soundly defeated them (14.32-33).

When Pompey himself arrived in the region, he too was visited by many delegations, including Jewish ones. Representatives of both Hyrcanus and Aristobulus approached him, and Pompey took it upon himself to adjudicate the dispute between them. While Pompey deferred his decision in the matter, Aristobulus incurred his anger by leaving and returning to Judea. The Roman general then marched into Judea and ordered Aristobulus to surrender the strongholds he held (14.37-53).

Aristobulus apparently tried to make peace with Pompey and to prevent war with him, but his efforts were frustrated by his own soldiers in Jerusalem. Pompey took him prisoner and set out to take Jerusalem. There Aristobulus's troops occupied the temple area and opposed Pompey, while the remainder of the city was handed over to him. After a siege of three months, the Romans captured the temple precincts and thus took control of the entire city. Hyrcanus had helped Pompey, and for this he received the reward of regaining the high priesthood. Pompey took a number of cities away from Judea and thus greatly reduced its borders. The city of Jerusalem fell to him in 63 BCE, the beginning of the fateful Roman rule that was to last for centuries. The Romans, who had for a long time been the allies of the Judeans, were now their masters (14.55-76).

THE ROMAN PERIOD (63 BCE AND BEYOND)

Roman control of Judea and other centers of Jewish population was to continue until the empire itself dissolved. We will survey only the first part of that long period.

The Early Years (63-37 BCE)

Pompey left Scaurus in charge of the area and turned toward Rome, taking Aristobulus and his family with him as his prisoners (14.79). Aristobulus's son Alexander managed to escape and in a short time, says Josephus, he was overrunning Judea — something the inept Hyrcanus could not prevent (14.82). The Romans were able to maintain order and control the family of Aristobulus, but it was not because the latter failed to oppose them. Some time after Alexander was defeated by the governor Gabinius, this Roman official put Hyrcanus in charge of the temple and divided Judea into five districts, each with its own sanhedrin (14.82-91). Aristobulus himself eventually escaped from Rome and attempted to regain his old position in Judea. He too was defeated by Gabinius and was brought as a prisoner to Rome for a second time, although, due to a promise Gabinius had made to his wife, Aristobulus's children were released (14.92-97). Later Gabinius had another opportunity to defeat Alexander (14.100-102). Because Aristobulus could be regarded as an opponent of Pompey, he became a pawn in Roman power politics. Julius Caesar gave him his freedom and even provided him with two legions to try to win support in the area of Syria. But Pompey's backers poisoned him and also beheaded his son Alexander (14.123-25).

In light of the pro-Roman policy pursued later by his son Herod, it is interesting to note that Antipater showed strong support for Caesar and reaped benefits from his stance. He assisted him militarily in Egypt and so impressed the noble Roman that Caesar began assigning him dangerous tasks. He made Antipater governor and confirmed Hyrcanus, who had also helped in Caesar's Egyptian campaign, in the high priesthood. Antipater and Hyrcanus continued to work together and were united in their support of the Romans (14.127-44). In fact, during the time of Hyrcanus the relation of goodwill and friendship with the Romans was again confirmed officially (14.145-48).

Antipater is credited with restoring order in the country, but, in view of Hyrcanus's listless ways, he appointed two of his own sons to high positions: he made Phasael governor of Jerusalem and the territories around it, and he "entrusted Galilee to his second son Herod, who was still quite young; he was, in fact, only fifteen years old" (14.158). Herod may actually have been somewhat older — perhaps twenty-five — at the time, ca. 47 BCE. Whatever his age, he quickly demonstrated that he was a capable and firm ruler by ridding the border area between Galilee and Syria of Ezekias (whom Josephus calls a bandit) and his men; he put them to death without trial (14.159-60). From that time on Herod cast a long shadow over Judean history. His public career would last more than four decades.

The power that Antipater and his sons had acquired and their willingness to use it aroused resentment, a feeling perhaps shared by Hyrcanus.

The Herodian Family

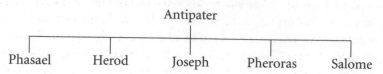

Antipater

Phasael   Herod   Joseph   Pheroras   Salome

Antipater's son Herod (Herod the Great [37-4 BCE]) had ten wives; through five of these he had children who were important in the history of the time.

1. Herod ——— Doris

   Antipater

2. Herod ——— Mariamne (Hasmonean)

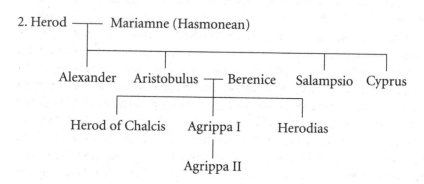

Alexander   Aristobulus ——— Berenice   Salampsio   Cyprus

Herod of Chalcis   Agrippa I   Herodias

Agrippa II

3. Herod ——— Mariamne

   Herod

4. Herod ——— Malthace

   Archelaus   Antipas   Olympias

5. Herod ——— Cleopatra

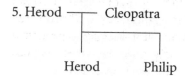

   Herod   Philip

Leading citizens persuaded Hyrcanus to take action, and, as a result, he summoned the youthful Herod to stand trial before the sanhedrin in Jerusalem. The sanhedrin in Jerusalem was a ruling and judicial body, consisting of seventy prominent men and headed by the high priest. The charge lodged against Herod was the murder of Ezekias and his band (14.168-69). The scene that Josephus depicts is a memorable one: Herod appeared before the judges surrounded by his troops and succeeded in intimidating them. It is not clear exactly what happened after this, but Herod, with powerful backing and before the sanhedrin could return a death verdict, managed to leave Jerusalem and even contemplated an invasion of the area before wiser counsel prevailed (14.172-84).

Herod continued to be the object of charges (see, e.g., 14.302-303; 14.324-26), but he always succeeded in escaping punishment (see 14.327-29). International events would soon come close to ending his career. In the year 40 BCE Parthians, a nation whose homeland lay north of Persia far to the east, invaded Syria and became involved in Jewish internal struggles. Another son of Aristobulus II, this one named Antigonus, accumulated strong support and, through bribery, he was able to win the backing of the invading Parthians. Antigonus wanted nothing less than to drive Hyrcanus and Herod from their positions and become king of the area. Herod and his brother Phasael succeeded in checking the Parthians (14.330-41), but at some point Phasael and Hyrcanus decided to deal with the Parthian commanders and while doing so were taken prisoner. The Parthians also had plans to do away with Herod. Herod fled with his family and some supporters, whom he left on top of the Judean desert fortress called Masada. Antigonus succeeded, but became concerned that the people would put Hyrcanus back in office. So, "he went up to him where he was being guarded by the Parthians, and cut off his ears, thus taking care that the high priesthood should never come to him another time, because he was now mutilated, and the law requires that this office should belong only to those who are sound of body" (14.366). Phasael apparently committed suicide while in Parthian custody (14.340-69).

Herod himself sailed for Rome, and there, with support from Mark Antony and Octavian, Herod was named king by the senate. We are told that he did not expect to receive the office but had come to request it for his wife's brother Aristobulus III who was from the Hasmonean line (14.370-87). Appointment of Herod served the need of the Romans to have an opponent of the Parthians in the office now occupied by Antigonus, who owed his position to the Parthians. Herod's appointment came in the year 40 BCE.

Appointment as king and actually ruling were two different matters, however. Herod returned to his home base in Galilee and with the military force he had mustered he advanced southward and rescued his family and friends from Masada.

Herod (37-4 BCE) and Archelaus (4 BCE–6 CE)

After many struggles, in the third year after his appointment as king, Herod, with Jewish and Roman forces, laid siege to Jerusalem. His forces took the city with massive loss of life to the defenders, who had offered powerful resistance. Antigonus was captured. Herod, who feared that many would want to restore the Hasmonean heir, bribed Mark Antony to kill Antigonus, the last of the Hasmonean rulers; Antony beheaded him (14.468-91; 15.8-10).

The aging and physically disfigured former high priest Hyrcanus, still in Parthian custody, was given his release. Although he was offered an opportunity to settle in Babylon where there was a large Jewish population (15.14), he declined and preferred to return to his homeland. According to Josephus, Herod pretended to receive him warmly when Hyrcanus actually returned to Judea, but fearing opposition, the king also appointed an undistinguished Babylonian priest as high priest in Jerusalem (15.21-22).

There seems to have been opposition to Herod's rule when he was established as king, just as there had been throughout his early career. Besides the opposition he aroused, Herod also had to contend with the fact that the former royal family, the Hasmoneans, were still prominent and enjoyed some loyalty from the populace. Herod himself, quite aware that he was from a non-royal line, was apparently reminded of the fact by others. He was forced to keep his suspicious eye on members of the Hasmonean family, and for good reason. His pro-Roman policy had stood him in good stead in his early years, and he continued his obedient behavior toward them when he was king. At first he courted the favor of the powerful Mark Antony whose influence had procured the kingship for him from the senate. Later, after the battle of Actium (31 BCE) he sagely turned his support to the winner Octavian, the future Augustus, with whom he was later to visit several times.

Through the influence of the Hasmonean Alexandra and her daughter Mariamne (Herod's wife), the king removed the high priest Hananel from office and gave it to Mariamne's brother Aristobulus in 35 BCE. Not long after his elevation, however, Herod arranged to have Aristobulus, the last Hasmonean to hold the office, drowned in a swimming pool (15.50-61). Herod's act caused him to be summoned before Mark Antony, but as always he contrived to avoid the appropriate punishment. Just four years later, in 31 BCE, Herod had the former high priest Hyrcanus executed (15.161-82). In fact, Herod killed quite a number of people who were members of his family well before his last years when his paranoia seems to have grown to exceptional levels. For example, he killed his brother Joseph (15.62-70, 80-87); his Hasmonean wife Mariamne, in 29 BCE (15.213-39); and his Hasmonean mother-in-law Alexandra, in 28 BCE (15.240-52).

One of the reasons for Herod's fame was that he was a great builder and benefactor. He is credited with paying for the construction of temples in cities outside his kingdom and for erecting whole cities (e.g. Caesarea) and fortresses (the most famous are Herodium and Masada) within his realm. In Jerusalem he built a theatre and amphitheatre as well as a palace for himself. His most famous architectural program was the Jerusalem temple itself (see 15.380-425). In 20 BCE work began on rebuilding and greatly improving the temple that had stood since 516/15 BCE. The work continued throughout the remainder of Herod's reign and long after it. In John 2:20, after Jesus had said "Destroy this temple, and in three days I will raise it up" (v. 19), the Jews responded: "This temple has been under construction for forty-six years." In fact, the work was not completed until the procuratorship of Albinus in 62-64 CE, shortly before it was destroyed in 70 CE. Interestingly enough, Herod did cut taxes twice, once by one third (20 BCE) and once by one fourth (14 BCE). One of the members of his court was Nicolaus of Damascus who became Herod's biographer and whose writings were the primary source for Josephus's extended and detailed account of the Herodian period.

The sources indicate that Herod's troubles mounted in the later years of his reign, particularly within his own family. Among his ten wives the most prominent seems to have been Mariamne, Hyrcanus's granddaughter (later he was to marry another woman named Mariamne). She and Herod were the parents of five children, two of whom — Alexander and Aristobulus — became the focus of domestic tensions. The sons were sent to Rome for their education for five or six years, at which time Herod brought them back from the capital (15.342; 16.6). The fact that the young men were Hasmonean on their mother's side inspired in them a feeling of superiority over their non-Hasmonean relatives, some of whom (especially Herod's sister Salome) responded with a campaign of slander against the two. The fact that Herod executed their mother in 29 BCE hardly improved relations with their father. To counter their influence, Herod set up another of his sons named Antipater as a likely heir to his throne. Charges against Alexander and Aristobulus eventually led Herod to denounce them before Augustus himself in 12 BCE (16.84, 87-135). They were later imprisoned by their father and accused of treason (16.320-34). Finally the two were strangled to death in 7 BCE (16.361-94).

Once the two Hasmonean princes were dead, friction between Herod and Antipater increased until Antipater too was imprisoned (17.93-141). To add to his woes, Herod was by this time ill with the physical maladies that would eventually claim his life, and the populace gave evidence that they were eager for his death. Herod received imperial permission to execute his son Antipater, which he did shortly before his own death (17.182-87). He named Archelaus, another of his sons, as his heir and also selected his son Antipas as ruler of Galilee and Perea and his son Philip as head of other territories in his kingdom (17.188-90).

Herod died in 4 BCE (17.191), in physical agony and with no love from family or nation. Josephus says that he was so concerned there would be no mourning when he died that he gave orders to have distinguished men killed at the time of his death so that the displays of grief he craved would take place. Mercifully the executions were not carried out (17.173-75). Herod himself was buried in his fortress Herodium.

Herod's death was followed by several periods of great difficulty for the Romans as they tried to maintain order in the volatile kingdom which had now lost its iron-fisted ruler. Before his son Archelaus could gain imperial confirmation of his appointment as outlined in his father's final will, he crushed a riot at the cost of many lives. The crowd had wanted Herod's counselors, who had been involved in the decision to kill two Pharisaic leaders late in Herod's reign, called to account for their action (17.206-18).

Archelaus traveled to Rome to have Herod's will confirmed, but his brother Antipas, who had been named king in an earlier will, also hastened to the imperial capital to plead his case. Other members of the Herodian family as well went to Rome to request that the kingdom be placed under direct Roman rule (17.218-27), that is, that neither brother be named king. While these groups and individuals were in Rome, troubles continued in Jerusalem. In the process of putting down one of the outbreaks of violence, the procurator Sabinus looted the temple treasury, keeping much of it for himself (17.250-64). It was at this time that Judas, a son of the Ezekias whom Herod had killed before becoming king, gathered support in Galilee and managed to steal a cache of royal weapons. His name is associated with the Zealots who were soon to play a major role in Judean history (17.271-72). Only the muscular intervention of Varus, governor of Syria, allowed the administration to crush the various uprisings in the land (17.286-98).

Augustus took his time in deciding on the succession to Herod. He heard all sides in the matter and finally confirmed Herod's last will. Much of the deceased king's territory he gave to Archelaus (4 BCE–6 CE), but he did not allow him to assume the title of king; rather, he was named an ethnarch or ruler of a nationality. Antipas (4 BCE–39 CE), who is often called Herod in the sources (e.g. Luke 13:31), was the one who executed John the Baptist (Matt. 14:6-11; Mark 6:21-28; Luke 9:9; *Ant.* 18.117-19); Jesus also appeared before him (Luke 23:7-12). He and Philip (4 BCE–33/34 CE) received the more limited territories that were named in the will and were given the title of tetrarch. In this way Herod's sizable kingdom was broken down into several smaller administrative units (17.317-23).

The reign of Archelaus was short and regrettable. His despotic, tyrannical ways eventually caused a delegation of Jewish and Samaritan nobles to journey to Rome where they complained to the emperor about his misrule. Augustus summoned Archelaus to the capital, removed him from his position as ethnarch, and banished him to Gaul (where Antipas would also be sent much later; 17.342-43).

Direct Roman Rule (6-66 CE)

At this point, in 6 CE, the government of Judea took on a rather different form. The territory was placed directly under Roman administration, and it was in some sense joined to the province of Syria. The Roman rulers in the area tended not to be sensitive to distinctive Jewish ways (something the Herods did at least understand); dire consequences followed for the fate of the region and its inhabitants. This period of Roman rule can be divided into two parts: during the first (6-41 CE) officials with the title prefect were placed in charge, while from 44-66 the territory was governed by procurators. Between those two periods there was a brief interlude when the Herodian Agrippa I served as king (41-44).

The prefects who governed from 6-41 were loosely under the control of the Roman legates in the province of Syria. They, and later the procurators, had their official residence in the seaside city of Caesarea, which served as the capital of Judea. They would, however, move temporarily to Jerusalem to boost the security of the area when the great festivals attracted large numbers of Jews to the holy city (which is why Pontius Pilate, a prefect, was in Jerusalem when Jesus was arrested and tried).

Six or seven men held the office of prefect between 6 and 41 CE. The best known of them is Pontius Pilate, who governed from 26 to 36. The Alexandrian Jewish philosopher Philo quoted a letter from King Agrippa I in which the king described Pilate as harsh, greedy, and cruel (*Legatio* 38.302). The sources credit him with a number of actions that reflected his failure to take Jewish views sufficiently into account. For example, he ordered his troops to enter Jerusalem at night with their standards (on which the emperor's image was found, a violation of the second commandment). Jewish pressure forced him to have the images removed a few days later (18.55-59). On another occasion he used temple funds to build an aqueduct that brought water to Jerusalem; his act led to strong opposition, which Pilate suppressed with much bloodshed (18.60-62; see Luke 13:1 for the time when Pilate mixed the blood of some Galileans with their sacrifices). In the end Pilate was removed from his post for the excessive cruelty with which he broke up a seemingly harmless crowd in Samaritan territory (18.87, 89).

An end came to this phase of Jewish history with the death of the deranged emperor Caligula (37-41), who had ordered that a statue of himself be erected in the temple in Jerusalem. Huge numbers of troops were moved to Palestine to enforce the edict (18.262), although the emperor's enthusiasm for the statue was not shared by Petronius, the governor of Syria, who would have to handle the violence it would spark. Petronius did manage to stall implementation of the edict, and not long thereafter — and to no one's sorrow — the emperor was murdered (18.263-72).

The new emperor Claudius (41-54) wasted little time in naming Agrippa, a grandson of Herod the Great, as king of Judea, Samaria, and all the territories that had belonged to his grandfather (actually Caligula had already appointed him to the post; see *Ant.* 19.274-77). Agrippa seems to have been a pious man, at least when he was in his own territory. He even read the appropriate portion from Deuteronomy during the festival of tabernacles, just as the book prescribed that the king was to do (see Deut. 17:18-20; see also Acts 12:1-19). The king remained in office only a short time, however; he died in 44, some time after he had been acclaimed as a god by a group of flatterers (*Ant.* 19.343-52; Acts 12:20-23).

Following his death the decision was made not to give his territories to his son Agrippa II but to place them once again under direct Roman control. From then on the officers whom the Romans appointed bore the title procurator. In general it can be said that these non-Jewish rulers failed to respect Jewish religious sensibilities sufficiently. In this volatile area the chief Roman goal was maintaining public order. Josephus writes about all of the procurators, and several of them are mentioned in the book of Acts. One of the first men to hold the office was Tiberius Julius Alexander (approximately 46-48) who was the Jewish philosopher Philo's nephew; he had rejected his ancestral religion and risen to high rank in the Roman world. The famine mentioned in Acts 11:28-30 occurred during his administration. While the procurators ruled, there were frequent outbreaks of violence for one reason or another, and just as frequent forceful reactions on the part of the Romans. For example, during the time of Felix (approximately 52-60) disturbances were nearly continuous, and he himself is roundly criticized in the sources for his cruelty in handling the situation. During his term the Zealots became more active; Josephus says that they agreed with the Pharisees but also refused to acknowledge anyone but God as ruler. An even more radical group was called the Sicarii after the name of the daggers they carried and used (20.185-87). Josephus credits "brigands" with murdering the high priest Jonathan, a man whose moderate views they refused to tolerate (20.161-63). And these were not the only religious groups who were strongly interested in ending Roman rule and oppression (see 20.167-72). The apostle Paul had an audience with this Felix (see Acts 23-24) who was eventually recalled to Rome in 60 CE. The troubles continued under his successor Porcius Festus (see Acts 24:27) whose term ended in 62 CE.

The next procurator, Albinus, is said to have been a rapacious tyrant who was open to bribery from anyone (20.197-215). The last of the procurators was a man named Gessius Florus (64-66) who, Josephus wrote, was the worst of all, a public bandit who plundered whole cities (20.252-58). At the end of his term of office, after a long period of unrest, tension, and violence — a time of provocations on both sides — the Jewish Revolt against Rome broke out. It was the spring of 66 CE.

The First Jewish Revolt against Rome (66-73 CE)

One of the procurator Florus's ill-advised acts may have been the trigger that started the largest, longest lasting Jewish attempt to throw off Roman rule. After the greedy governor had removed a large amount of money from the ever inviting temple treasury, the predictable Jewish opposition was aroused. In this case, the opposition included personal abuse of Florus, whose poverty, the crowd suggested, had led him to rob the temple. In his rage at being mocked for his greed he allowed his troops to sack parts of Jerusalem (*War* 2.293-308). Around this time a group of Sicarii seized the mighty fortress of Masada.

In a momentous step, one that was opposed by many Jewish leaders, the practice of offering a sacrifice daily at the temple for the emperor was stopped under the influence of Eleazar, the son of the high priest (2.408-21). Rebels managed to take over the entire city of Jerusalem, massacring the last detachment of Roman soldiers (to whom they had promised safe passage; 2.449-56). Fighting between Jews and non-Jews also broke out in a number of other cities.

The initial Roman response came from Cestius Gallus, the governor of Syria, who invaded the land with a large force. When he reached Jerusalem, he attacked the temple mount but was unable to take it. For unknown reasons he then retreated, and as he withdrew toward Antioch he was attacked by rebel forces who succeeded in capturing large amounts of war materiel from him. Josephus observes that the jubilation over this victory deprived the Jewish peace party of any chance of persuading the rebels to desist. In the days that followed, prominent Jews, including Josephus himself, were placed in charge of the resistance to the expected Roman response. Josephus was assigned the position of military commander in Galilee (the likely place for a Roman invasion), but he was so strongly opposed there by one John of Gischala (a town in Galilee) that he barely succeeded in saving his life and new job.

In the year 67 the emperor Nero placed responsibility for suppressing the Jewish uprising in the hands of the veteran general Vespasian, assisted by his son Titus. They commanded three legions and many other troops. Large parts of Josephus's northern army apparently deserted him even before the Romans came into sight, although Vespasian and Titus did have to subdue a few fortified cities in the region, among which was Jotapata, north of Sepphoris. There Josephus and the forces that remained with him held out for a couple of months before the place was taken amid much carnage and the enslavement of the Jewish survivors. Josephus claims that he was saved (or saved himself) almost miraculously. He and forty companions agreed, after Josephus had wanted to surrender, to kill one another in an order determined by casting lots; as it turned out, Josephus was the last one designated by the lot, and now freed from his companions he surrendered as he had originally intended. He writes that he was brought before Vespasian and predicted that the general would become emperor, a prediction that did not win him his immediate freedom but did gain him more gentle treatment (3.340-408). Vespasian also took the city of Gamala after suffering heavy losses. The result of these and other victories was that the northern part of the country was under firm Roman control by the end of the campaigning season of 67 CE.

One would think that such ominous news from the north would unify the rebel leaders in Jerusalem, but just the opposite occurred, according to Josephus. The Zealots, now led by John of Gischala (he had escaped from that Galilean city just before the gates were opened to the Romans), gained sufficient numbers and influence to take control of the situation in Jerusalem. They killed a number of prominent Jews who opposed them and even appointed their own high priest. The Zealots increased their strength by inviting Idumean forces into the city, and in this way the more aristocratic early leaders of the revolt lost power, and frequently their lives as well.

Josephus presents a picture of disorganization in the capital, but, whoever was in charge, coins were minted by Jewish authorities throughout the war. None of the Jewish coins bears the name of a leader, but they have paleo-Hebrew inscriptions. In years one through three it is "Jerusalem the holy" (some bronze coins have "the freedom of Zion"), but in the fourth year one reads "for the redemption of Zion," perhaps expressing hope for divine intervention.

Early in 68 CE Vespasian's forces subdued Perea on the east side of the Jordan River and moved easily through other parts of the country. Once the land was largely under his control, Vespasian prepared to lay siege to Jerusalem. But at that time (June of the year 68) he received the news that Nero was dead; since he was an astute and powerful man, he decided to await further developments. As it turned out, developments came swiftly, as several men held the imperial office in a single year. In 69 Vespasian resumed his military operations and again turned his attention to Jerusalem, after taking several other places. Inside the city a new power had arrived in the wake of a violent period of Zealot rule, Simon Bar-Giora. The result was that the city now had two harsh masters rather than one.

On July 1, 69, Vespasian was acclaimed emperor by the legions stationed in Egypt, and their nomination was soon seconded by the legions in Syria and Palestine. As he was now the major player in the struggle for the throne, the war effort in Judea slowed. It was not until the year 70 that he sent Titus from Egypt to Palestine. During the time when Vespasian was preoccupied with the imperial issue, the situation in Jerusalem had worsened. It turns out that Simon Bar-Giora's son Eleazar had formed a third group that vied with his father's men and with the Zealots for control of the city. In their hatred for one another the groups burned large amounts of the precious and dwindling food supply in the city so that their opponents would not get control of it.

In 70 CE Titus laid siege to Jerusalem with his four legions and several other contingents of troops. There were some surprisingly successful attacks by Jewish groups, although the factional bloodletting is supposed to have continued unabated in the city. Titus and his forces systematically took each of Jerusalem's three walls by smashing away at them with their battering rams. In this time of extreme peril, says Josephus, the fighting between Jewish groups in the city finally gave way to a unity of purpose. As resistance continued, Titus ordered that a stone wall be raised around Jerusalem to prevent import of supplies to an already starving population. Once the Roman forces made their way into the city, the temple compound became the site of intense fighting. Josephus (who was in the Roman camp) says that at a Roman council of war a decision was made to spare the temple itself. Nevertheless, in the course of the conflict the building was burned. It had been finished only a few years before during Albinus's procuratorship. Once they had destroyed the temple, the Roman forces completed the conquest by taking the upper city as well. In this way the second temple period ended.

The defeat of Jerusalem had the expected result: the survivors were sent off to such fates as gladiatorial combat or the mines; others were executed. The surviving leaders, Simon and John and others, were saved to be paraded in Titus's triumph in Rome. The triumph was celebrated by Titus, his father Vespasian, and his brother Domitian in 71. At that point Simon Bar-Giora was executed. In the triumphal procession the table of show bread and the menorah from the temple were also put on display. The Romans struck an unusual number of coins to broadcast their victory over the Jews.

The work of the Roman forces did not entirely cease with the destruction of Jerusalem because three fortresses remained in rebel hands. Herodium and Macherus fell quickly, but Masada remained a holdout. The new governor of the area, Flavius Silva (73/74-81), was given the unenviable task of taking the virtually impregnable mountain fortress located in the boiling Judean wilderness. As noted earlier, Masada had been occupied by a band of Sicarii very early in the revolt; their leader was a man named Eleazar ben Yair. The Romans pitched their camps around Masada and began building up the western spur so that they could move a battering ram into position to attack the wall around the fortress. Eventually they breached the wall and burned another one that defenders had hastily erected. Eleazar is supposed to have given two speeches to the defenders, urging them that it was the honorable thing for each of the men to kill his family and then himself to escape the horrible fates that awaited them all at Roman hands. Josephus reports that some nine hundred died in this fashion, so that when the Romans reached the top of Masada they were greeted by a mass of dead bodies (and a mere handful of survivors who had hidden and thus avoided execution by their kinsmen). Masada was taken in the year 73 (possibly 74).

Jerusalem now lay in ruins. Its spectacular temple was only a memory, and the holy city became the base for a detachment of the tenth Roman legion. Little is known about events in Judea after the war, but it is safe to say that an old way of life, in which the temple and its priests and the sanhedrin played a central role, had come to an end. The sources do report that a number of Jewish scholars gathered as a kind of academy in the city of Yavneh (Jamnia) under the leadership of Rabbi Yohanan ben Zakkai and later Gamaliel II. Their discussions and decisions were to have a great effect on Judaism as it redefined itself in the postwar years as a community centered on the Torah, not on the temple and the sacrificial cult.

The events of 70 CE presumably had a profound impact on the survivors, although we have little information other than what Josephus tells us. The human toll was enormous and the religious implications proved to be massive. One way in which we can gauge the religious trauma is by looking at two apocalypses which were written in response to the loss of Jerusalem and the temple: 4 Ezra and 2 Baruch. Both of these books purport to be written by the biblical characters for whom they are named, and both give as their setting the aftermath of the Babylonian destruction of Jerusalem and the first temple. It soon becomes clear in reading them, however, that they are responding to the disaster of 70 CE and raising searching questions about it. The very existence of these books shows that the apocalyptic mentality which may well have played a role in fanning enthusiasm for the revolt did not perish with the flames of 70 CE, but the two apocalypses also demonstrate that the destruction strongly influenced the contents of such works. In them the revelations concern that destruction, the reasons for it, and what is to follow it. Both may have been written around the year 100 CE, about thirty years after the tragic events.

Fourth Ezra is the name given to a sixteen-chapter book which actually incorporates three independent works: chapters 1–2 (called by scholars 5 Ezra) and chapters 15–16 (called 6 Ezra), both Christian compositions, sandwich a Jewish apocalypse in chapters 3–14. In that apocalypse a character named Salathiel, who is identified as Ezra, has seven visions while he is in Babylon. In the visions Ezra raises anguished questions about the destruction of Jerusalem and about divine justice, and the angel Uriel attempts to handle his concerns — not always to Ezra's full satisfaction. In the first vision (3:1–5:20) he contrasts the prosperity of wicked nations with the humbled condition of God's covenant people, but his queries soon turn to the end and when it will be. Uriel assures Ezra that he does not understand God's ways but does tell him some signs of the end. Visions 2 (5:21–6:34) and 3 (6:35–9:25) continue these themes, although there is some development in them as Ezra comes to accept more of what the angel says. With vision 4 (9:26–10:59) a change of content occurs. Ezra sees a woman who is mourning bitterly in a field away from the city (9:38–10:28). When he asks why she is weeping so, she explains that after thirty years of desperately wanting a child she gave birth to a son and raised him with great care but he died at his wedding. As a result she plans to fast and mourn until she herself dies. Ezra scolds her for focusing on her private grief when mother Zion has lost so many of her children. After a time the weeping woman is transformed before his eyes so that he no longer sees a woman but a shining city. Uriel interprets the vision (10:29-59) by identifying the woman as Zion. After three thousand years from creation (= the woman's thirty barren years) Solomon began the sacrificial cult in the temple, and the lifetime of the child was the time the cult continued. His death symbolized the destruction of Jerusalem. The miraculously transformed woman was the new Jerusalem of the future, a woman made by a divine miracle, it seems, not by dint of human effort.

Ezra's fifth vision (chaps. 11–12) illustrates for us how the author has reflected on an earlier apocalypse (Dan. 7) and interpreted it in light of his experiences. In the vision (11:1–12:3) he sees an eagle, "which had twelve feathered wings and three heads" (11:1). It emerged from the sea and ruled the entire earth. The wings rule one after the other but finally disappear leaving only the three heads and some smaller wings. Eventually a lion comes forth, identifies the eagle as the fourth beast (that is, of Daniel's vision), and announces his complete destruction due to his unjust and violent reign. In 12:3b-9 a frightened Ezra requests an interpretation, which he receives in 12:10-39. The angel tells him that the eagle is indeed the fourth kingdom of Daniel's vision (12:11). That a reinterpretation of the danielic vision is here taking place the angel admits: "But it was not explained to him as I now explain or have explained it to you" (v. 12). The twelve wings are kings, the second of whom rules longer than any of the others. The three heads are another group of kings who "shall rule the earth and its inhabitants more oppressively than all who were before them; therefore they are called the heads of the eagle. For it is they who shall sum up his wickedness and perform his last actions" (12:23-25). The lion, says the angel, is the messiah from the line of David who will first criticize and then destroy the eagle. He will also "deliver in mercy the remnant of my people" (v. 34) and rule them during a temporary messianic kingdom until the final judgment (v. 34). Not all details in the vision correspond with our information about Roman history, but the three heads do indeed appear to be the three Flavian emperors, Vespasian, Titus, and Domitian, the first two of whom were of painful memory to the Jewish people, while Domitian (81-96) may still have been ruling when 4 Ezra was written. The point that emerges from the vision, one that arises from study of an older apocalyptic text, is that God had foretold all the events of the Roman period, including the horrors of 70 CE, to Ezra centuries before. But, even more importantly, he also located the future destruction of Rome in that same plan, a plan that he will carry out through his messiah.

Some of the teachings in the fifth vision come to further expression in the sixth (chap. 13) which speaks of one like a man who comes from the sea (the danielic tradition continues here as well). In it the one like a man is attacked by a great multitude. He makes a mountain on which he stands and from which he destroys his enemies with flames from his mouth. He then gathers another multitude who are peaceful. According to the divine interpretation, the man like being is God's son (that is, the messiah) who from Mt. Zion defeats the nations with the law (= the fire) and gathers the ten tribes from afar to join those in Zion.

The final vision of Ezra (chap. 14) involves a scene in which the seer, empowered by a drink "of something like water, but its color was like fire" (14:39), dictated ninety-four books to five scribes within a Moses-like period of forty days. Those books were the twenty-four of the Hebrew Bible and seventy others from the tradition. The twenty-four were for all to read, while the seventy were only for the wise. Thus, after the destruction, the scriptures are restored by inspiration through a second Moses, and the traditions of the people are also preserved but under more guarded conditions. All is in place for the nation to carry on.

These visions in 4 Ezra assure the seer that the end has been planned, will be preceded by certain signs, and will result in the deliverance of the righteous and the destruction of the wicked. The exact time is not foretold, but Ezra is also informed that it is not far away (e.g., 14:10-12). In the context in which the text was written another theme may have been even more dominant to the reader: deliverance will come, the Roman beast will be destroyed, but that destruction will not come about through another armed uprising. Rather, in his good time God will effect it through his son the messiah. The future victory would be miraculous, not the result of weapons and military strategy.

That message finds an echo in a number of passages in the contemporary apocalypse called 2 Baruch, a work that parallels 4 Ezra in many ways. In it the apocalypse of the forest, vine, fountain, and cedar (35–40) resembles the eagle vision (4 Ezra 11–12). Its apocalypse of clouds (53–74) surveys the twelve parts of history and predicts the destruction of the last great oppressor before the judgment and rule of the messiah. Again, this will come about by divine action effected through God's messiah.

The voice that sounds in 4 Ezra and 2 Baruch was to be drowned out a few decades later when the second revolt broke out.

The Bar Kokhba Revolt (132-135 CE)

Although it occurred after the end of the second temple period, brief mention should be made of the Bar Kokhba Revolt. During the reign of the emperor Hadrian (117-38) a second, large-scale rebellion broke out in Palestine. The causes for it are not clear, although there is some evidence that Hadrian had banned the practice of circumcision. His official act seems not to have been directed at the Jews alone, as other peoples also practiced the rite. Hadrian may have banned circumcision because it was considered barbarous and similar to castration, another practice that had earlier been proscribed. In addition, the emperor was planning to build a new city (something he did frequently) on the ruins of Jerusalem. The city, Aelia Capitolina as it was to be called, would include a temple to Jupiter Capitolinus. The evidence of coins now suggests that the foundation of the city was a cause for the revolt. Opposition by the Jews was kept in check while Hadrian was traveling in the east, but when he departed a revolt broke out in the year 132 CE. Perhaps it is pertinent that this was sixty-two years after the destruction of the temple. It is possible that some Jews thought that, like the second temple which was completed seventy years after the first was destroyed, a third temple would be constructed at a similar remove from the catastrophe of 70 CE. Some of the coins struck during the revolt show the facade of the temple on them; perhaps this too reflects an interest in erecting another temple.

The leader of the Jewish forces was a man whose name was Simon Bar Kosiba, as we now know from a number of documents dating from his time, found in sites in the Judean desert (at Naḥal Hever and other places). It is said that the influential Rabbi Akiba called him the son of the star (Bar Kokhba), referring to the prediction in Numbers 24:17 that a "star shall come out of Jacob." The passage was understood messianically, and thus Akiba would have been recognizing the leader of the revolt as a messiah. Bar Kokhba took the title "prince of Israel" and was associated with a priest named Eleazar (both are mentioned on coins of the first year). It may be that the rebels took the area of Jerusalem early in the revolt; they certainly minted their own coins (many have been found) and dated them by "year one of the redemption of Israel," "year two of the freedom of Israel," and "for the freedom of Jerusalem" (years three and four). Simon's name continues to appear on the coins throughout the revolt.

Bar Kokhba and his forces eventually made their last stand against the Romans at a fortress called Bether, located southwest of Jerusalem. It fell in the year 135 CE, and there Bar Kokhba met his death. The devastation brought on by the violence of the revolt and the efforts to smash it was again immense. Once again thousands of lives were lost and numerous people enslaved. Jerusalem itself continued to be Aelia Capitolina, and the Jews were not permitted to enter it. A temple to Jupiter Capitolinus was in fact built on the old temple site.

APPENDIX ON EGYPTIAN JUDAISM

Since it was not convenient to incorporate the history of the Jews in Egypt into the preceding survey of the last two centuries BCE and the first century or so CE, it will be useful to add a short sketch of it at this point. At earlier places in the narrative we examined the Elephantine community, the story about the translation of the law, and the Tobiad Romance for the information they gave about the Jewish community in Egypt and relations between Jews of the Holy Land and those of Egypt. Although our evidence remains spotty for Egyptian Judaism in later periods, it is obvious that some Jews gained high positions in Egypt and some made intellectual contributions that have in part survived. The rich harvest of papyri from Egypt have cast surprising light on the lives of Jews from various places and social strata. From early Hellenistic times Jews served in the Ptolemaic army and bureaucracy, and in Alexandria they were at some point given their own quarter of the city (see Josephus, *War* 2.488). It may be that the Jewish chronographer Demetrius wrote during the reign of Ptolemy IV Philopator (221-204 BCE). The surviving fragments of his work indicate that he set biblical history within the chronological framework of Greek mythology and history.

When the high priest Onias III was removed from his post (175 BCE) and later executed, his son Onias IV went to Egypt (*Ant.* 12.387) where he was well received by the monarch, Ptolemy VI Philometor (180-145 BCE). Onias settled in Leontopolis at the southeastern tip of the Nile delta, and there he gathered troops around himself and also built a temple where sacrifices were offered until it was destroyed in 73 CE (see *War* 7.421-36; *Ant.* 13.62-73). With his army Onias played an active role for some time in Egyptian power politics. Josephus even claims that Ptolemy and his wife Cleopatra II entrusted the kingdom to the Jews and placed the entire army under the command of Onias and a fellow Jew named Dositheus (see *Against Apion* 2.49). When Philometor died in 145 BCE, a war broke out between Cleopatra II with her allies and Philometor's brother and long-time rival Ptolemy VII Euergetes II Physcon. Onias led his troops to Alexandria in support of the queen, but Physcon won out and the Jews of Alexandria who had sided with Onias suffered reprisals for their stand (*Against Apion* 2.49-56; this has been suggested as the historical kernel behind 3 Maccabees, which places the events at an earlier time). Later, Onias's two sons Chelkias and Ananias led the Oniad troops during another dynastic quarrel (*Ant.* 13.349). The same Ananias advised Cleopatra III not to invade Judea in the time of Alexander Jannaeus (*Ant.* 13.352-55). The Jews from Leontopolis offered support to the side of Julius Caesar in 48-47 BCE, when he was in difficult straits in Alexandria (*War* 1.187-92; *Ant.* 14.127-32).

Several Jewish writers were active in this period. In the reign of Ptolemy VI Philometor, Aristobulus philosophized about the nature of God, dealt with the date of passover, and claimed that Greek philosophers such as Plato borrowed ideas from the Torah. According to 2 Maccabees 1:10, he was a teacher of the king (if the same Aristobulus is meant). Artapanus wrote about Jewish heroes such as Abraham, Joseph, and especially Moses who were associated with Egypt. His dates are unknown, but he was active before 100 BCE. Finally, Ezekiel at some point in the second century BCE recast the exodus story in the form of a Greek tragedy.

The Roman period was to bring some difficult moments for the Jews of Egypt, although it began well under Augustus's rule, when they enjoyed a secure status. However, in 38 CE a major conflict erupted between the Alexandrian Greeks and Jews at the time when Flaccus was the governor. He was thrust into a difficult political situation when Gaius Caligula became emperor in 37 CE, and the opponents of the Jews apparently exploited his weakness. The trigger for the riots was the visit of the Jewish king Agrippa I to Alexandria. The Greeks of the city humiliated him by staging a mock parade for the king. The ensuing violence led to many deaths and much destruction of property including desecration of synagogues, in which images of the emperor were installed. The governor abrogated Jewish rights, flogged some of their leaders, and had others tortured to death. Flaccus was eventually arrested, and both the Greeks and the Jews were allowed to send delegations to plead their cases before the emperor. This was the delegation headed by Philo of Alexandria, who is our major source of information for the events of this period. The leader of the Greek delegation was the Homeric scholar Apion, who authored a five-volume work against the Jews (Josephus responded to it in *Against Apion*). As the delegations awaited an imperial audience, they received news of the emperor's desire to have a statue of himself erected in the Jerusalem temple. But the emperor soon died and thus defused that crisis. The new emperor Claudius (41-54 CE) was met by a second Jewish delegation from Alexandria. He was annoyed to have to deal with two opposing groups representing the Jews of Alexandria. Claudius's decision in the matter is preserved in *Antiquities* 19.280-85, and another version has been preserved on a papyrus found in Egypt. He seems to have allowed the Jews to follow their own practices but may have excluded them from citizenship — a terrible and costly blow to high-ranking individuals like Philo.

There were more clashes between the Jews and their opponents in 66 CE when the first revolt broke out in Judea and Galilee. This time Philo's nephew Tiberius Julius Alexander was the governor, and he suppressed the outbreak with huge numbers of casualties (*War* 2.494-98). In the next decades tensions continued until they finally exploded into a violent war in 116-17 CE, coinciding with revolts in different parts of the diaspora. The

Jewish revolt in Egypt spread throughout the country and was put down only with great effort on the part of the administration. The vehemence of the rebellion was matched by the ruthlessness with which it was defeated. As a result the once populous Jewish community of Egypt was reduced to a small band of survivors.

CHAPTER 2

Jewish Literature
of the Second Temple Period

A vast and relatively unknown literature has survived from the second temple period — texts written by Jews living in the land of Judah and in the far-flung diaspora. The earliest of these works are in the Bible, while most of them were not admitted into the canon of scripture and thus have experienced varied textual histories.

SECOND TEMPLE TEXTS
IN THE HEBREW BIBLE

The oldest surviving literature of the second temple period became a part of the Hebrew Bible itself. There is considerable debate among scholars regarding the dates of some scriptural texts. For example, many experts assign the priestly literature in the Pentateuch (e.g., Leviticus) to the time after the exile, while others argue that it comes from a much earlier time. Many would also place the so-called Third Isaiah (Isa. 56–66) in the period of the return, and perhaps other texts were written at roughly the same time. Additonal books — for example, Ruth, Joel, and Jonah — have been terribly difficult to situate historically, as have wisdom compositions such as Proverbs and Job with their more timeless themes.

There is, however, another series of biblical books that undoubtedly originated while the second temple stood, because they describe that time or presuppose conditions and characters from it. These books are (using the order of English Bibles): 1–2 Chronicles, Ezra, Nehemiah, Esther, some Psalms, Ecclesiastes, Daniel, Haggai, Zechariah, and Malachi. Since there are many fine introductions to these biblical books, they will not be included in the following survey. The historical information that can be derived from them was summarized in the first part of this book.

While there is debate about when various parts of the Bible may have been written, one does not have to read very far into second temple Jewish literature to become aware that there was a shared body of older written material which was very important to Jewish authors of varied times and places. This is apparent already in early second temple texts such as Nehemiah, where actions are taken on the basis of what was written in Moses' law (see, e.g., Neh. 8).

THE CLASSIFICATION OF SECOND TEMPLE LITERATURE

There are some practical problems that arise in canvassing the extensive Jewish literature of the second temple period. One problem concerns the traditional categories that have been used to classify the texts. The voluminous writings of the Jewish scholars Philo and Josephus have always been treated as a category of their own, while substantial sets of other texts have been subsumed under the headings *Apocrypha* and *Pseudepigrapha*. Modern discoveries have added exponentially to this already sizable corpus. Because they are still widely used today, it will be useful to clarify the meaning of the terms *Apocrypha* and *Pseudepigrapha* and also to mention some of the difficulties inherent in retaining the categories.

Apocrypha

This word has been applied to different books over the years. There are at least two senses that can be distinguished.

The Catholic Deuterocanonical Books

Protestants sometimes term these book the Apocrypha. They are found in the present Catholic Old Testament but not in the Hebrew Bible (= the Protestant Old Testament; for convenience, just the term Hebrew Bible will be used to designate the Protestant Old Testament hereafter). The deuterocanonical books, each of which will be treated separately in the survey below, include:

1. *Tobit*
2. *Judith* (Tobit and Judith appear after Nehemiah in the Catholic Old Testament)
3. *1 Maccabees*
4. *2 Maccabees* (1-2 Maccabees appear after Esther)
5. *Wisdom* (or *Wisdom of Solomon;* placed after Song of Solomon)
6. *Ecclesiasticus* (or *Sirach;* after Wisdom)
7. *Baruch* (after Lamentations; the sixth chapter is sometimes given a separate title, *Epistle of Jeremiah*)

In addition to these seven books, two works found in the Hebrew Bible have different forms in Catholic Bibles:

- *Esther* (the version of Esther in the Catholic Old Testament has all of the text of Esther in the Hebrew Bible plus six additional sections scattered throughout; it appears after Judith)
- *Daniel* (placed after Ezekiel; the version of Daniel in the Catholic Old Testament has all of the text of Daniel in the Hebrew Bible plus three extra compositions: *Susanna, The Prayer of Azariah and the Song of the Three Young Men,* and *Bel and the Dragon*).

Works in Greek Bibles but Not in the Hebrew Bible

The term *apocrypha* can also be used for the extra books found in Greek manuscripts of the Old Testament. Included are all of the Catholic deuterocanonical works, plus a few more. For example, the most widely used edition of the Greek Old Testament, *Septuaginta* edited by A. Rahlfs, is primarily based on three great ancient codices: Codex Vaticanus, Codex Sinaiticus, and Codex Alexandrinus. In it one finds all of the books in the Hebrew Bible and all of the Catholic deuterocanonicals plus:

- *3–4 Maccabees*
- *1 Esdras* (a work combining and supplementing material from the end of 2 Chronicles, Ezra, and Nehemiah)
- *Psalms of Solomon*
- *Odes* (a collection of hymns drawn mostly from the Bible, e.g., Hannah's song, Simeon's song)

These compositions, with the exception of *4 Maccabees* and *Odes* (which date from a later time), will be included in the survey below.

If these two senses of apocrypha are not carefully distinguished, confusion may result. Part of the potential confusion is due to the fact that the official list of the deuterocanonical books was not established for Catholics until the Council of Trent (1545-63); before that time it was less clear which books were included in Christian Bibles beyond the ones in the Hebrew Bible.

Pseudepigrapha

The word refers, literally, to writings that have a false name placed over them. That is, a pseudepigraph claims as its author a famous, usually ancient person who did not actually write the book (Adam and Enoch are examples). It could be called a reverse form of plagiarism — writing something oneself and crediting it to someone else. However, this feature of pseudepigraphy is not found in all books that scholars have assigned to the category Pseudepigrapha; in fact, the word has been used rather loosely to encompass a great variety of books from various times and places and belonging to sundry literary types. To add to the confusion, Catholic authors at times call these works Apocrypha, and a book like the Wisdom of Solomon is actually a pseudepigraph though it is classified among the deuterocanonicals/Apocrypha.

For the last century or so in the western world there has been a set of Jewish texts that people have regarded as *the* Pseudepigrapha. These are the texts included in the great collections compiled by R. H. Charles in English (*The Apocrypha and Pseudepigrapha of the Old Testament in English* [Oxford: Clarendon Press, 1913]; volume 2 contains the Pseudepigrapha) and E. Kautzsch in German (*Die Apokryphen und Pseudepigraphen des Alten Testaments* [Tübingen: Mohr (Siebeck), 1900]; volume 2 has the Pseudepigrapha). Charles's collection included the following books (with the categories under which he arranged them):

Primitive History Rewritten from the Standpoint of the Law
> *The Book of Jubilees*

Sacred Legends
> *The Letter of Aristeas*
> *The Books of Adam and Eve*
> *The Martyrdom of Isaiah*

Apocalypses
> *1 Enoch*
> *The Testaments of the XII Patriarchs*
> *The Sibylline Oracles*
> *The Assumption of Moses*
> *2 Enoch, or the Book of the Secrets of Enoch*
> *2 Baruch, or the Syriac Apocalypse of Baruch*
> *3 Baruch, or the Greek Apocalypse of Baruch*
> *4 Ezra*

Psalms
> *The Psalms of Solomon*

Ethics and Wisdom Literature
> *4 Maccabees*
> *Pirkē Aboth*
> *The Story of Aḥiḳar*

History
> *The Fragments of a Zadokite Work*

These seventeen texts, because of the wide influence and circulation of the volume that Charles edited, became modestly well known; what was less often considered was that Charles's purpose was not to be exhaustive but selective. Some of the works he included were curious choices indeed. For example, it is difficult to see how the *Letter of Aristeas* could be called a pseudepigraph, while *Pirke Avot* is a rabbinic text, and the *Fragments of a Zadokite Work* is a largely legal work (hardly history) that has now also been found among the Dead Sea Scrolls. Kautzsch's collection contained all of the same texts less *2 Enoch*, *Pirke Avot*, and the *Story of Ahiqar*.

A more recent and also very widely used collection has been edited by J. Charlesworth under the title *The Old Testament Pseudepigrapha* (Garden City, NY: Doubleday, 1983, 1985). It is a two-volume work that includes sixty-three texts (all of those in Charles except *Pirke Avot* and *Fragments of a Zadokite Work*, and many more). These volumes have the advantage that they allow the reader to see more of the full extent of surviving second temple literature, but the definition of *pseudepigrapha* that underlies the collection is so vague that the word has become almost a catch-all for whatever is left after one eliminates the books of the Bible, the writings of Philo and Josephus, and the Dead Sea Scrolls.

A difficulty involved in using the traditional categories Apocrypha and Pseudepigrapha is that they are artificial in the sense that they were later imposed on a literary corpus for which they are not always entirely appropriate. Moreover, they involve value judgments: to term a book *biblical* places it on one level (which not everyone would define in the same way), while to place it among the Apocrypha is to cast some doubt on it, to distinguish it from a book that is more authentic in some sense. The term *Pseudepigrapha* contains within it the idea of falsehood and can lead to a denigration of such texts without considering their purposes(s) and the level of authority ascribed to some of them by at least some people in the second temple period.

In view of the difficulties involved in employing the categories Apocrypha and Pseudepigrapha, it seems wiser to survey the Jewish literature of the second temple period in chronological order. This approach allows us to dodge some pitfalls associated with the traditional categories. However, there are often disputes about the date or dates of material in a composition; these debates arise because insufficient information about the author and/or situation of a work has survived. Nevertheless, it is often possible to suggest a rough chronological order, and where there are questions or unresolved difficulties these will be noted.

The approach adopted here is to survey the texts by literary types, following chronological order within each category if possible. We have also decided to treat the great modern discoveries of texts separately, although where they overlap with the other categories, this will be indicated. The section on the discoveries follows the survey of the literature.

JEWISH WRITINGS OF
THE SECOND TEMPLE PERIOD

Narrative Works

Histories

> *(1) 1 Esdras (neither deuterocanonical nor apocryphal; it is considered authoritative by the Eastern churches and is therefore often included in translations of the Apocrypha)*

There are several books that circulate under the name of Ezra (Esdras in Greek). There is, of course, the familiar biblical book of Ezra that tells of the return from exile and rebuilding of the temple (538-516/15 BCE) and of Ezra's later mission (458 BCE). But in copies of the Septuagint there are two books with the name Esdras:

- *1 Esdras:* a work combining 2 Chron. 35:1–36:23, the book of Ezra (to which a new section [chaps. 3:1–5:6] has been added), and Neh. 7:38–8:12 (the Ezra sections in the book of Nehemiah)
- *2 Esdras:* the books of Ezra and Nehemiah combined

However, in the Vulgate, Jerome's Latin translation of the Bible, there are four books bearing the title Esdras:

- *1 Esdras:* the book of Ezra
- *2 Esdras:* the book of Nehemiah
- *3 Esdras:* the 1 Esdras of the Septuagint
- *4 Esdras:* an apocalyptic work from ca. 100 CE. Later it acquired an extra opening section (chaps. 1–2 = *5 Esdras*) and a concluding section (chaps. 15–16 = *6 Esdras*)

In the following paragraphs the *1 Esdras* of the Greek Bible (the *3 Esdras* of the Vulgate) will be examined.

The story begins with King Josiah's celebration of the passover in 622 BCE as part of his religious reform based on the book of the law that had been found in the temple (see 2 Kings 23:21-23). This and the story about the last days of Judah are related in chapter 1 (2 Chron. 35:1–36:23, with some small changes). At chapter 2:1 the text of the book of Ezra begins, with Cyrus's decree allowing exiles to return to Jerusalem, there to build a new temple. This decree is a fulfilment of God's word through Jeremiah (Jeremiah's prophecy about the exile concluded 1 Esdras 1). First Esdras 2:1-15 corresponds with Ezra 1:1-11, and the events are placed in Cyrus's first year (538 BCE). However, rather than continuing after this with Ezra 2, the text of 1 Esdras 2:16-30 reproduces Ezra 4:7-24, a section that is clearly out of chronological order in Ezra; it deals with events in the time of King Artaxerxes (465-24), some seventy years later than the events in the preceding and following sections. In his summary of this section of 1 Esdras, the historian Josephus claimed that the Persian monarch involved was Cambyses, who reigned at the more appropriate time of 530-522 BCE.

At 1 Esdras 3:1–5:6 there is a section that is not found in the book of Ezra. It is set in the time of King Darius, who did indeed follow Cyrus (after Cambyses who is not mentioned in the Bible) and ruled from 522-486 BCE. First Esdras 5:6 says the events happened in the king's first year. Three young men among the king's bodyguards decided to hold a contest: "Let each of us state what one thing is strongest; and to the one whose statement seems wisest, King Darius will give rich gifts and great honors of victories" (3:5). Each of them wrote out their views, and the documents were placed beneath Darius's pillow so that when he awakened he could read them. He and his nobles would decide who made the best case.

The first argued that wine was the strongest (3:17b-24), noting that it was a great leveler as it affected all alike and made them do unusual things that they forgot once they became sober. The second championed the king as the strongest (4:1-12). The monarch commands and people obey. Soldiers bring him the spoils of war, and farmers give him the produce of their fields. The third, who is identified as Zerubbabel in 4:13 (he is known from Ezra 2–5 as the prince of the early postexilic Jewish community), maintained that women are the strongest (4:14-32). They give birth to all men, "men cannot exist without women" (4:17), and men prefer a beautiful woman to anything. They leave parents for wives whom they love more than their fathers and mothers, and they bring their profits to women. Indeed Apame, Darius's concubine, does as she pleases to the king.

The reader expects the decision to be rendered at this point, but Zerubbabel proceeds to claim that truth is even stronger than women (4:34-41). Truth "endures and is strong forever, and lives and prevails forever and ever. With it there is no partiality or preference, but it does what is righteous" (4:38-39a). His last speech carries the day (4:41).

Zerubbabel was then invited to request whatever he wished. He reminded Darius of the vow he had made on the day of his coronation to re-build Jerusalem and to return the temple vessels that Cyrus had set apart when he took Babylon (4:43-46). Darius gave exceptionally generous or-ders that his requests be carried out and even more; all was to be paid for from the royal purse (4:47-57). Zerubbabel thanked God for giving him wisdom (4:58-60), brought the good news to his kin, and formed a group that would return to Jerusalem under armed escort. After naming the lead-ers of the group, including Jeshua the priest and Zerubbabel (though the text is a little confused), the section reaches its conclusion.

From this point on 1 Esdras returns to the biblical text:

- 1 Esdras 5:7-46 − Ezra 2:1-70
- 1 Esdras 5:47-73 = Ezra 3:1–4:5
- 1 Esdras 6:1–7:15 = Ezra 4:24–6:22
- 1 Esdras 8:1–9:55 = Ezra 7:1–10:44; Neh. 7:73–8:12.

Thus 1 Esdras describes the late preexilic situation and the beginning of the exile, the return from exile, the Zerubbabel episode, the rebuilding of the temple, and the Ezra story. A good case has been made that the Zerubbabel episode (3:1–5:6) was translated from an Aramaic base, so that all of the material in 1 Esdras would be a translation from Semitic texts, Hebrew for most of it or Aramaic for smaller parts. That is, the time when the Greek translation was made is clearly not the time when the original was composed. In those many places where 1 Esdras parallels Ezra-Nehemiah, it tends to have a shorter, superior text, one that has been of in-terest to text-critics; and if the section 1 Esdras 2:16-30 = Ezra 4:7-24 did belong in the time of Cambyses, as Josephus says, then 1 Esdras would pre-serve a better order than Ezra does. Also, one could argue that it makes better sense to have the Ezra material brought together rather than to sep-arate it as the biblical version does, with some of it in Ezra (chaps. 7–10) and the rest in Nehemiah (7:73–9:37). But the last point is a weak argu-ment in support of 1 Esdras: it seems more likely that an editor found it as strange as readers do today that the Ezra sections are separated and de-cided to unite them. Another point against 1 Esdras is that, for some rea-son, only the first part of the Ezra story from the book of Nehemiah is pre-served in it.

So what is 1 Esdras and what did the writer/editor/compiler accom-plish by producing it? Some have argued that it is a truncated version of a longer composition that included all or large parts of 1–2 Chronicles, Ezra, and Nehemiah, but there is no textual evidence for a large work of this kind. The book as we have it begins with a festival (passover) and ends with another (the festival of booths), both celebrated at the temple, with priests and Levites leading in the celebration. Between these two holidays there is reference to another passover (7:10-15) where the priests and Levites are also prominent. So, one accomplishment of the compiler was to relate the story from the last time a joyful festival at the temple is mentioned before its destruction to the time when holidays were again held at the temple as the law required. The book obviously is made up of ancient material, all of which is translated from Semitic texts, but seems more likely to be an editorial combination of existing texts than an abbreviated form of a once longer work.

(2) 1 Maccabees (deuterocanonical/apocryphal)

It is widely agreed that 1 Maccabees was written in Hebrew not far from the year 100 BCE, since the last event to which it alludes may be as late as 104 BCE. It has received its name from the fact that Judas Maccabeus is the protagonist in it (he is given the epithet "Maccabee" in 2:4, 66; it is often thought to mean "hammerer" as a tribute to his military prowess). The book is an extremely important historical source for events in Judea in the second century BCE.

After swiftly relating the conquests of Alexander the Great and his death (1:1-7), the writer moves to Alexander's successors and mentions in particular "a sinful root, Antiochus Epiphanes" who took the Seleucid throne in 175 BCE (1:10). In this age of Hellenism, some Jewish renegades received permission from the king to "observe the ordinances of the Gentiles" (v. 13), which meant erecting a gymnasium, the central institution in the Greek educational system, in Jerusalem, removing the marks of circumcision, and abandoning the covenant (vv. 14-15). In his arrogance Antiochus invaded Egypt, took it, and then marched home. He visited Jerusalem on the way, looted the temple, and left. His action seems unmotivated in 1 Maccabees because the author has mentioned only Antiochus's first campaign to Egypt (in 170 BCE), not the second (169 BCE) in which he was repulsed by Roman authorities. After being humiliated by the Romans, he took out his rage on the Jerusalem temple. Antiochus increased his oppression of Israel two years later when he sent an agent who again plundered the city and resorted to all sorts of violence. At that time (167 BCE) "they fortified the city of David with a great strong wall and strong towers, and it became their citadel" (1:33). The citadel was to remain the center of Seleucid control in Jerusalem for the next twenty-five years. Moreover, the king is reported to have written to his entire realm "that all should be one people, and that all should give up their particular customs" (1:41-42). Some in Israel accepted his proposal. The king's religious policy involved prohibiting sacrifices at the temple, profaning sabbaths and festivals, defiling the sanctuary and priests, erecting altars and shrines for other gods, sacrificing pigs and other forbidden animals, and leaving sons uncircumcised. All of this was enforced on pain of death for offenders.

"Now on the fifteenth day of Chislev, in the one hundred forty-fifth year [= 167 BCE], they erected a desolating sacrilege on the altar of burnt offering" (1:54a); the "desolating sacrilege" was apparently some sort of statue. Copies of the Torah were destroyed, and on the 25th of the month they offered sacrifice on the altar, which had been built above the old one. But, the author notes, "many in Israel stood firm and were resolved in their hearts not to eat unclean food. They chose to die rather than to be defiled by food or to profane the holy covenant; and they did die" (1:62-63). The remainder of the book is the story of one family who stood firm and changed the nation for generations to come.

The first member of the family to lead the resistance was the father Mattathias (2:1-70). Josephus (*Ant.* 12.265) says that one of his ancestors was named *Asamonaios* (= Hashmon), and from this the family name Hasmonean is derived. Mattathias was a priest who refused to participate in a pagan sacrifice when asked to do so and who instead killed a Jew who was about to participate in the offering. Mattathias then sounded the alarm to arouse all those zealous for the law and the covenant, and he and his five sons went to the hills. They and their forces decided that defensive warfare on the sabbath was permissible after another band of Jewish rebels was slaughtered when they would not defend themselves on the sabbath. Mattathias's forces tore down pagan altars and enforced Judaism in various ways. A short time later, after he gave a testamentary speech about heroes of Israel's past, he died and was succeeded by arguably the chief character in the book, his third son "Judas called Maccabeus" (2:4) who is the protagonist from 3:1–9:22. He won victories over several Seleucid armies, using knowledge of the terrain and surprise as key weapons. These efforts allowed him to enter Jerusalem and there, while his men defended them, select priests cleansed the neglected sanctuary, rebuilt parts of it, and constructed a new altar. They offered the first sacrifices on the new altar exactly three years after the first pagan offering had been made at that place. They rededicated the temple and celebrated a festival in connection with it. The group then decided that in the future Jews should always do as they had done and celebrate an eight-day festival of (re-)dedication (Hanukkah), marking the reconsecration of the altar (164 BCE).

Judas and his men campaigned in surrounding areas and won territory for the Jews, but at this time the religious decrees of Antiochus were still in force. The king died, possibly around the time of the first Hanukkah, but it was not until 162 BCE that his successor revoked the decrees banning Judaism. One important act that Judas performed, apart from his continual warfare, was to send an embassy to Rome to establish a treaty of friendship with the Romans. The Roman connection would prove extremely important as the Jewish community in Judea attempted to maintain themselves against the Seleucids. Judas himself died in battle against the Seleucids.

Leadership of Judas's forces then fell to his brother Jonathan (9:23–12:53), Mattathias's fifth and youngest son (2:5). He too fought a number of battles, but the most significant event during the years when he led the Maccabean forces was that Jonathan became the high priest. First Maccabees mentions only one earlier high priest: Alcimus, who is roundly condemned for his impiety and the damage he did to the sanctuary. He died in 159 BCE and Jonathan became high priest in 152 BCE when two contenders for the Seleucid throne offered the position to him. He accepted the offer of the contender who actually gained the throne (Alexander Balas). Thus, ironically, a member of the family who had led the revolt received appointment as Jewish high priest from a Seleucid king. The family of the Hasmoneans was to retain the position until 37 (or 35) BCE.

In 152 BCE Jonathan died in Seleucid hands after being captured by them. His older brother Simon (13:1–16:24; he is listed as the second of Mattathias's sons in 2:3) succeeded him as military commander of the Maccabean forces and as high priest. Early in Simon's reign his troops succeeded in driving out the Seleucid forces from the citadel in Jerusalem, thus removing this center of Seleucid power and influence and giving a form of liberty to the Jews. A great assembly granted Simon (and his line) perpetual rule as high priest and leader of the nation. Simon was assassinated by his son-in-law in 134 BCE and succeeded by his son John Hyrcanus who was leader and high priest from 134-104.

First Maccabees is a serious work of historiography based on sources that are at times quoted (e.g., 8:23-32; 10:18-20). The writer takes care to date events precisely according to the Seleucid era, which began in the Fall of 312 (or Spring of 311 BCE), and he mentions many documented names and events as he tells the exciting story of how Judaism nearly perished, only to be saved through God's raising up the family of Mattathias, who brought the Jewish people from near ruin to nationhood with the right to practice the traditional religion. The focus of the book on the family of Mattathias is its most obvious characteristic; note the defeat of the non-Hasmonean leaders Joseph and Azariah who "did not belong to the family of those men through whom deliverance was given to Israel" (5:62). The earlier chapters are more focused on issues related to religion — Hellenization, the ban on the practice of Judaism, and regaining the temple — while the later ones (from chap. 5 on) are more a military history of three famous brothers. The writer expresses no concern that Jonathan and Simon became high priests although they were not from the traditional high-priestly family. The piety expressed in the book (especially the earlier chapters) consists of careful keeping of the covenantal laws; nothing is said about eschatology. The reference at the end to John Hyrcanus and in particular the phrasing of it — "The rest of the acts of John and his wars . . . are written in the annals of his high priesthood, from the time that he became high priest after his father" (16:23-24) — suggest that the author was writing after his reign had ended (as do similar examples from the books of Kings, e.g., 2 Kings 10:34) in 104 BCE. How much later is not known, but the pro-Roman attitude certainly implies that it was written before 63 BCE when the Romans conquered Jerusalem.

(3) 2 Maccabees (deuterocanonical/apocryphal)

The second book bearing the name Maccabees is not a continuation of the first, as, say, 2 Kings is the sequel to 1 Kings. Rather, it tells the story of Jewish history from the time of the Seleucid king Seleucus IV (187-75 BCE) and the high priest Onias III to the defeat of the Seleucid general Nicanor by Judas Maccabeus in 161 BCE. To this history are prefaced two chapters that contain two letters addressed to the Jews in Egypt. The first (1:1-9; in v. 7 the writers refer to an earlier letter from the year 143 BCE) is from the Jews of Jerusalem and Judea and was written in the year 124 BCE; in it they report on their deliverance from distress and call on the Egyptian Jews to "keep the festival of booths in the month of Chislev," that is, Hanukkah. The second letter is in 1:10–2:18. This longer missive is said to be from the people of Jerusalem, Judea, the senate, and Judas (apparently Maccabeus) to Aristobulus, "who is of the family of the anointed priests, teacher of King Ptolemy" (Ptolemy VIII [145-116 BCE]), and the Egyptian Jews. The second letter also urges them to keep the new festival of Hanukkah, and in it they recall amazing events in Nehemiah's time, when the fire from the altar of the first temple was conveyed to the altar of the second and when the items from the first temple hidden by Jeremiah were rediscovered for use in the second. This emphasis on the temple and the reference to its purification establish the sanctuary as a central topic in the book. Even if the letters are from a different author than the remainder of the book, they do share some themes with it. The hope that "God will gather us from everywhere under heaven into his holy place" (2:18) is not, however, echoed elsewhere in 2 Maccabees.

Second Maccabees tells us more about itself than most ancient writings. The author, or rather the epitomizer, prefaced a section to the history explaining the nature and purpose of his work (2:19-32). He tells us that one Jason of Cyrene had written a five-volume account of Judas Maccabeus and his brothers, the purification of the temple, the wars against Antiochus IV and his son, and abolishing and reestablishing the laws; all of this "we shall attempt to condense into a single book" (2:23). As he says, "[i]t is the duty of the original historian to occupy the ground, to discuss matters from every side, and to take trouble with details, but the one who recasts the narrative should be allowed to strive for brevity of expression and to forego exhaustive treatment" (2:30-31). At the end of the book he addresses the reader once more: "If it is well told and to the point, that is what I myself desired; if it is poorly done and mediocre, that was the best I could do" (15:38).

The story that the anonymous abridger tells begins at an earlier point than the detailed narrative of 1 Maccabees and does not pursue the history beyond the time of Judas. Second Maccabees is our only source of information about some important events in Jerusalem during the 180s and 170s BCE. It begins with Onias (III) who was serving as high priest during the reign of Seleucus (IV), that is, between 187 and 175 BCE. After a story about an unsuccessful effort by Heliodorus, a Seleucid official, to confiscate money from the Jerusalem temple (the story should be compared with the one about King Ptolemy's visit to the temple in 3 Maccabees, see below), the writer tells about the successful bid by the high priest's brother Jason to purchase the high priesthood from the new king, Antiochus IV. His bid was accepted, and for the first time in centuries (as far as we know) the high priesthood was taken from one person (Onias, who was later murdered) and sold to another. During Jason's time in office (175-172 BCE) Hellenization, including the building of a gymnasium, was officially promoted in Jerusalem. Soon another individual, Menelaus, paid a higher price to the royal coffers for the supreme office and became high priest in Jason's place (in 172 BCE). After Antiochus's second invasion of Egypt, when the Romans turned him back, and at the time when Jason was trying to regain Jerusalem by force, the king came to Jerusalem, plundered the temple, and eventually tried to suppress Judaism.

The first we hear of the Maccabees is in this context. Nothing is said about Mattathias; Judas is the first to be mentioned, and is given the name Maccabeus (5:27). He remains the protagonist to the end of the story. It is remarkable in comparison with 1 Maccabees that Jonathan and Simon are hardly mentioned at all in 2 Maccabees (Judas appoints both as commanders in 8:22) and that where they are named it is in a negative way. Simon has venal men in his employ (10:20-22) and is unsuccessful in fighting Nicanor (14:17). After mentioning Maccabeus but before beginning the tale of the revolt, 2 Maccabees devotes a lengthy section to describing several cases of martyrdom that resulted from the prohibition of Judaism. One was the death of Eleazar, an elderly scribe, who was being forced to eat pork. He was offered the opportunity to pretend that he was eating the flesh of swine while actually eating something kosher, but he refused, citing the example it would give to the youth and declaring: "Even if for the present I would avoid the punishment of mortals, yet whether I live or die I shall not escape the hands of the Almighty" (6:26). Seven brothers were arrested with their mother and an attempt was also made to compel them to eat the forbidden pork, this time in the presence of the king. One, speaking for all, said they would rather die than disobey the laws. Each of the brothers in succession was horribly tortured but would not submit to the king's will. One confessed as he was about to lose his tongue and hands: "I got these from Heaven, and because of his laws I disdain them, and from him I hope to get them back again" (7:11) — that is, he expressed the belief that he would experience the resurrection of his body. The fourth brother not only embraced this hope but also declared that for the king there would be no resurrection (7:14; cf. the mother in 7:23, 29, the seventh brother in 7:36, and Razis in 14:46). The last brother explains that they were giving up their lives for the laws of their ancestors and were asking that God have mercy on the nation. God would make the king confess him as the only God, and through the seven brothers God would bring an end to the anger that he had justly directed against his people (7:37-38). Last of all the mother died.

After this martyriological interlude, the writer returns to Judas Maccabeus and his companions. As in 1 Maccabees, we read about several victories by Judas and his forces, especially his victory over Nicanor. Second Maccabees 9 tells about the death of Antiochus IV during an ill-fated attempt to rob temples in the eastern part of his kingdom. As is the author's custom, he describes Antiochus's loathsome end in detail and adds that, in his last moments when he could not endure the horrid stench of his own rotting body, he vowed to become a Jew and proclaim God's power everywhere. In this way one of the purposes of the martyrdoms by the seven brothers was achieved. After the king's death Maccabeus and his forces took Jerusalem and rededicated the temple. In this way 2 Maccabees reverses the order of the two events as they are presented in 1 Maccabees (there, Antiochus's death follows the rededication). The remainder of 2 Maccabees is given over to accounts of Judas's further campaigns, highlighting another victory over Nicanor. The victors decreed that the date on which it occurred, the thirteenth of the month Adar (the twelfth month), was forever to be celebrated in memory of the event.

The first letter prefixed to the book indicates that the present form of 2 Maccabees was not completed before 124 BCE. Exactly when after that the epitomizer condensed and edited Jason's multivolume work is difficult to say. It seems likely that 2 Maccabees was composed before the Romans took control of Judea in 63 BCE because in 15:37 the writer/epitomist says that ever since the defeat of Nicanor "the city has been in the possession of the Hebrews."

Second Maccabees has been identified as an example of "pathetic" historiography, that is, a history that places emphasis on emotions (of the characters and of the readers) and describes people and events in graphic, at times painful detail. The writer has chosen a particular style — one far different from 1 Maccabees — as the vehicle for expressing his convictions about the way that God had worked in sacred history and again had operated in the events narrated in the book. His theology is deuteronomistic: God punishes his people when they are disobedient and may use the nations to do so, and he blesses them when they are faithful to the covenant. The oppressive foreign rulers such as Antiochus IV were instruments through which God chastised his people for their sins, such as their adoption of Hellenistic ways and rejection of the law and covenant. The deity does, however, hear the prayers of characters such as Judas and the seven brothers who recognize his sovereignty and the deuteronomistic way in which he conducts affairs.

The temple is clearly central in the book. It is the theme that bridges the prefixed letters and the body of the work. Both of the letters call for the celebration of Hanukkah, the festival of the rededication of altar and temple, and the second recalls miraculous events surrounding the second temple and how features of the first temple survived with divine aid to become part of the second. Within the narrative, the attempt by Heliodorus to enter the temple is divinely thwarted, and the defiled temple is later regained by Judas and his forces. After this Judas continues to be active around the temple, and the story ends with the death of Nicanor who had threatened to destroy it. The epitome itself falls into two parts that have to do with the temple: the first involves the profanation of it, the death of the enemy (Antiochus IV) after martyrdom (Eleazar, the seven brothers, the mother), and the festival of Hanukkah; the second includes the threat to it from Nicanor, the death of Nicanor after the martyrdom of Razis, and the festival of Nicanor. The author wrote in Greek; the book is not a translation. Presumably the epitomizer did his work in some part of the diaspora, perhaps in Egypt.

Tales

Several Jewish narratives from the second temple period are novelistic. That is, they are stories with no serious claim to historicity but aim to inculcate wise teachings through the stories and the speeches they narrate. The wisdom that they teach is thoroughly Jewish: there are exhortations to pious behavior, trust in the one God, and obedience to his revealed will. If one does these things God will bless in his own good time and way.

(1) Tobit (deuterocanonical/apocryphal)

The Book of Tobit was written in the Aramaic language. Four fragmentary copies of the Aramaic version have been found in Qumran cave 4 (4Q196-99) and one in Hebrew (4Q200); it seems therefore that the book was translated into Hebrew at an early time. It was later rendered into Greek and is included in copies of the Greek Bible. Though the Qumran copies are fragmentary, in combination they offer parts of every chapter in the book and show that the longer Greek version is closer to the original text of the book than the shorter one.

There is no incontrovertible evidence for the date of the book, but a third century date is not unlikely. The earliest of the Qumran copies (4Q199) dates from approximately 100 BCE; how much earlier the book was written is more difficult to determine. The survey of the future in Tobit 14:3-11 refers to the rebuilding of the temple (520-15 BCE) as the last event predicted; it says nothing about the arrival of the Greeks and does not mention the desecration of the temple carried out by Seleucid forces in 167 BCE. The nature of the forecast suggests that at least the defiling of the sanctuary would have been mentioned had the author known about it. Consequently, Tobit may have been written in the Persian period, possibly a little later.

The Book of Tobit combines stories about two families with the purpose of showing that God works behind the scenes to bless his faithful people even in the most painful trials. The pious actions that are commended in the book include giving alms and showing mercy generally, praying, marrying within kinship bounds, and praising God for his goodness.

The protagonists in the story are Tobit, his son Tobias, and a distant relative named Sarah. Tobit is introduced as an exemplary person from northern Israel (from the tribe of Naphtali) who went into exile when the Assyrian king Shalmaneser deported Israelites. Though he entered the employ of the king, Tobit continued to practice his piety by caring for needy Israelites and burying the abandoned corpses of his fellow countrymen who were executed by the king. Such devotion eventually cost him his job and his belongings, although he had the foresight to deposit some money with an acquaintance far away in Media. Tobit, who was under a death sentence, was later restored through the intercession of his kinsman Ahiqar (see the section below on the Elephantine texts), but he remained impoverished. Soon after, he lost his eyesight and plunged into even deeper despair. He had the misfortune of resting under a tree in which there were sparrows whose droppings fell onto his eyes, formed a white film, and blinded him. Under the circumstances it is understandable that Tobit prayed for death to come.

At the same time a second tragic story was playing out in Ecbatana, Media. Lovely young Sarah, Tobit's relative, also was praying for death. She had been married seven times, but each husband had died on the wedding night. It turns out that each was killed by the demon Asmodeus; however, the women servants accused Sarah of killing them.

The remainder of the story shows how God worked things out for the good of these righteous Israelites after they had suffered misfortunes in exile. Tobit dispatched Tobias to retrieve the money he had deposited in Media, and providentially the angel Raphael, whose name means "God has healed," was hired to accompany him. Raphael hid his identity from Tobit and Tobias and went under the assumed name of Azariah (= the Lord has helped). As the two traveled, they caught a fish from which they removed the heart, liver, and gall, all of which had wonderfully convenient medicinal powers: the heart and liver, when burned, would produce a smoke that drives demons away; and the gall, when applied to eyes, would remove white films from them. They visited Sarah's home where Tobias, as nearest of kin, married her. To avert the fate of his seven predecessors, he burned the heart and liver of the fish, and the special smoke emanating from them drove Asmodeus away. Tobias and the angel (still disguised) then traveled on to obtain the money Tobit had deposited in Media and returned with it and with Sarah to Tobit's home. Once there, they applied the gall to his eyes and his sight was restored. It is not until this point in the story that Raphael revealed who he was.

Some time later, on his death bed, Tobit looked prophetically to the future and foresaw the destruction of Nineveh and Jerusalem, the return of Judeans from their exile, and the rebuilding of the temple in Jerusalem. In fact his vision extended even beyond those events to the return of all God's people to Jerusalem, a new temple (the one the prophets had foreseen), and the conversion of all nations. Evil would then vanish from the earth.

The wisdom advanced in the book is that the righteous should persist in their pious behavior and praise the God whom they trust despite the suffering they may undergo. Their lives should be marked by the virtues exercised by Tobit, Tobias, and Sarah: observing the festivals, almsgiving, good deeds (like burying the dead), eating kosher foods, honoring parents, marrying within ethnic bounds, praying, and praising God. In a few sections of the book characters expound their teachings. The first (4:3-19) contains Tobit's set of instructions to Tobias when sending him on his travels. Later Raphael himself teaches Tobit and Tobias about giving alms (12:6-10). Near the end Tobit again instructs Tobias and his sons before he dies (14:8-11), once more stressing the giving of alms.

The book envisages a blessed future for all in Jerusalem and at the temple. Its picture of the new age involves no destruction of the earth or messianic leader. The scheme of world empires that underlies the apocalyptic section in chapter 14 has intrigued scholars; it seems to reflect an old pattern in which Assyria is followed by Babylon and then Media (the Greeks are not mentioned). The form of the list is another factor favoring a date for the book in the Persian period.

71

(2) Judith (deuterocanonical/apocryphal)

The style of the book makes it very likely that it was composed in Hebrew, but the Hebrew text is no longer available. The earliest extant text is in Greek and is found in copies of the Greek Bible.

Judith is a story about how an extraordinarily pious and capable lady of means used her intelligence, feminine charms, and trust in God to kill Nebuchadnezzar's all-conquering general Holofernes and thus to save her city and people from destruction. It is a work of considerable verbal artistry, visible in the delightfully ambiguous language used by Judith (especially her ambiguous use of the word "lord/Lord") and employed unwittingly by Holofernes during the failed seduction scene in chapter 11.

As scholars have attempted to place the book in its historical context, they have been struck by the fact that it can be read as reflecting two different historical periods. First, much in the book suggests it comes from Persian times (that is, before ca. 330 BCE), even though Nebuchadnezzar is the king of Assyria according to the author. Persian features include: (a) names such as Holofernes and Bagoas; (b) the demand for earth and water as a symbol of submission (2:7); (c) the Jews have recently returned to their land and rebuilt their temple (4:3); and (d) local leaders may be called satraps (if Greek *stratēgoi* is a translation of this term). Countering these features, however, are others that have made experts think of Maccabean times (that is, after 167 BCE). Among these are: (a) worship of the divine king Nebuchadnezzar which echoes a practice in Hellenistic times when the ruler cult was widespread (see 3:8, for example), although it is attested for earlier periods (see Isa. 14, Ezek. 28); (b) the defiling of the Jerusalem temple feared by the Jews which reminds one of what Seleucid forces did to the temple from 167-164 BCE (4:12; 9:8); and (c) aspects of the story (especially Holofernes' fate) that parallel the battle between Judas Maccabeus and the Seleucid general Nicanor who had threatened the temple and was later decapitated (1 Macc. 7:33-50; his army, like that of Holofernes, panicked when he was the first to fall). In view of these two sets of evidence, some have proposed as a compromise solution that Judith is a tale from the Persian period that was (re)written in Maccabean times. Also, since the area of the Samaritans is the central theatre of the action, the story may have originated there, although if it did it later was altered to give Jerusalem a central position.

At many points the narrative reminds one of stories in the Bible: Manasseh, Judith's husband, dies like the son of the Shunnamite woman in

2 Kings 4:18-20; the land has peace all the days of Judith's life (16:25) just as it did in the age of the judges; and her song (16:1-17) seems modeled on the poem in Exodus 15.

Anyone familiar with Assyrian, Babylonian, and Persian history is likely to be baffled by the opening of the book. Nebuchadnezzar, we are told, is king of Assyria and rules in Nineveh. He holds sway there in the postexilic period because the Jews have already rebuilt the temple when the events are supposed to have taken place. One recognizable feature of Nebuchadnezzar in the confused setting is, however, his pretension to be a god and his demand that all in his kingdom so honor him (see Dan. 3). He is called the great king, lord of the whole earth (2:5), and claims he will carry out his mighty design by his own hand (2:12). Rather than reading it as a quasi-historical work, Judith is better seen as a novel meant to extol the value of obedience to and trust in the one true God who is powerful to save in whatever way he chooses and against any foe. As the author tells the exciting tale, he succeeds in entertaining the reader with his narrative and artistic skill.

Nebuchadnezzar is pictured as organizing a military campaign against the entire west in order to punish the nations there for failing to assist him in his fight against Arphaxad the Mede. Holofernes, second in command only to Nebuchadnezzar himself, leads 120,000 foot soldiers and 12,000 cavalry in a devastating attack that crushes all opposition and terrifies others into surrender. All are forced to worship Nebuchadnezzar. Oddly enough, however, the immense war machine pauses to collect supplies for one month before attacking the small nation of Israel, situated in the mountains. It turns out that there is one crucial pass through which, Thermopylae-like, only two can wedge their way at a time. That pass was located near the city of Bethulia. If the attackers managed to force their way through it, they would be able to overrun the entire country including Jerusalem. The high priest Joakim organizes the Jewish resistance, and all fast, wear sackcloth, and cry out to the Lord, who hears their plea. Holofernes becomes angry when he hears about the Jewish resistance and asks neighboring peoples in his army for a report about these Israelites. The Ammonite Achior provides a remarkably well informed survey of biblical history and declares that if the Israelites have sinned they will be defeated but if they are obedient to their God no one can conquer them. In anger, Holofernes declares that Achior will not see his face again until he gets his revenge. He then commands that he be handed over to the Jews. They receive Achior, and he is invited into the home of one of their leaders.

The seemingly invincible army then surrounds Bethulia, takes the springs in the area, and subjects the city to a siege. As the residents contemplate surrender because their supplies would run out in five days, Judith makes her first appearance in the story. She is a beautiful, rich, and pious widow who has withdrawn from the life of the city until this moment (she has been fasting virtually every day). But she conceives a plan and criticizes the local authorities for putting God to the test by giving him five more days to save them before they surrender. Her theology is that of the author: "Do not try to bind the purposes of the Lord our God; for God is not like a human being, to be threatened, or like a mere mortal, to be won over by pleading. Therefore, while we wait for his deliverance, let us call upon him to help us, and he will hear our voice, if it pleases him" (8:16-17). Judith has an unusual plan, but she is permitted to try it out. The leaders allow Judith and her maid to leave the city and go to the enemy camp. Once she comes in contact with the Assyrian army, her beauty causes a sensation and she is brought to Holofernes himself. Although Judith is offered his rich food and drunk his wine, she has brought her own food and drink and feeds herself with them. She establishes a pattern for her activities which requires that she go out of the camp at a very early hour every morning in order to pray. Holofernes, however, determines to seduce her and invites her to a banquet; at the appropriate time all others leave. But Holofernes has drunk more that night than ever before and is dead drunk. Judith then takes his sword, cuts off his head, puts it in her food bag, and leaves the camp with her maid, just as they had done other mornings. They return to Bethulia where Achior confirms the identity of the head (so he does see Holofernes' face again, but in unexpected circumstances). Achior the Ammonite is circumcised and joins the house of Israel.

After Judith and her maid return, the troops of Bethulia act as if they were going to attack, making the Assyrians run to summon Holofernes. When his fate is discovered, they all panic, just as Judith said they would. They and the other Israelites win a great victory that day. They plunder the Assyrian camp, with Judith receiving Holofernes' belongings. Judith is praised and lives out her life full of honors.

There are several aspects of the book that should be highlighted. Judith has been called a nationalistic romance or a historical novel. There is no doubting that it has a nationalistic side, as it tells the story of how a tiny nation withstood a world empire headed by a king who claimed to be a god. The writer made use of historical figures in writing his story, but the transparent deviations from historical precision lead one to think that he was less interested in historical figures and places than his more immediate goal of teaching a lesson.

The city name Bethulia is an example of how the author proceeds. There is no city by this name in any historical record, and the position given it in the book would be more appropriate for a site that would be guarding the city of Samaria than for one protecting Jerusalem. The name may well be symbolic: it could reflect the Hebrew term for virgin *(betulah)*. Bethulia would, then, be a representative of Israel, the virgin Israel whom the enemy desired to ravage, just as Holofernes wanted to have Judith, a name that means "Jewess." As God saved Judith, so he saved Bethulia = the virgin Israel from enemy hands.

The role of the Ammonite Achior is another intriguing feature in the story. His role is contrasted and yet paralleled with that of Judith. The two are opposites in many ways (male/female, foreigner/Jewish; soldier/secluded widow; enemy/potential victim, in the Assyrian camp/in Bethulia), and at first they move in opposite directions (he from the Assyrian camp to Bethulia, and she the reverse). Yet they parallel each other in that both make speeches evoking Israel's history and emphasizing the power of Israel's God to save, if he is obeyed (that is, both present a deuteronomistic theology). In fact Achior has more confidence in Israel's God than do the Bethulians (who planned to surrender). In the end Judith and Achior are in the same place, Achior is circumcised, and he joins the house of Israel. His becoming a proselyte is in itself remarkable because he should have been excluded from Israel by the law that "[n]o Ammonite . . . shall be admitted to the assembly of the Lord" (Deut. 23:3). It may be that he qualified under the ten-generation statute of limitations (Deut. 23:3), but his admission to a Jewish leader's home and entry into the religious community seem contrary to the policies of leaders such as Ezra and Nehemiah. That is, the book of Judith seems to represent a dissenting opinion.

Like Tobit, Judith deals with a time of deepest distress, but even under those circumstances the heroine maintains her trust in God, with her informed understanding of his nature. She simply refuses to compromise her principles. Due to her courage and trust, God delivers his people from the enemy's great power "by the hand of a woman" (13:15).

(3) Susanna (deuterocanonical/apocryphal)

Susanna is one of the three additions to the book of Daniel in the Greek versions of the book. There is no clear evidence for dating this entertaining tale other than to say it was written at some point in the last centuries BCE because it is a part of the Greek translation of the Bible. The study of the story is complicated by the existence of two rather different Greek versions. The more familiar of the two is that of Theodotion which has been used as the basis for all translations into English. The other is the Old Greek version (the Septuagint) which was replaced in the manuscript tradition by the Theodotionic form and thus nearly disappeared. These Greek versions of Daniel place Susanna in different locations relative to the older Semitic book (Daniel 1–12): the Old Greek version places it as a fourteenth chapter (after Bel and the Dragon, another of the Greek additions), while the Theodotionic version logically positions it before chapter 1 as the beginning of Daniel's amazing career in Babylon.

The longer Theodotionic version is a sapiential story that launches young Daniel on his career and that, like Esther and Judith, involves a beautiful, rich, and pious Jewess. Within the Jewish community in Babylonian exile there was a wealthy man named Joakim who married the lovely and devout Susanna. Their estate, with its garden, was a gathering place for the Jews in the area. In a certain year two evil men assumed the office of judge for the Jewish people in Babylon; it is thought that this motif arose from Jeremiah's reference to Ahab and Zedekiah, two false prophets in Babylon who "have perpetrated outrage in Israel and have committed adultery with their neighbors' wives, and have spoken in my name lying words that I did not command them; I am the one who knows and bears witness, says the Lord" (Jer. 29:23). Those judges developed a lustful passion for Susanna and took to spying on the lovely lady as she promenaded through the garden. One day as they were watching from hiding she dismissed her servant girls to get the articles necessary for her to bathe. As she was alone and they could no longer contain their passion, the two dashed up to her and said: "'Look, the garden doors are shut, and no one can see us. We are burning with desire for you; so give your consent, and lie with us. If you refuse, we will testify against you that a young man was with you, and this was why you sent your maids away'" (vv. 20-21). Susanna refused their proposition and the two did as they had threatened: they testified against her, she was sentenced to death for adultery, and led off to her execution. At that moment God stirred up the spirit of a young man named Daniel who stopped the proceedings, charged that the judges had perjured themselves, and brought the court back into session. Daniel questioned the two judges separately and caught them in a contradiction. One claimed that Susanna and the young man had been intimate beneath a mastic tree and the other that they were under an evergreen oak. Daniel pronounced sentences on each one; the sentence involved a pun on the name of the tree that each had designated. Susanna was exonerated while the two false witnesses suffered the fate she was to undergo (as Deut. 19:18-19 commands). All survivors were happy and Daniel became famous.

The Old Greek version begins at what is verse 5b of the Theodotionic text. It thus lacks the opening description of Susanna. While there are many smaller differences throughout the text, the variant endings sound different notes.

Old Greek	Theodotion
For this reason the young are the beloved of Jacob in their simplicity, and we are to be on guard that the young become mighty sons. Then the young will be pious and the spirit of knowledge and understanding will be in them forever.	Hilkiah and his wife praised God for their daughter Susanna, and so did her husband Joakim and all her relatives, because she was found innocent of a shameful deed. And from that day onward Daniel had a great reputation among the people.

From the endings it appears that the Old Greek is a story about the danger that corrupt leaders posed for the Jewish community which was saved from a terrible miscarriage of justice by Daniel (to whom an angel, at God's command, had given a spirit of understanding, v. 45). It concludes with a plea for training the young properly. The Theodotionic version is a more romantic story with its fuller description of Susanna and her circumstances. It ends as it began with naming the members of her family, joy that her reputation was saved, and a notice about Daniel's fame.

Since antiquity there has been a debate about the original language of the story — Greek or Hebrew/Aramaic. The point around which the argument has turned is the set of puns in vv. 54-55 and 58-59. They involve the name of the tree and the punishment on the judge who specified that tree: *schinon — schisei* and *prinon — kataprise* (Old Greek; they are virtually the same in Theodotion). Note that these are not only puns, but the two tree names rhyme as do the verbs related to them. Julius Africanus (third century CE) argued that these word plays worked in Greek and that this fact pointed to Greek as the original language. An objection to his argument has been that the Greek translator could have fashioned the puns, while different word plays may have existed in the

Semitic original. Though this is possible, no likely candidates for Semitic puns have emerged.

> *(4) 3 Maccabees (neither deuterocanonical nor apocryphal; it is authoritative in the Eastern churches and is thus often included in translations of the Apocrypha)*

The title of 3 Maccabees is curious because the book has nothing to do with the Maccabees (who are never mentioned in it). The principal feature that it shares with 1–2 Maccabees is that it is a story about a situation when the Jewish people, this time in Egypt, were in danger of being annihilated by a Hellenistic monarch, in part for their religious convictions and practices. The book was composed in Greek and relates a story set in the time of Ptolemy IV Philopator (221-203 BCE).

After his victory over Antiochus III (223-187 BCE) in the battle of Raphia (217 BCE), Ptolemy, according to our story, visited the cities in Coele-Syria (the area that Antiochus was trying to take from Ptolemy) to boost their morale and give gifts to their temples. Naturally he came to Jerusalem. While there, he was so impressed with the temple that he wanted to enter it, including the holy of holies. The Jews desperately tried to stop this violation of their law. Amid the great uproar that broke out in the city, the high priest Simon offered a prayer in which he appealed to past cases of divine deliverance from danger and to the promise that if his people prayed in their distress from the temple God would hear them (see 1 Kings 8:33-34, 48-50). The Lord answered his prayer swiftly by striking King Ptolemy with temporary paralysis that forced him to withdraw from Palestine and return to Egypt, though he went uttering curses and vowing revenge for such humiliating treatment.

His plan for revenge involved the Jews of Alexandria. The king decreed that they were to be subjected to a registration that involved a poll-tax and reduction of status to the level of slaves. In addition the registration included being branded with an ivy leaf shape, a symbol of the god Dionysus. The monarch also decreed through a letter that the many Jews outside Alexandria were to be delivered to the city in chains after undergoing other forms of harsh treatment. Those who handed Jews to the authorities were to be given substantial monetary rewards. During the process of registering this large number of Jews, the second divine intervention in the story occurred: God made the writing materials used by the scribes run out so that the registration was impeded.

When Ptolemy saw that his plans were being frustrated by exhaustion of scribal materials, he angrily commanded that his five hundred elephants be given an intoxicating drink and that, when drunk, they be let loose to trample the Jews who were bound and held within the enclosed hippodrome. On the day when the plan was to be carried out, the king miraculously overslept so badly that the event had to be postponed until the next day. However, on the next day God plagued the king with forgetfulness so that he was unable to remember his plan, reversed himself, and defended the Jews as loyal subjects. Indeed he claimed it was only his own benevolence that kept him from letting loose the elephants on his own employees who had made them drunk to trample Jews. Later the king did another about-face and vowed irrevocably to kill the Jews the next day and swore that he would also level Judea and its temple. When it seemed that all was lost, Eleazar, an elderly Jewish priest, prayed; like Simon the high priest, he cited biblical examples of past deliverances and asked God to intervene on behalf of his people in these dire circumstances. Once more God responded by sending two angels (unseen by the Jews) who terrified the elephants and made them turn back on the soldiers (and on Ptolemy) who were conducting them to the hippodrome.

Astonishingly, the king changed his mind yet again and chided his subordinates for how they had treated the Jews. He released the imprisoned Jews and provided the resources so that they could celebrate a seven-day festival of deliverance. He then dismissed them and wrote a letter to governmental officials in Egypt. He blamed all the misfortunes suffered by the Jews on malicious friends of his, and credited their salvation to his own actions and his awareness of the true situation. Some sentences in the letter are thematic for 3 Maccabees: "Since we have come to realize that the God of heaven surely defends the Jews, always taking their part as a father does for his children, and since we have taken into account the friendly and firm goodwill that they had toward us and our ancestors, we justly have acquitted them of every charge of whatever kind" (7:6b-7; see also v. 9). The Jews requested and received permission from the king to execute any Jews who had apostatized to save themselves from the king's earlier edicts; they killed about three hundred and also kept that day as a holiday. The Jews from the countryside were then transported home, where there was more celebrating and all regained their confiscated property.

Several themes stand out in the book, and they are presented with motifs found elsewhere in the Jewish literature from the diaspora. One theme is the all-powerful God served by the Jews, and his willingness to intervene on behalf of those Jews who faithfully served him by obeying the law. Another is the loyalty of the Jews, which is recognized by people of good will and by kings when they are in their right minds. Among the stock motifs in this kind of literature is a king who is very powerful but also, like Nebuchadnezzar and Xerxes, foolish and given to excesses, and enemies who make unjust charges against the Jews relating to their particular practices.

Third Maccabees resembles 2 Maccabees in that it is a type of storytelling in which emotions are emphasized. The author resorts to a verbose and pompous style as he describes the terrible conditions into which the Jews were placed and the frightful anger of the king and the enemies of the Jews. Yet it does offer itself as an account of events that are supposed to have occurred. There is no external confirmation of the actions that 3 Maccabees relates, although Josephus tells a similar story but places it in the time of Ptolemy VIII Euergetes II (Physkon) who ruled from 146-117 BCE (see *Against Apion* 2.49-55). In his account, during a struggle for control of Alexandria, the king "arrested all the Jews in the city with their wives and children, and exposed them, naked and in chains, to be trampled to death by elephants, the beasts being actually made drunk for the purpose. However, the outcome was the reverse of the intentions. The elephants, without touching the Jews at their feet, rushed at Physkon's friends, and killed a large number of them." An apparition was involved, as was the plea of the king's favorite concubine not to carry out his original intentions; both elements occur in 3 Maccabees also. Josephus says that the king relented, and this occasion was the origin of a festival the Alexandrian Jews celebrated on that day. In Josephus's version the story lacks the pathetic element that is so overwhelming in 3 Maccabees. Both stories may be legendary accounts, perhaps with some basis in fact, regarding how it came about that the Jews in Egypt celebrated a particular festival of deliverance. Third Maccabees is certainly not devoid of historical truth (Ptolemy IV's promotion of the cult of Dionysus, his cruelty, his interest in architecture, etc.), but as it stands it seems unlikely to be a reliable account of events in the reign of Ptolemy IV.

The date when 3 Maccabees was written is not known. One pointer to its time may be the word *laographia* used for the registration of the Jews. Augustus ordered that such a registration be made in Egypt so that a poll-tax could be implemented; this act, dating to 24 or 23 BCE, made a distinction between citizens of Greek cities and others, reducing the latter to the level of slaves. Perhaps the laographia of 3 Maccabees is a literary reflection of that event. Others have noted close similarities between 3 Maccabees and the Additions to Esther; the relations between the two works suggest that 3 Maccabees is earlier and thus it would have been written before 77 BCE, the latest possible date for these Additions. Perhaps 3 Maccabees was composed at some time in the first century BCE.

(5) Letter of Aristeas (Aristeas to Philocrates; pseudepigraphal)

The *Letter of Aristeas* owes its fame to the fact that it purports to tell how the Torah was translated from Hebrew into Greek. As a matter of fact, this subject occupies only a small part of the finished text, but its presence there has attracted the attention of readers since antiquity. The work was written in Greek and is usually dated to some time in the second century BCE, but there are really no firm grounds for assigning it to a particular period. The first undisputed reference to it by a later writer is in Josephus's *Antiquities* (written in the 90s CE) where he quotes and summarizes large parts of it. It is also possible that Philo knew the book.

Aristeas presents himself as someone in the court of Ptolemy II Philadelphus (283-246 BCE; the king's name is not given but can be inferred from references to his father), who had been sent by the king on an embassy to the high priest Eleazar in Jerusalem in connection with the translation of the Torah. His book is a report (it is often called a letter) to his brother Philocrates about this and other experiences (paragraphs 1-8).

The king had appointed Demetrius of Phalerum as keeper of the new royal library in Alexandria. He "aimed at collecting, if possible, all the books in the world" (9). In a conversation with the king he reported that he wished to increase the current holdings from 200,000 to 500,000 and added: "Information has reached me that the lawbooks of the Jews are worth translation and inclusion in your royal library" (10). The king ordered that a letter be sent to the high priest in Jerusalem so that work on the translation could begin (10). Aristeas said he seized this moment, when Jewish people were on the king's mind in a favorable way, to ask the monarch to release from slavery the approximately 100,000 Jews whom his father had deported from Judea. In line with the spirit of the book, he told Ptolemy that the Greeks and the Jews worshiped the same God but under different names (16). The gracious sovereign ordered their release (and others') with a massive outlay of money besides (12-27). The next section contains a copy of the documents involved in arranging the translation. In a much-disputed passage referring to the Jewish law and other works, Demetrius is quoted as saying: "But they have been transcribed somewhat carelessly and not as they should be [the terms rendered "transcribed" and "should be" are the debated ones], according to the report of the experts, because they have not received royal patronage. These books must be in your library in an accurate version, because this legislation, as could be expected from its divine nature, is very philosophical and genuine. Writers therefore and poets and the whole army of historians have been reluctant to refer to the aforementioned books, and to the men past (and present) who featured largely in them, because the consideration of them is sacred and hallowed . . ." (30-31). His recommendation was that six learned men from each of the twelve tribes should be brought to Alexandria "in order that after the examination of the text agreed by the majority, and the achievement of accuracy in the translation, we may produce an outstanding version in a manner worthy both of the contents and of your purpose" (32). Aristeas also reproduces the letter which the king sent to the high priest Eleazar requesting these translators and mentioning the release of slaves and the lavish gifts that the king was sending to him (35-40). Eleazar's reply is found in 41-46 and the names of the seventy-two translators are listed in 47-50. The king's gifts are detailed in 51-82 (especially the table for the temple) and paragraphs 83-120 provide a description of Jerusalem, the temple, the priestly service, the high-priestly vestments, and the citadel in Jerusalem.

The surpassing wisdom and virtue of the seventy-two translators, six from each of the twelve tribes, are of great interest to the writer. Aristeas tells us that the high priest chose "men of the highest merit and of excellent education due to the distinction of their parentage; they had not only mastered the Jewish literature, but had made a serious study of that of the Greeks as well. They were therefore well qualified for the embassy, and brought it to fruition as occasion demanded; they had a tremendous natural facility for the negotiations and questions arising from the Law, with the middle way as their commendable ideal . . ." (121-22; 121-27 are concerned with the translators).

After describing the surpassing qualities of the men who were to do the translating, Aristeas devotes a long section to the answers the high priest gave to questions about the law that he and his companion Andreas had posed (128-71). In particular they asked about the amount of concern shown in the law about matters clean and unclean. Among the statements of the high priest was this remarkable explanation: "Do not take the contemptible view that Moses enacted this legislation because of an excessive proccupation with mice and weasels or suchlike creatures. The fact is that everything has been solemnly set in order for unblemished investigation and amendment of life for the sake of righteousness" (144). The details of the law pointed to and embodied higher principles.

The translators were at last sent, and the king received them immediately — something not done even for ambassadors from other kings — thus showing the status that Ptolemy accorded to the high priest who had sent them (see 175). He invited them to a banquet where they would be served food in harmony with their custom; the king himself would eat the same fare (181). The oldest priest among the translators was invited to offer the prayer in which he asked for God's blessing on the king, his family, and all who were like-minded (195).

Paragraphs 187-294, one third of the work, are devoted to a rather overlong (Aristeas apologizes for its length in 295) account of the seven successive banquets at which the king asked questions of all seventy-two translators and all answered him wisely — ten at each banquet, with eleven at each of the last two. The questions and especially the answers are often on the subject of kingship. The king himself acknowledges this in 294: "I have been assisted a great deal by your giving me essential teaching on kingship." The translators stressed royal virtues such as impartiality, liberality, and justice. Sections 295-300 give Aristeas's personal reactions to the brilliance of the men from Israel.

By this time the reader may have forgotten about the translation, but it is treated in the next section (301-7), although more attention is devoted to the accommodations and daily routine of the men than to their work. The translation itself occupies one sentence: "They set to completing their several tasks, reaching agreement among themselves on each by comparing versions" (302; see also 306 which mentions their reading and explicating each point). The work took seventy-two days "just as if a result was achieved by some deliberate design" (307). The translation, in Demetrius's fair copy, was then presented to the Jews living in the area (308-11). They agreed that, "as this version has been made rightly and reverently, and in every respect accurately, it is good that this should remain exactly so, and that there should be no revision" (310). Anyone who changed it in any way was to be accursed (311). The product was also presented to the king, who read the whole. He marvelled at the lawgiver and gave orders for the careful preservation of the books. At last the translators were allowed to go home, laden with gifts from the king and with an open invitation to return (318-21).

The Letter presents a defense of Judaism and especially its law as the greatest wisdom coming from God through the most extraordinary lawgiver Moses. That law could not only take its place among the highest examples of Greek culture but exceeded them all. The high priest Eleazar, otherwise known only as a name in the list of the chief religious leaders of second temple Judaism, was a man of great wisdom who not only knew the details of the law but understood the great principles that underlay them. In addition he dealt comfortably with the greatest Ptolemaic monarch, who treated the Jewish high priest's messengers with more deference than those of other kings. The translators, drawn from all the tribes, were men of culture, well educated both in their native Hebrew and in Greek letters. The king admired the Jewish law and the men who were learned in it, and the philosophers present at the banquets led the way in appreciating the replies by the translators. When the king said: "I think that these men excel in virtue and have a fuller understanding, because when asked questions of this sort unexpectedly they give appropriate answers, all making God the basis of their argument" (200). To this the philospher Menedemus of Eritrea gave hearty consent (201). At a later banquet, after another round of questions and answers, the king again complimented them, as did the audience, "especially the philosophers, for these men far surpassed them in attitudes and eloquence, their starting point being God himself" (235).

Not only are Judaism, its scholars, its law, and its cult presented in a most favorable light but there is also a positive attitude toward the best of Greek culture. Demetrius learned of the excellence of the law, and the cultured, limitlessly wealthy king arranged for and financed the translation of it. He also freed more than 100,000 Judeans who had mistakenly been enslaved by his father, and during the banquets received many compliments from the translators. For the author, these two — the Hellenistic kingdom and the Jews — could live in harmony and mutual appreciation.

There has been a long debate among scholars regarding whether the Letter tells us anything historically reliable about the translation of the law into Greek. It is not impossible that the process happened or started in Philadelphus's reign since use of the translation is attested by ca. 200 BCE. It seems unlikely on general grounds that it all transpired just as the Letter claims. It is possible that the Letter was written in part to defend the validity of the Torah in Greek in face of claims made for the sole sufficiency of the Hebrew version. In later Christian retellings of the story about the translation found in the Letter, the tale expanded so that eventually the entire Hebrew Bible was involved (so Justin Martyr, *Dialogue with Trypho*

68:6-7); indeed, all the translators worked on the entire project independently, and when they compared their results at the end, wonder of wonders, every one of them was exactly alike (Irenaeus, *Against Heresies* 3.21.2).

(6) The Greek Esther (the Additions are deuterocanonical/apocryphal)

The Greek versions of the book of Esther contain not only a rendering of the nine chapters of the Hebrew book (with some differences) but also an extra 107 verses divided into six units scattered throughout the book and conventionally designated by the letters A-F. Esther resembles the book of Daniel in that it attracted additional sections over time. Most of the six Additions (A, C, D, F) were composed in a Semitic language (Hebrew or Aramaic), while Greek may have been the original language of B and E. Addition F, which is appended to the end of the original book, concludes with a colophon that explains the circumstances of at least that Addition: "In the fourth year of the reign of Ptolemy and Cleopatra, Dositheus, who said that he was a priest and a Levite, and his son Ptolemy brought to Egypt the preceding Letter about Purim, which they said was authentic and had been translated by Lysimachus son of Ptolemy, one of the residents of Jerusalem." It may be that the "Letter about Purim" refers to the entire book of Esther and at least Addition F (with which the book ends). There is some dispute about which Ptolemy and Cleopatra are meant, since several of such pairs are known. The most likely candidates are Ptolemy IX Soter II (114 BCE) and Ptolemy XII (77 BCE).

The six Additions were moved to the end of the original book by St. Jerome when he made his Latin translation of Esther. The result has been that the Additions have also been given chapter numbers which do not reflect their true locations in the book but the order in which they were assembled at the end. The locations of the six Additions relative to the original Hebrew text are these:

Addition A	(11:2–12:6)	precedes Esther 1	Mordecai's dream
Addition B	(13:1-7)	between 3:13 and 3:14	a letter of Artaxerxes
Addition C	(13:8–14:19)	after chap. 4	prayers of Mordecai and Esther
Addition D	(15:4-19)	after Addition C	Esther risks her life
Addition E	(16:1-24)	between 8:12 and 8:13	a second letter of Artaxerxes
Addition F	(10:4–11:1)	after 10:3 (end of the book)	Mordecai's dream interpreted

That is, the Greek Esther presents the story with a new introduction and a new conclusion, reinforced by other supplements in three places: within chapters 3 and 8, and a double one between chapters 4 and 5. A survey of these Additions will give the reader some idea of what effect they have on the original book.

Addition A: The section opens by identifying Mordecai and his circumstances, making some implausible historical claims in the process. Mordecai, according to the text, was taken captive during Nebuchadnezzar's first conquest of Jerusalem when he deported King Jeconiah (598 BCE), yet he was still serving in the court of King Artaxerxes more that 100 years later. Mordecai had a dream in which he saw two dragons who were poised to fight. As they roared in anticipation, all nations prepared for war against "the righteous nation" (11:7). When the righteous nation was about to perish, they cried to the deity; ". . . and at their outcry, as though from a tiny spring, there came a great river, with abundant water; light came, and the sun rose, and the lowly were exalted and devoured those held in honor" (11:10-11). Mordecai recognized that the dream predicted what God would do, but at this point he did not understand what it meant. He also overheard two eunuchs plotting an attack on the king, informed the king about it, and received a reward (while the eunuchs were executed). For some reason, all of this made Haman angry, and he "determined to injure Mordecai and his people because of the two eunuchs of the king" (12:6). The entire episode looks very much like the story in Esther 2:21-23.

Addition B: Esther 3:12-13 refers to the letter that Artaxerxes ordered to be drafted and in which he commanded that Haman's wish to exterminate the Jews be carried out; it does not, however, reproduce the text of the letter. Addition B supplies the text of the king's lengthy epistle in which he maintains that the Jews stand in the way of peace in his empire and should be killed on the fourteenth of Adar (the twelfth month).

Addition C: As Esther prepared to risk her life by entering the king's presence unsummoned, Mordecai prays. He acknowledges God as Lord and creator of all and declares that it was not pride that made him refuse to bow to Haman. Rather, he wished to show that he would bow to no one but God. He asks the God of Abraham to spare his people so that they could live to praise him. Next Queen Esther offers a prayer out of her great anxiety. Before doing so she removes her royal clothing and puts on the apparel of a mourner. For her, she says, God alone is king. She had heard as a child how the Lord had taken Israel from among the nations for an eternal inheritance, but sin had led God to hand Israel to the enemy. The queen prays that he will reverse the current enemy's plan and also asks for eloquent speech to turn the king against Haman. As she pleads for help she says: "I hate the splendor of the wicked and abhor the bed of the uncircumcised and of any alien" (14:15). She also hates the sign of royalty that she wears on her head. Her words address the problem raised by the original book that Esther seemingly had no qualms about the way in which she was selected and about her marriage to the Persian king. She ends by begging: "O God, whose might is over all, hear the voice of the despairing, and save us from the hands of evildoers. And save me from my fear!" (14:19).

Addition D: Following immediately after Addition C, Addition D tells the story of how Esther in great fear took the risk of entering Artaxerxes' presence without having been summoned. It is an expanded version of Esther 5:1-2, which it displaces. The Addition heightens the drama by describing Esther's extraordinary beauty, her great apprehension, and the king's terrible majesty. At first he was enraged when he saw her and Esther fainted, but God transformed the king into a kinder, gentler husband who tried to help and comfort her. He explained that she was not to die as the law required, since it applied only to their subjects. Esther flattered the king by saying he looked like an angel, yet she soon fainted again, causing quite a disturbance in the royal court. Addition D is followed directly by Esther 5:3.

Addition E: Esther 8:9-12 describes another letter from Artaxerxes, this one countering his earlier one. In it he allows the Jews to live by their laws, to defend themselves, and to do as they wished to their enemies on the thirteenth of the twelfth month. As with Addition B, Addition E cites the text of the letter. The king begins by speaking of honored people who become proud and evil and adds that from now on he will administer his kingdom more carefully. He condemns Haman and his request that Mordecai, Esther, and their people be destroyed. In the letter the king calls Haman a Macedonian who wanted to hand the Persian empire back to his people! Artaxerxes praises the Jews, their law, and their God; he even credits the God of the Jews with having always directed the kingdom. The royal governors are commanded not to enforce the earlier letter; rather, the Jews should be allowed to live by their laws and should be given reinforcements to help defend themselves on Adar 13. He also gives orders that the day is to be a festival for Jews and loyal Persians.

Addition F: As Additions B and E (the two letters) and C and D (which are placed one after the other and connected in content) are paired, so A and F belong together. In the last of the Additions Mordecai recalls the dream described in Addition A and realizes that it has now been fulfilled. The little spring that grew into a river was Esther, and the dragons were Haman and Mordecai. God had rescued his people Israel and had performed mighty signs. Alluding to the festival of Purim (= Lots) that memorializes the events of the book of Esther, Mordecai says there is one lot for Israel and one for all the nations. Hence, Adar 14 and 15 were to be celebrated with joy forever. The colophon noted above concludes Addition F.

What do these Additions do to the book of Esther? First, the many references to God, the prayers to him, the references to Israel's saving history and apostasy from the Lord all lend a strongly religious cast to the book which, in the original form, lacks it almost entirely. The Greek translation also has references to God in places where it is translating the Hebrew but where the Hebrew fails to mention him. Second, the Additions fill in what is missing from the Hebrew version (e.g., the letters) and add intriguing details such as Haman's being a Macedonian. Third, the Additions at times heighten the drama in the already dramatic story; this happens especially in Addition D. And fourth, the dream at the beginning shows that everything that happens in the book was known beforehand to God and foreordained by him.

Rewritten Scripture

While the narrative books tell stories of different kinds, whether historical or novelistic, there is another series of works that often take narrative form but which seize upon some hero from the Hebrew Bible and expand upon scriptural stories about him. In some instances one can make a good case that one such story has influenced another; in fact, they may all stand in a common, broad tradition.

1 Enoch (pseudepigraphal)

One of the oldest texts from the second temple period is the long and complex work known today as *1 Enoch*. As it now stands, the collection is made up of five booklets, each of which was composed at a different time and all of which present themselves as revelations made to Enoch, the seventh patriarch from Adam according to the genealogy in Genesis 5 (see vv. 21-24). In the following paragraphs the two oldest parts of *1 Enoch* will be treated: chapters 1–36 and 72-82. The other sections will be reserved for later study. Chapters 83–90 and 37–71 are analyzed in the apocalyptic section, and chapters 91–108 (less the Apocalypse of Weeks in chapters 93 and 91) can be found in the wisdom section.

(1) The Astronomical Book of Enoch (1 Enoch 72–82)

The Astronomical Book (AB) was written in the Aramaic language, as we now know from the four copies of it found among the Dead Sea Scrolls (4Q208-11). From Aramaic it was translated into Greek (there are only a few small remnants that have survived) and from Greek into Ethiopic. Judging from the script, the oldest of the Aramaic copies (4Q208) dates from a time not far from 200 BCE; consequently, the book itself was composed no later than that and probably earlier, although we do not know how much earlier. The Aramaic copies that have survived indicate that the Ethiopic version of the booklet, the only complete one that exists, is a condensed form of the AB in that its text lacks some of the long, table-like sections attested for the beginning of the book in two of the Aramaic copies.

The AB presents itself as a revelation to Enoch by the angel Uriel, whose name appropriately means "God is my light." He does not simply tell Enoch the contents of the book but rather takes him on an immense tour, showing him the workings of the sun, moon, stars, the heavenly gates through which they pass, and some of the major geographical features of the earth. The book itself is actually supposed to be Enoch's first person report about these matters to his son Methuselah, after he had returned from his journey. The AB is the earliest known work that associates Enoch with astronomical phenomena and with the length of the year — something that may already be implied by his biblical age of 365 years at the time when God "took" him (Gen. 5:23-24). The revelations contain a large amount of descriptive (though often inaccurate) data, in which Uriel advances the unscientific claim that angels run the universe on God's behalf. The laws depicted in the book, we are told, will be in effect until the new creation.

The first chapter of the surviving text describes a solar year consisting of 364 days. Uriel shows Enoch that the sun rises through six gates in the east and sets into six in the west. The moon and stars too rise and set through them. As the sun progresses from one gate to another from month to month, the amount of daylight increases or decreases. At the solstices the ratio of darkness/light in a day is 2:1. The first month in the year has thirty days as does the second but the third has thirty-one; this pattern is repeated in each quarter of the year. Several times the writer notes that people err by not including the four extra days in calculating the year.

First Enoch 73:1–74:9 (see also chap. 78) provides information about the movements of the moon in relation to the sun, and also begins to describe the increasing illumination of the lunar surface facing the earth in the days after the new moon. Each night the amount of the surface that is lighted increases by one fourteenth until it reaches full moon, and after that it decreases by the same percentage each night until the moon is invisible from the earth. The systematic presentation of such information is abbreviated, however, in the Ethiopic version. It seems that in the original Aramaic form of the booklet, the writer gave detailed accounts of such matters for each day in the year in what must have been a long and tedious section. The Ethiopic has preserved the data only for a few days. We are also told that the lunar year lasts 354 days, with alternating months of twenty-nine and thirty days.

After treating the sun and moon for several chapters, the writer turns to geographical topics in chapters 76–77. Here he mentions features such as seven exceptionally high mountains, seven rivers, and seven large islands. These topics may seem strange in an astronomical book, but we know that ancient astrology had a geographical side to it because certain signs or configurations were believed to predict what would happen in certain parts of the earth. The AB thus seems to be combining two topics of astrological interest.

Most of chapters 80:2–82:3 deal with unexpected subjects. They predict that in the coming days of the sinners the years will grow shorter, the crops will be late, the moon will change its pattern, and people will consider stars to be gods. In chapter 81 Enoch reads the deeds of all people from heavenly tablets. As these chapters appear to be in conflict with the remainder of the book, where the laws of nature are supposed to be in effect until the end, it is not clear why they are in the text.

The AB allows us to see clearly that ancient Jewish writers thought of Enoch as an expert in astronomy, one who had an unimpeachable source of information. Enoch, as the seventh man from Adam, has been compared with Enmeduranki, who was the seventh antediluvian king in some versions of the Sumerian king list. Enmeduranki was king of Sippar, the city of the sun god, and was the ancestor of a certain kind of diviner. The gods had disclosed secret information to him. The Enoch of the AB seems to embody some similar traits as the Jewish hero who associates with divine beings and is perfectly informed about the movements of the heavenly bodies.

The AB presents two schematic calendars for the year. It does not evaluate them, or prefer one to the other; rather they are both revealed to Enoch. The calendars, however, have nothing distinctively Jewish about them. Although the 364-day solar year is divisible by seven (it has exactly fifty-two weeks), the sabbath is never mentioned, nor is any other biblical holiday dated by it. In fact, there are only a few places in which the AB is clearly based on the Hebrew Bible (one being the choice of Enoch as the hero). It is rather a "scientific" teatise which exercised a considerable influence on the authors of the *Book of Jubilees* and the Qumran literature.

(2) The Book of the Watchers (1 Enoch 1–36)

The second early booklet connected with the name Enoch was also written in Aramaic. It too has been identified in several copies from Qumran cave 4 (4Q201-202, 204-206), the oldest of which (4Q201) dates from between 200 and 150 BCE. As a result, it may be another third-century text. The Book of the Watchers (BW) is best known for introducing the strange story (or stories) about the angels who sinned by marrying women and fathering giants. The story in various forms became a major theme in the Enoch tradition and in a surprisingly large number of other works both Jewish and Christian.

The BW is a composite work, containing at least five sections which may not always have been joined.

Chapters 1–5: These chapters serve as an introduction to the booklet and set the theme of divine judgment for human sin. The author writes that the composition is the blessing with which Enoch blessed the righteous and a vision shown to him by the holy angels for the benefit of a distant generation. Most of the first chapter is a poetic theophany, a description of God's descent to Mt. Sinai for the final judgment (Jude 14-15 quotes the end of it, *1 Enoch* 1:9). This impressive poem precedes a section in which nature's obedience to the laws established by the creator is contrasted with human disobedience to God's commands. Enoch tells the sinners about the curse awaiting them, and the chosen are promised life and peace (chaps. 2–5).

Chapters 6–11: These chapters, in which Enoch plays no explicit role, offer the earliest forms of the story about heavenly angels (Watchers) who sinned by marrying women and fathering children from them. It is based on Genesis 6:1-4 (some words from it are quoted here): the sons of God in that passage are understood to be angels and the daughters of men are, of course, women. The section includes at least two versions of the myth. In one Shemihazah is the leader of some two hundred angels who descended from heaven after seeing and desiring the lovely ladies of the earth. They married some of them and taught them magical arts. The women bore giants who ate all the crops and finally ate humans and one another. A second version features Asael (Azazel) as chief angel; he is credited with teaching people how to make weapons, telling women how to use cosmetics, and disclosing information about precious stones. All of these are considered illicit disclosures which led people into sin. The violence and evil that resulted from the angelic incursion into the world caused humans to cry out for help. Their cry reached four righteous angels who had remained in heaven; they brought it before God who assigned to each of them a task in undoing the damage done. Uriel was dispatched to warn the son of Lamech (= Noah) of the approaching flood. Raphael was to bind Asael and throw him into darkness until the day of judgment, when he was to be transferred into fire; Raphael was also to restore the earth. The angel Gabriel was sent to punish the children born from the illicit unions by having them engage in a war of mutual destruction. Michael had as his assignment to tell Shemihazah and his angels that they were to witness the battle between their sons, and then to be bound until the judgment when they too would be led to a fiery prison. The section concludes with a description of the blessed conditions that would follow after wrong was destroyed from the earth.

While the angel stories may have served different purposes, one aim was to explain why God took the drastic step of sending a flood. Genesis speaks only generally about the evil of mankind as the cause, but *1 Enoch* provides greater detail which explains the exponential growth of wickedness before the flood that forced God's hand into an extraordinary punishment.

Chapters 12–16: Presupposing a story about angels who sinned, chapters 12–16 introduce Enoch into the action from which he was previously missing (although the events narrated here are understood to have occurred during the action of chaps. 6–11). Here the Watchers ask Enoch to intercede on their behalf before the God into whose presence they can no longer enter. That is, there is a reversal of roles: angels should bring human petitions before God (as they do in chap. 10), but now a special human brings the case of angels to the deity. Enoch receives an answer to the petition in a spectacular vision in which he sees the heavenly temple-palace, which is made of ice and fire. Unlike biblical worthies such as Isaiah, who from below saw the Lord enthroned, Enoch not only sees him but is brought into heaven and summoned by God into his presence. The Lord rejects the Watchers' request, sentences them to everlasting punishment, and decrees the destruction of their children. God charges them with violating their natures: procreation was for mortals, not for immortal angels. This section also introduces a new cast of unsavory characters: demons or evil spirits, who are said to emerge from the corpses of the giants and who carry on their evil influences in the world, thus explaining why evil continued even after the angels and giants were removed.

Chapters 17–19: As they are located in the text, these chapters resume the narrative directly after Enoch's visionary encounter with God in his heavenly home. Now angels, primarily Uriel, conduct Enoch on a tour of intriguing parts of the world as imagined by the author, especially at its limits. They first bring him to the west and then to the south where, among other phenomena, he sees seven great mountains (perhaps in the northwest corner of the world): three were aligned toward the east and three to the south, with one in the middle reaching to heaven like the throne of God. On his tour Enoch sees the horrible place where the angels who sinned are imprisoned until the judgment takes place. The section ends with Enoch declaring: "(So) I, Enoch, I saw the vision of the end of everything alone; and none among human beings will see as I have seen" (19:3).

Chapters 20–36: Chapter 20 is an interlude which names the six (or seven in Greek) angels who keep watch and lists their functions. Once their names have been presented, the text continues with another tour for Enoch that in some respects parallels the one in chapters 17–19 but which contains a number of allusions to the Genesis stories about the garden of Eden. One of the more interesting passages in this section is chapter 22 where the angel Raphael shows Enoch the four places where different kinds of souls are to be gathered: one place for the righteous, one for the sinners who were not punished during their lives on earth, one for the righteous who became martyrs (like Abel, who figures prominently in the chapter), and one for the souls of the unrighteous who apparently did receive punishment during their lives. Enoch thus sees that such places are part of the presently existing structure of the universe.

Another site that Enoch inspects (perhaps in the east) also has seven mountains, distributed in the same way as the ones in chapter 18. The middle mountain has many trees around it, one of which, Michael explains, no creature may touch until the end. Then its fruit will give long lives to the righteous, as long as those of Enoch's ancestors. That tree will be planted next to the Lord's house. The reference here is clearly to the tree of life from the garden of Eden.

Enoch then travels past the center of the earth (the area of Jerusalem) and moves toward the northeast where he again sees seven mountains covered with fragrant trees. Eventually he reaches the garden of righteousness which has within it the tree of wisdom. Raphael explains that it was the one from which Adam and Eve had eaten, gained wisdom, but realized their nakedness. His tour finally takes him around the ends of the earth where he sees more wondrous sights, including the gates through which the stars and winds move. There are a number of points of contact in chapters 33–36 with the Astronomical Book. At the end of it all, as he does at several points during his travels, Enoch blesses and praises the great God who has made all these wonders.

By the end of *1 Enoch* 1–36 the reader should be impressed with Enoch's encyclopedic knowledge which was revealed to him by God and his angels. These teachings, unlike those of the Watchers, were legal and beneficial. In the course of his contacts with heavenly beings and tours of the universe, Enoch learns not only interesting and at times exotic details but also becomes aware that God has not forgotten the righteous nor has he overlooked the evil of the angels and other sinners. He has already created separated places where the different kinds of souls will receive their due rewards. Presumably such teachings were to reassure suffering people that God was in control and would rescue them while also punishing those who oppressed them and who had filled the world with overwhelming violence and evil.

Aramaic Levi

Aramaic Levi differs from the previously considered texts in that no complete copy exists and it is included in none of the traditional categories. Rather it has been reconstructed by modern scholars from a series of fragmentary witnesses in two languages and from several different time periods, ranging from the second century BCE (4Q213) to the medieval period. Consequently, the order of the text, especially at the beginning, has been a matter of debate among experts. The order that is given below seems the most likely, but is not the only possible one.

Aramaic Levi appears in this section of the present book because it is probably a very old text and one that influenced others in the tradition. The earliest copy, found in Qumran cave 4 (4Q213), dates from perhaps the middle of the second century BCE; it is likely that the work was written earlier still. Also, it very likely served in some way as a source for the *Book of Jubilees* (see below), which was written ca. 160-150 BCE. It is not impossible that Aramaic Levi is a third century work.

The following appears to be the most reasonable order of sections in Aramaic Levi.

The Shechem Story (preserved in very fragmentary form): In Genesis 34 Shechem, the son of the ruler of the city Shechem, desired Dinah, Leah and Jacob's only daughter, and raped her. He then requested through his father that she be given to him in marriage. That marriage was to be part of a program of intermarriage between the people of Shechem and the family of Jacob, but Jacob's sons objected that no such alliance could occur while the men of Shechem remained uncircumcised. Shechem convinced the men of the city to become circumcised; however, on the third day after the operation, "when they were still in pain, two of the sons of Jacob, Simeon and Levi, Dinah's brothers, took their swords and came against the city unawares, and killed all the males. They killed Hamor and his son Shechem with the sword, and took Dinah out of Shechem's house, and went away" (Gen. 34:25-26). Their other brothers then plundered the city. In Genesis 49:5-7 Jacob cursed the violent deed of these two sons of his, but in the later tradition presented here their effort was applauded as a praiseworthy expression of zeal, one that gained the priesthood for Levi who was, according to the Bible, the ancestor of the priests.

Levi's Prayer (well preserved): At some time after the Shechem episode Levi prayed that an unrighteous spirit would be removed from him, that he would be shown the holy spirit, and that he would be given counsel, wisdom, and strength. He also asked that God would draw him and his sons close to him so that they should be his servants forever in the cause against evil.

Levi's Vision (fragmentarily preserved): Levi sees heaven and apparently ascends to it; there he receives a warning against marrying outside the clan (an issue in the Shechem episode). There he is also proclaimed as priest, and priestly sovereignty is presented as superior to that of the sword (that is, the secular government).

Levi's Meetings with Isaac and Jacob (brief and well preserved): Isaac blesses his grandson Levi. Levi then officiates as priest, and Jacob gives him a tithe of everything. This happens at Bethel where Jacob had vowed that he would give a tenth of all to God (= to a priest; Gen. 28:22); now he pays that vow. Jacob also consecrates Levi as priest, and Levi offers sacrifice and blesses his father and brothers. All of them take up residence near the aging Isaac.

Isaac's Instructions to Levi about Sacrifice (well preserved): This appears to have been the longest section in the work, perhaps occupying about one third of the entire text. Isaac, who like all the great patriarchs of Genesis acts as a priest, informs Levi about the law of the priesthood. He stresses that Levi is to keep himself pure from uncleanness and fornication (again warning about exogamy). When sacrificing he must wash his hands and feet before and after, use only the twelve acceptable kinds of wood for incinerating the victim, and be extremely careful about covering and washing blood. A fairly large amount of space is devoted to the proportions of items that accompanied burnt offerings (e.g., wine, salt). These cultic instructions are traced to Abraham's teachings, drawn from a book of Noah about blood. Levi is to have an eternal priesthood.

Levi's Autobiography (well preserved section): Levi relates how old he was when various events in his life occurred. For example, the Shechem episode happened when he was eighteen and he became priest at age nineteen. He mentions his children and explains their names.

Levi's Testamentary Address to His Children (well preserved): In the year that Joseph died and Levi was 118 years of age (he would live to be 137), he speaks to his children and their children. He stresses various virtues to them, such as justice, truth, and especially wisdom (reading, writing, and instruction in wisdom). He also predicts that they will turn aside from the path of righteousness and mentions, in a poorly preserved context, an accusation that Enoch had uttered in his day.

The work serves to elevate Levi, who is a curious character in the Bible. In Genesis he is mentioned, apart from lists of Jacob's sons, only in the Shechem story of chapter 34 and in the curse Jacob pronounced on him in chapter 49; nevertheless, as the patriarch of the tribe of Levi he was the ancestor of the priests. Aramaic Levi draws motifs from Exodus 32, where the Levites zealously slaughter those who worshiped the golden calf, and Numbers 25 where the priest Phinehas is given a covenant of eternal priesthood for his zeal in executing an Israelite man and the Moabite woman with whom he was having sex. Levi is described in glowing terms in Malachi 2:4-7 which mentions a covenant with him, and that he revered God, stood in awe of him, and walked in integrity and uprightness; Malachi may even call him a messenger of God. The Aramaic Levi text thus reads the priesthood back to an earlier time in biblical history and rehabilitates the rather questionable character of Levi. It also presents a view of priestly duties and certainly warns strongly against marrying outside the clan. This portrait of Levi was to prove influential in the *Book of Jubilees* and in the *Testaments of the Twelve Patriarchs*.

The Book of Jubilees (pseudepigraphal)

Jubilees is a work that draws upon the early Enoch booklets (which it mentions) and Aramaic Levi. It is a retelling of the biblical stories from creation to the scene at Mt. Sinai, often reproducing parts of Genesis-Exodus but also adding to or subtracting from them. The original language of the book was almost certainly Hebrew, since all of the fourteen or fifteen fragmentary copies of it found at Qumran are in that language. The oldest of these copies (4Q216) can be dated to approximately 125-100 BCE; consequently, the book was almost certainly written before that time. As the author seems to know the Enochic Book of Dreams (*1 Enoch* 83–90; see below) which was written in the late 160s BCE, a date of around 150 BCE seems likely for *Jubilees*. The Hebrew text of the book was translated into Greek and possibly Syriac and later lost until the Dead Sea Scrolls were found. The Greek version (also lost) served as the basis for translations into the Latin and Ethiopic languages. The only complete text of the book is in Ethiopic, but comparison of the Ethiopic text with the Hebrew fragments shows that it is a reliable rendition.

Jubilees begins with the Lord's command that Moses come up to him on Mt. Sinai on the day after the covenant was made there (see Exodus 24). As he speaks with Moses, the Lord predicts that Israel will stray from the covenant it has just made, and Moses tries unsuccessfully to intercede for the nation. God then orders an angel of the divine presence to dictate the course of history to Moses from the heavenly tablets (an image which suggests that all has been preordained). This he does in *Jubilees* 2–50, which are another form of the material in Genesis 1–Exodus 19. By prefacing his own chapter 1 to the biblical story, the writer stresses the importance of obeying the covenantal laws for maintaining a proper relationship with the God of the covenant.

There is no need to rehearse the contents of *Jubilees*, since the book retells the stories of Genesis and, more briefly, the first half of Exodus. Yet there are a number of traits that distinguish *Jubilees* from its biblical base.

The covenant: Covenants are tremendously important in Genesis-Exodus, but *Jubilees* presents the agreements with Noah, Abra(ha)m, and Moses in a somewhat different light. Each of the pacts, beginning with the one directly after the flood, is considered the same covenant; it is renewed and updated as time moves along. Also, each covenantal ceremony takes place in the third month of the year, and all of them are associated with the festival of weeks (all but the one with Noah transpire on the fifteenth of the third month, the date of this festival in *Jubilees*). The coupling of covenant and the festival of weeks (called *pentecoste* in Greek) was to continue at Qumran where the annual covenant renewal and admission of new members seems to have occurred on this date. In *Jubilees*, the single agreement between God and the chosen line had more laws added to it as more renewals occurred. Fidelity to the laws of the covenant, insofar as those laws had been revealed at a particular time, was essential to maintaining a proper relation with God.

Antedating: Jubilees teaches that a number of laws or practices which in the Bible are introduced only in Moses' time, were already revealed to and practiced by the patriarchs of Genesis. So, for example, the rules in Leviticus 12 for the times of a woman's impurity after bearing a boy or a girl (these times determine how long she is to stay away from the sanctuary and avoid touching holy objects) are based on the separate times when Adam and Eve were introduced into the garden of Eden (3:8-14; Eden is presented as a sanctuary in *Jubilees*). Also, all of the pilgrimage festivals, first mentioned in Exodus 23, are said to have been practiced by Abraham, and Noah was the first human to celebrate the festival of weeks (6:17-22). In *Jubilees*, therefore, the patriarchs are pictured as careful practitioners of the law.

Separating from gentiles: Jubilees mentions the divine election of Jacob and his descendants already in the creation story and draws some parallels between Jacob and the sabbath. It insists that members of the chosen line avoid those outside of it, and it is especially insistent that they not intermarry with the nations (as Esau did). The paradigmatic story is in *Jubilees* 30 (see Genesis 34) where Levi and Simeon prevent large-scale intermarriage between Jacob's family and the Shechemites by killing the men of Shechem. In *Jubilees'* retelling of this story there is a lengthy exhortation from the angel of the presence against such marriages, and Levi is rewarded for his zeal by being given the priesthood. The ultimate problem with such marriages was that they involved mixing the pure with the impure and greatly increased the danger that a gentile spouse would lead a member of Jacob's family into idolatry.

Chronology and calendar: Jubilees dates a large number of events using a heptadic system in which the key unit is a jubilee of years (= a forty-nine-year period). Each jubilee unit (hence the name of the book) consists of seven weeks of years (a week is a seven-year span), and each year lasts 364 days, a total exactly divisible by seven. Thus *Jubilees* has the same solar year as the Astronomical Book of Enoch, with each of the twelve months having the same numbers of days as in the Enochic text. Unlike it, however, *Jubilees* forbids use of the moon in calculating the month or year (6:23-38).

Jubilees uses creation, not some other starting point, as the beginning of its chronological system. The exodus from Egypt occurred in the year 2410 from creation (= forty-nine jubilees, one week, and two years; see 50:4). The writer notes that the entry into Canaan lay forty years in the future, that is, it would take place in the year of the world 2450 (the end of exactly fifty jubilee periods). As a result, the author places two crucial events in this fiftieth jubilee period: the freeing of the Israelite slaves from Egypt (the exodus) and restoration to them of their ancestral land (Canaan; in *Jubilees* Canaan was given to Shem, Noah's son, and later stolen by Canaan [see chaps. 8–10]). These events parallel on a national level what was supposed to happen for the individual Israelite in the fiftieth or jubilee year: the Hebrew slave was released from bondage, and the alienated ancestral property was restored to its original owner (see Leviticus 25).

Problem-solving: As he retells the biblical story, the author solves some difficulties that arise from the scriptural text. For example, in Genesis 2:17 the Lord God said to the first man: "but of the tree of the knowledge of good and evil you shall not eat, for in the day that you eat of it you shall die." However, the man does eat from the fruit of the tree but, rather than dying on that day, he lives until a goodly age of 930 years. *Jubilees* solves the difficulty by interpreting the word *day* in the light of Psalm 90:4 where one thousand years are said to be "like yesterday when it is past." For the writer of *Jubilees* this implied that, as the writer of 2 Peter 3:8 was to put it later, "with the Lord one day is like a thousand years, and a thousand years are like one day." Read in that sense, Adam did die during the "day" of his sin by living only 930 years. Or, to mention one other example of problem-solving, Jubilees removes some of the troubling implications of Genesis 22 where God commands Abraham to sacrifice his son Isaac. Our author says that the prince of Mastema, the leader of the forces of evil, had challenged God to test Abraham in this way, just as the satan challenged him to try Job. Hence the order to sacrifice Isaac is to be seen within a larger context in which the guilt is transferred to the prince of Mastema.

Jubilees seems to have been an important book for the people associated with the Dead Sea Scrolls, as the number of copies of it found in the caves testifies. Its calendar was used there, and its dating of the festivals was adopted by the men of Qumran who also renewed the covenant on the festival of weeks.

The Testaments of the Twelve Patriarchs (pseudepigraphal)

The *Testaments of the Twelve Patriarchs* is the name given to a collection of shorter compositions that are supposed to be the last wills and testaments of Jacob's twelve sons, each ending with an account of the death of a patriarch. The composite work which survives in Greek is related to biblical scenes such as Genesis 49 where Jacob, at the close of his life, gathers his twelve sons "that I may tell you what will happen to you in the days to come" (49:1). He then addresses words to each of his sons, moving from oldest to youngest (vv. 2-28), gives instructions about his burial, and then dies in his bed (vv. 29-35). The editor of the *Testaments of the Twelve Patriarchs* has adopted the same format for his compositions, except that each of the twelve components has one of Jacob's sons, beginning with the eldest (Reuben) and continuing through the youngest (Benjamin), gather his sons around him as he is about to die. The elderly man mentions an event or events from his life (drawn from Genesis or other sources [the *Testament of Asher* is an exception]), gives moral instructions that arise from his experiences, predicts what will happen to them, exhorts them once more, dies, and is buried by his sons. Eight of the testaments are relatively short while four are more extensive: Levi, Judah, Joseph, and Benjamin. Levi and Judah are prominent because they were the ancestors of the priests and kings, and Joseph and to a lesser degree Benjamin are important because of the larger roles they play in Genesis.

It is debatable whether the *Testaments of the Twelve Patriarchs* should be included in a book about the second temple period because, as it now exists, it is clearly a Christian work. Although almost all of it reads like a Jewish composition, a series of passages have been identified as Christian in origin, some of them more obviously than others (see *T. Benj.* 9:3 for an unmistakable example). This has led to two major options for understanding the development of the work. One is that a Jewish writer compiled a collection of testaments connected with Jacob's twelve sons and that a Christian editor or copyist (perhaps more than one) added a few sentences in the predictive sections to relate the forecasts more directly to Jesus Christ. The other is that a Christian compiled the testaments, using Jewish sources. Given the small number of demonstrably Christian passages, it seems more likely that the *Testaments of the Twelve Patriarchs* is a Jewish work with some Christian additions. Moreover, at Qumran texts that may be related to two of the testaments have been found: the Aramaic Levi text (treated above) has a large amount of the material that appears in the *Testament of Levi,* and a *Testament of Naphtali* (4Q215) shares some points with the Greek work of the same name. In light of the uncertainties about the genesis of the *Testaments,* it is very difficult to date. Suggestions have ranged from the second century BCE to the second century CE.

Though there are twelve compositions involved, they share a number of themes and thus suggest that they have undergone a shared editorial process.

1. Throughout the work the superiority of Levi and Judah is reiterated. The other patriarchs exhort their children to obey them and predict that eschatological leaders will arise from those two tribes. This is a clue that the *Testaments* belongs in the same tradition as Aramaic Levi and *Jubilees.* The latter stresses the importance of Levi and Judah and incorporates a scene in which Isaac blesses both of them and predicts bright futures for their descendants (*Jubilees* 31). Other indications that the work belongs in the *Enoch-Levi-Jubilees* tradition are the several references to the angelic Watchers and their sin, to Enoch's writings (although the passages in question cannot be found in *1 Enoch*), and calling the leader of evil Belial. The testaments of Levi and Judah are well developed. That of Levi contains accounts of two visions, and deals at length with his virtuous conduct at Shechem (Genesis 34) and his appointment to the priesthood. The *Testament of Judah* highlights his role as ancestor of the kings but it differs from the *Testament of Levi* in that Judah has more to confess (marrying a Canaanite woman and having children with his daughter-in-law Tamar whom he mistook for a prostitute; see Gen. 38). Judah himself recognizes the superiority of Levi. His testament also contains several stories about his military prowess (some of which are paralleled in *Jubilees*) and about his problems with drunkenness.

2. Joseph plays a prominent role throughout the *Testaments* because his brothers have to confess their role in the mistreatment of their annoying younger brother and acknowledge that he treated them virtuously when they came to him in Egypt. In his own testament Joseph appears as a paragon of virtue, primarily because of his success in withstanding the unrelenting sexual advances of the Egyptian woman whose husband owned him (see Gen. 39:6b-18). His success in this regard served as a strong counterexample to the difficulties that two of his brothers — Judah and Reuben (see Gen. 35:22 where Reuben has sexual relations with Bilhah, Jacob's concubine) — experienced in this area of life, and thus as a source and model of what the younger generation was called upon to do.

3. The *Testaments* are filled with warnings against various vices and with recommendations of different virtues. The dangers of sexual impurity are frequently held before the younger generation's eyes; also condemned are envy, arrogance, greed, anger, lying, hatred, and double-mindedness. Virtues encouraged are simplicity, mercy, goodness, chastity, and a pure mind.

4. As the patriarchs predict what will happen to their descendants, they regularly forecast a time of sin, exile as punishment for that sin, and eventual return. In these sections there are predictions about future messiahs, and in such passages a number of Christian additions appear. The *Testaments* speak of a resurrection and also of salvation for the gentiles as well as for the offspring of the patriarchs.

5. The patriarchs often exhort their sons to obey the law, and *T. Asher* 2:10 even makes reference to a specific law in the Pentateuch (see Lev. 11:6; Deut. 14:7). This is strange, given the fictive setting of the book in patriarchal, pre-Mosaic times. However, it should be recalled that *Jubilees* too retrojects a number of Mosaic laws into the stories of Genesis; the author of the *Testaments* may be assuming a similar situation.

Apocalypses

The apocalypses are among the most interesting kinds of texts composed in the second temple period. These works have received their name from their resemblance to the New Testament book of Revelation (whose Greek title is *apokalupsis*). The apocalypses normally have these generic elements: (1) they are revelations (2) by a supernatural being such as an angel (3) to a human recipient. They may contain disclosures about the heavenly world (that is, what is beyond normal human knowledge) and/or the future. The

Jewish apocalypses are pseudepigraphs, that is, they are attributed to famous figures of the past (e.g., Enoch). An implication of this practice is that the apocalypses which survey biblical history present it in the form of prediction, since most of biblical history transpired after the time of, say, Enoch. These "predictions" of the past are not distinguished formally from parts of the apocalypses that are actual predictions for the real author. Apparently his accuracy in "predicting" the past was supposed to give the reader confidence that he would get the actual future right as well. The apocalypses arose among Jews in perhaps the late third century and certainly in the second century BCE and were written to console the readers with information about the true nature of the present situation, not limited to what humans normally perceive. The Astronomical Book of Enoch is sometimes called an apocalypse, although the reality it discloses is largely what is accessible to human observation. The Book of the Watchers is also termed an apocalypse by some; this would be true especially of Enoch's throne vision in chapter 14 and his tours in chapters 17–36.

The first historical apocalypses, that is, ones with surveys of history and the future, first appear in the second century BCE. The material in Daniel 7–12 belongs in this category, and these chapters are usually dated to approximately 165 BCE. However, since they are in the Hebrew Bible, they will not be treated here. The first historical apocalypses come from the fourth and fifth books of *1 Enoch*.

The Apocalypse of Weeks (1 Enoch 93:1-10; 91:11-17; pseudepigraphal)

The oldest surviving historical apocalypse in Jewish literature is probably the short composition known as the Apocalypse of Weeks. The fact that it does not mention the persecution of Jews and the ban on Judaism by Antiochus IV in 167 BCE implies that it was written before these events, that is, perhaps in approximately 170 BCE. It has accidentally been divided into two parts in the Ethiopic version of *1 Enoch* and the order of the two parts reversed; an Aramaic manuscript from Qumran preserves much of the apocalypse and has the parts in the correct order (4Q212). The apocalypse takes the form of Enoch's report to Methuselah regarding a vision he had seen; the text also mentions words of the angels and the contents of the heavenly tablets as the sources of the revelation disclosed to him. In the report he quickly sketches history from beginning to end, with almost all of it packaged as a prediction. History and the different stages of the judgment are divided into ten units called "weeks." These seven-part units are suggestive for several reasons: they are one of a number of references and allusions to "sevens" in the apocalypse (e.g., Enoch is the seventh patriarch); the ten "weeks" total seventy units, itself a highly significant number in light of Jeremiah's prediction that Jerusalem would be desolate for the seventy years of Babylonian control (see Jer. 25:11-12; 29:10; Dan. 9:2, 24-27); and the decisive "week," that is, the one in which the actual author lives and when the great turning point in history will begin is the seventh. As 7 × 7 = 49, the total brings to mind associations with the biblical jubilee (which the author of *Jubilees* and others understood as a forty-nine-year unit).

The sentences about each of the ten "weeks" center around an important character or event, sometimes groups of them. The author has taken some pains to group the weeks. Weeks one and ten parallel each other in that the Watchers appear in both, and they are the times of the first and second creation. Weeks two and nine are also paired by the shared theme of judgments over the whole earth, the flood in week two and a phase of the final judgment in week nine. Weeks three and eight are similar in that each refers to an event at the "weekend." In the first week Enoch is said to be the seventh, in the second Noah and the flood are noted toward the end, in the third Abraham, in the fourth the giving of the law, and in the fifth the davidic monarchy are placed at the conclusion. The descriptions of the next few "weeks" are more complicated. In the sixth there is a time of wickedness, the ascent of Elijah, the destruction of the davidic monarchy, and the exile. The pivotal seventh "week," the time of the author, witnesses the rise of an apostate generation, the gift of sevenfold wisdom to the chosen, and the destruction of sinners. The eighth "week" is the time for righteousness and righteous judgment on the sinners, while a house is built for God. In the ninth righteous judgment is revealed to the entire world and evil vanishes, and in the tenth judgment is executed on the Watchers, the old heaven vanishes, and a new one appears. After this there will be, predicts Enoch, numberless weeks forever and in them sin will have no part.

A noteworthy feature of the apocalypse is its periodizing of history, implying that all is already predetermined in heaven, supposedly long before most of the predicted events took place. Also, the writer never mentions a resurrection before the judgment but consoles the readers with the thought of judgment on evil and a future life forever free of its influence.

The Book of Dreams
(1 Enoch 83–90; pseudepigraphal)

Here too Enoch tells his son Methuselah about his predictive dream visions. In this section he reports two such experiences. In the first and shorter one (83–84) he sees the heavens thrown down on earth, the earth swallowed up, and everything sinking into the abyss. His grandfather Mahalalel explains to him that the vision concerns the wickedness of the earth and its approaching destruction (the flood). He urges Enoch to pray that a remnant be left to him on the earth. He does pray for the remnant, and, after seeing the sun rise on a new day, blesses and praises the Lord.

The second and longer section is called the Animal Apocalypse (chaps. 85–90). Interpretation of the last historical allusions in the vision, especially the character who appears to be Judas Maccabeus (the ram with a horn in 90:9, etc.), has led scholars to date it to the late 160s BCE. The apocalypse has received its name from the fact that in it biblical characters are described symbolically as animals. Colors and types of animals express character evaluations. In the text Enoch surveys all of scriptural history and moves beyond it to the time of the actual author and the end. The symbols and the language are usually clear enough so that the biblically literate reader can follow the course of the story.

The patriarchs at the beginning of Genesis are portrayed as bulls; those in the chosen line are pictured as white, and the others as black bulls. The story about the angels who sinned looms large in the text. These celestial beings are called stars, and are distinguished from virtuous angels who are called men. One star fell from heaven first (apparently Azazel) and his arrival among the bulls was accompanied by sexual evils and mixings of different kinds of bulls and cows. He was followed by many others. The stars began mating with the cows and fathered three kinds of giants. Enoch saw seven angels descend to address the problems on the earth. One of them raised Enoch onto a high tower from which he could observe what happened on the earth. The punishments familiar from 1 Enoch 6–11 were then meted out to the evildoers, and Noah and his family alone survived the flood. His three sons (bulls of three different colors) repopulated the earth after the flood; their children are depicted as various wild or negative animals (e.g., a pig) and birds (e.g., ravens).

With Jacob the image changes from a bull to that of a sheep. His descendants are a flock of sheep, while the enemy nations are represented as the sorts of wild animals or birds who attack sheep. For example, the Egyptians are wolves. Under such imagery the survey continues to follow the biblical story line, including the Joseph story, enslavement in Egypt, the exodus, and the deliverance at the sea. It seems significant that, while the Sinai episode plays a role in the story, nothing is said about giving the law (Moses, however, is called a man, which symbolically implies that he was an angel). When the story reaches the beginnings of the monarchy, Saul and David are called rams. The temple is said to be a tower and the davidic kingdom a house. We are reminded that Enoch is the narrator of the story when he relates that Elijah was brought up to him.

At the close of a section about the sin and punishment of the flock during the divided monarchy, the author introduces the third part of the apocalypse with a new image: seventy shepherds (from 89:59 on). God assigns them the task of punishing the sheep but also appoints a recorder to note what each of them does in obedience to the command and what they do in excess of it, because the deity knows they will destroy more than he permits. However, the shepherds are not to be told about the record keeping until the end, when the full report is to be submitted to God. The seventy shepherds — the number derives from the traditional number of non-Israelite nations (see Genesis 10) — afflict the sheep during four successive periods consisting of the rule of 12, 23, 23, and 12 shepherds respectively. Their time begins shortly before the destruction of Jerusalem and the temple (noted in 89:66) and continues through the exile, the return and rebuilding of the temple (its sacrificial cult is condemned as impure in 89:73), and the entire postexilic period until the author's day in the second century BCE and the expected judgment. Thus the ages of their dominion included the times of the Babylonians, Persians, Ptolemies, and Seleucids. At some point late in this period (apparently around 200 BCE) a new group, described as small lambs born from white sheep, arises and tries in vain to call the other sheep back to the right way.

Around the end of the shepherd section the reader meets a ram/sheep with a large horn who certainly seems to be Judas Maccabeus. When the animals and birds attack him, God strikes the earth with his staff and the attackers fall into the hole that results from the blow. The reference should give a clue about the time when the apocalypse was written because it is the last historical event reflected in it (about 164 BCE). The judgment then transpires in stages, with Azazel, the other angels, and the seventy shepherds being pitched into an abyss of fire. Blind sheep (apostate Israelites) are treated in a similar way. When a new Jerusalem replaces the old, God takes up his residence in it, though there is no temple. To that city the scattered Israelites as well as people from other nations come. A white bull is then born; he seems to be a messiah (90:37). The image for him is the same as for the patriarchs with whom the story began; we have come full circle, with conditions reverting to those at the beginning. Once the white bull is on the scene, all are transformed into white bulls. And here the story ends; Enoch awakes and quite understandably weeps.

The Animal Apocalypse resembles the Apocalypse of Weeks in covering all of history, but the author focuses his attention primarily on the last part of it and on the seventy shepherds. That image and others as well derive from Jeremiah 25 with its prophecy about the seventy years of Babylon. But the author understands those seventy years more in the way that we find in Daniel 9 where they are explained as seventy weeks of years and where they also cover the entire period from the fall of Jerusalem to the author's time in the second century BCE. Jeremiah 25, like the Animal Apocalypse, speaks about shepherds who punish Israel excessively and who will eventually be judged. The author's failure to mention the revelation of the law at Sinai and his negative attitude toward the second temple are remarkable features of this entertaining apocalypse, as is the presence of a messiah, although he does not play an overly prominent role.

Sibylline Oracles (pseudepigraphal)

It may be that the next Jewish apocalypses — or rather apocalyptic-like works — are to be found embedded in a lengthy Greek work entitled the *Sibylline Oracles*. Modeling their works on the famous oracles uttered by an aged prophetess (whether in classical Greece or elsewhere), the authors of these compositions placed predictions pertinent to Jewish concerns in the mouth of the Sibyl, who speaks in hexameters. The twelve books of the *Sibylline Oracles* (oddly numbered as 1–8 and 11–14 in the editions) are presented as a Christian collection. The writer of the Prologue says that he assembled these oracles into one book because they expound important, beneficial subjects such as the Trinity. He also comments: "In manifold ways they tell of certain past history, and equally, foretell events, and, to speak simply, they can profit those who read them in no small way." The resulting work is a combination of Jewish, Christian, and other materials that were composed in different times and places and for varied purposes.

Here it will suffice to discuss the oldest Jewish material in this large and assorted collection of texts: the third oracle. A study of it will provide some indication of what the oracles are like, and the form of Judaism that is expressed in them. Simply the fact that a Jewish writer chose to express his thoughts through the medium of a prophetess popular in the pagan world should lead one to expect something intriguing, and the reader is not disappointed. The mixture of Greek and Jewish elements here is a marvel to behold. The third oracle shares with the others a pattern of predicted disasters followed by a fundamental change in the world.

The main component of the third oracle may be divided into five oracles, all of which belong to a single composition and date from approximately the mid-second century BCE.

1. 97-161: After poetically relating the story about the tower of Babel, the author devotes a section to the rule and conflicts of Cronos, Titan, and Iapetus after the flood (the third name closely resembles that of Noah's third son Japheth). These are transparently divine characters from Greek mythology, but here they are called "the first of articulate men" (112). The section ends with a list of eight kingdoms, thereby introducing the subject of kings and kingship that is important in the subsequent sections.

2. 162-95: These verses prophesy the rise of a series of kingdoms, including the Macedonians (Alexander and others) and the Romans. Here one meets the topic of homosexuality, which the oracles repeatedly condemn (185-86). The predictive survey culminates in "the seventh reign, when a king of Egypt, who will be of the Greeks by race, will rule. And then the people of the great God will again be strong who will be guides in life for all mortals" (193-95). There are other references to this seventh king in 318 and 608. Given the description, he must be a Ptolemy, probably Ptolemy VI Philometor (the seventh, counting Alexander; he reigned from 180-145 BCE). Philometor had favorable relations with Egyptian Jews, and his army was led by two Jewish generals, Dositheus and the priest Onias IV (Josephus, *Against Apion* 2.49, 53-55), the rightful heir to the high priesthood who had to flee when his father Onias III was deposed and lost his life. Philometor gave him land and permission to construct the Jewish temple at Leontopolis. We probably have here the best clue to the date of the third oracle during the reign of Ptolemy VI Philometor.

3. 196-294: The third section opens by predicting woes on various nations before turning to the Israelites. Beginning with Abram in Ur of the Chaldees, the sibyl praises him and his descendants for rejecting the divinatory practices of their environment and for their concern with righteousness and protection of the poor and weak. She predicts the rise of Moses, the exodus, and the law-giving at Sinai, but skips over the nation's

history in the promised land to tell of the exile, which resulted from disobedience to the law revealed at Sinai. After seventy years, however, there would be a change and a new temple would be built.

4. 545-656: The sibyl questions the Greeks about their idolatry and calls on them to revere the great God. She next turns to the Jews and praises them for making proper offerings in their worship of the true God. God gave to them alone "wise counsel and faith and excellent understanding" (584-85). She also lauds them for their sexual morality. A section on those who worship idols contains a reference to the time when "the young seventh king of Egypt rules his own land, numbered from the dynasty of the Greeks, which the Macedonians, wondrous men, will found" (608-10). The reference is followed by a prediction of the invasion by a king who may be Antiochus IV (or Antiochus as the latest in a series of Asiatic kings who fought against Egypt) who twice attacked Egypt in Philometor's time. The writer, after describing terrible times, says that "God will send a king from the sun who will stop the entire earth from evil war" in obedience to God (652-56). Presumably the king from the sun is also the seventh king.

5. 657-808: The sibyl prophesies that kings will seek to destroy the temple but God will annihilate them, shake the earth, and cause incredible carnage. But God's people will live in peace around the temple, protected and blessed by the deity. As a result, the inhabitants of the islands and cities will wish to serve God at his temple and ponder his law. The Greeks are exhorted to entreat God and not attack his people. There follows a picture of eschatological bliss, with plenty and peace among people and animals. There will be just one temple to which all will bring gifts.

In a concluding section the sibyl identifies herself as the daughter-in-law of Noah (827).

If the parts of the third sibylline oracle sketched above are a mid-second-century Jewish work from Egypt, it seems quite reasonable to suppose that a Jewish supporter of Philometor such as Onias may have had something to do with the work. Sibylline oracles in antiquity had a decidedly political import, and the same would be the case with this one. It may seem strange that a Ptolemaic king would be hailed in what appear to be quasi-messianic terms, but the third sibylline oracle is a good reminder of what at least some Jews may have understood a messianic leader to be: a human king who would effect God's will in the perilous and frightening times of the author. It is not entirely clear that the third oracle qualifies as an apocalypse because the picture of the end is not developed very far beyond biblical teachings, but it is a revelation that deals with the last times and promises salvation to the faithful people of God and a life of peace around his temple.

The Similitudes or Parables of Enoch (1 Enoch 37–71; pseudepigraphal)

Tucked between the two oldest parts of *1 Enoch* is an apocalypse that goes under the name the *Similitudes* or *Parables of Enoch*. In it Enoch receives a series of revelations that are called *parables;* the first is in chaps. 38–44, the second in 45–57, and the third in 58–69. Around these three units the author/editor has placed introductory and concluding chapters (38 and 70–71). The focus in the *Similitudes* is on the eschatological punishment of sinners and the blessing of the righteous; a strong element of reversal is also involved. The downtrodden righteous do not realize that their salvation is already prepared, while the oppressive sinners at present fail to understand what awaits them. The text discloses that at the end the righteous will enjoy bliss while the mighty sinners will be punished and destroyed. In this work Enoch is termed a "son of man," and he is deeply involved in the final judgment of the wicked and reward of the righteous.

It is likely that the *Similitudes of Enoch* experienced a different history than the other Enochic booklets. Its emphases differ somewhat from the earlier works, and the lengthy *Similitudes* are the only part of *1 Enoch* that has failed to turn up among the thousands of fragments from the Qumran caves. Unless this is simply an accident, the text may have been written and transmitted in Enochic circles other than the one(s) represented at Qumran. The work also was composed at a later time than any of the other components of *1 Enoch*. It seems to have been written in a Semitic language, but it survives today only in the Ethiopic language; presumably it had first been translated into Greek and from Greek into Ethiopic. Although its allusions are not always decipherable, it is possible that the writer refers to circumstances in the time of King Herod (37-4 BCE): there may be allusions to the Parthian invasion of 40 BCE (56:5-8), and the hot springs used by Herod and others may be what is meant by 67:4-13. There are no clear references to later events. As a result, the *Similitudes* may have been written at the end of the first century BCE or early in the first century CE. The fact that a Jewish work from approximately this date speaks at length of an eschatological son of man who will come to judge has made the *Similitudes* an object of many studies by

New Testament scholars, who have compared the son of man Enoch in the *Similitudes* with the son of man Jesus in the gospels, especially as he is presented in Matthew.

In *1 Enoch* 37:1 the work is called a "second vision" seen by Enoch, perhaps to distinguish it from the Book of Watchers (*1 Enoch* 1–36; see 1:2). Already in this same chapter the three-parable structure of the text is mentioned (37:5), and Enoch addresses his words to all mankind from his pre-flood vantage point. He receives the revelations from "the Lord of the spirits," a title for God that seems to be a modification of the biblical "the Lord of hosts" (see 39:12); yet he continues to be in angelic company (e.g., 40:2). Enoch sees the place prepared for the righteous where they will be with the angels and views the blessings that await them; he also sees that he has been destined to dwell there. His visions include sights of judgment and of natural phenomena, as in the earlier Enochic booklets (see chaps. 41, 43). The short first parable also has a brief chapter (42) about wisdom's inability to find a place to live among mankind and her return to her heavenly dwelling — a view contrasting with the more positive one found in the Wisdom of Ben Sira and Wisdom.

The second parable (chaps. 45–57) continues the book's focus on the last judgment. At several points (chaps. 46–48; see 55:1; 60:2 for allusions in the third parable) it uses the contents and characters of Daniel 7, with its ancient of days and one like a son of man, to picture what will happen in the final court scene. The reader learns that the son of man was named before the Lord of spirits prior to creation (48:2-3, 6) and that the righteous will lean on this one who is also termed the light of the nations (see Isa 42:6; 49:6) and the hope of those who mourn. The kings and mighty people of the earth will be most distressed when they are judged for having denied the Lord and his anointed (46:8-10; see Ps 2:2). The chosen one will sit on his throne and judge the mighty people of the earth through his spirit of wisdom and understanding (49:3-4; 51:3; 55:4). In this section we also find mention of the old Enochic theme of Azazel and his hosts (54:5-6; see also chap. 64).

The third parable elaborates similar themes of judgment and destruction for the wicked but vindication and life for the righteous. We also learn how the mighty oppressors will be called upon to acknowledge the chosen one who had been hidden from the beginning but revealed by God only to the chosen; they will beg him for mercy but to no avail; rather, they will receive their just reward for what they have done to God's children, his chosen ones. The righteous will live forever with the son of man and with the

Lord and will never see the wicked again (chaps. 62–63). Within the third parable are several chapters that seem to belong to a book or books of Noah: chap. 60, where the five hundredth year of the hero's life must refer to Noah's days, not Enoch's; in fact, Enoch is called his great-grandfather (60:8); and chaps. 65–69, where the flood as a sign of God's judgment comes in for extended treatment and where the secrets are written down by Enoch in a book that he gives to Noah. The final chapter of this section (chap. 69) provides an extended list of angel names many of which are familiar from *1 Enoch* 6–11 and which remind one of the story about the angels who sinned. The same chapter contains a description of the oath through which creation occurred and by which it maintains its orderly operation. At the very end (69:26-29), the son of man is pictured pronouncing judgment from his throne and the sinners are destroyed.

As this summary shows, the *Similitudes of Enoch* hold before the reader's eyes an extraordinary leader of the righteous who, while hidden for a long time and always under God's ultimate control, is the hope of the chosen and will save them in the end, even as he will condemn the mighty evildoers who have treated them harshly. The author attributes four titles to this one leader: in just a few cases he is called the righteous one or the anointed one (messiah); in the vast majority of instances he is termed the son of man or the chosen one. The titles are drawn from biblical passages such as Daniel 7, 2 Isaiah, and Psalm 2, as noted above. As his titles show, he closely identifies with the suffering righteous and chosen ones and will lead them to victory at the last judgment. Who is this remarkable character who was chosen and hidden before creation? The last part of the *Similitudes* identifies him as Enoch (71:14), whose elevation is pictured in several stages in chaps. 70–71. There are some textual problems in these chapters, and the identification of Enoch as the preexistent son of man has seemed implausible to some scholars, but this is the way the book presents him. Enoch is the son of man who judges (Daniel 7) and the chosen of the Lord who is a light to the nations (Isaiah 40–55), a servant of the Lord who does not himself suffer but who delivers those who do suffer in this life. In him the chosen hope, and with him they will enjoy eternal life, free at last from their persecutors. Such teachings were meant, it seems, to encourage the author's community to believe that circumstances would change in the future and that they would be rescued at the end. In the *Similitudes of Enoch* the lofty status of Enoch himself is heavily emphasized, becoming a central point of interest to a greater extent than in the earlier Enochic texts.

The Testament of Moses (pseudepigraphal)

As the name indicates, the book purports to be Moses' final words, addressed to Joshua. The situation presupposed is the one found in the last chapters of Deuteronomy on which the *Testament of Moses* draws for other motifs. Moses "predicts" the course of biblical history in rather negative terms and continues the story through subsequent times, including the reign of Herod the Great and beyond. The *Testament of Moses* is more than a little frustrating to read because it is available in just one Latin copy (the Latin is a translation of a Greek text that may in turn have been based on a Semitic original) which is missing both the beginning and end, as well as some smaller sections throughout the text.

The *Testament* is set in the year 2500 from creation (a chronology only fifty years longer than for the comparable time according to the *Book of Jubilees*). The author tells us that "this is the prophecy which was made by Moses in the book of Deuteronomy" (1:5). Joshua will receive books from Moses that he is to place in earthenware jars for preservation until the time of judgment. The early post-Mosaic biblical period is described with some chronological indicators: the era of the united nation is said to last eighteen years (apparently one year per judge with one year each for Saul, David, and Solomon as well) and the divided monarchy receives nineteen years (for the kings of Israel) and twenty years (for the time of the temple and the kings of Judah). A king from the east will destroy the city and temple and exile the two tribes around it. In exile they will speak with the ten tribes who had been removed from their land at an earlier time. All will lament together and call on God to remember the covenant with the patriarchs. They will also recall in their distress that Moses had predicted such a fate for Israel. The captivity of the two tribes will last, says the writer, about seventy-seven years.

At this point an unnamed leader prays for the people and God remembers and has compassion on them, restoring them to their land. As a result, the two tribes will live in a secure place but will be unable to offer sacrifices — apparently another negative comment on the cult of the second temple (see the Animal Apocalypse above). Rather than inspiring the people to faithfulness, return to their land leads to more sin and punishment. Priest-kings (the Maccabees) will then arise; they will commit "great impiety in the Holy of Holies" (6:2). The "wanton king" who follows them is clearly Herod the Great because he is credited with a reign of thirty-four years (6:6; he reigned from 37-4 BCE). In 6:7-9 the survey advances to

Herod's death and to the time of his successors; it also mentions a partial destruction of the temple which occurred shortly after Herod's death.

Chapter 7 has an eschatological ring to it, as it depicts what appear to be the last, terrible times. According to 7:1, "the times will quickly come to an end," but the chapter goes on to describe wealthy, corrupt individuals whose evil is followed by unprecedented punishment and divine wrath. A king then arises who has some of the qualities attributed to Antiochus IV. In fact, one could read all of chapter 8 against the backdrop of the Antiochan suppression of Judaism, even though that occurred more than 125 years before Herod ascended the throne. This curious sequence has led some scholars to the conclusion that chapters 6–7 were inserted into the text at a later time. In chapter 9 we meet Taxo, a Levite who tells his seven sons that in the present evil circumstances they must fast for three days and enter a cave on the fourth. "There let us die rather than transgress the commandments of the Lord of Lords, the God of our fathers, For if we do this, and do die, our blood will be avenged before the Lord" (9:6b-7). We are not told whether they met a martyr's death, but that may be the implication. The next chapter contains a poem that predicts the destruction of the devil and the cataclysmic events that will transpire when God comes to the earth to execute judgment on the nations and their gods (see the theophany of Deut. 33:2 and *1 Enoch* 1). Perhaps the deaths of Taxo and his sons were the catalyst for the decisive divine intervention. At that time God will "raise you to the heights" and "fix you firmly in the heaven of the stars" (10:7). Israel will rejoice over their enemies from on high.

Echoing the year of his address to Joshua (2500), Moses predicts that there will be 250 times between his burial and God's advent (10:12). Chapters 11 and 12 deal with the despair felt by Joshua at the prospect of Moses' approaching death, and his great sense of inadequacy to lead the nation without Moses serving as their advocate. Moses does reassure him, however, that God is in control and sees everything from beginning to end.

There our manuscript ends. It would be especially helpful to know how the composition concluded because in other ancient sources there are references to a Moses text which included a dispute between Michael and the devil over Moses' body (see, for example, Jude 9). It is possible that a story of this sort once stood at the end of the *Testament of Moses,* but there is no way to be sure.

The fact that the predictions extend well into the first century CE means that the *Testament of Moses* as we have it was not written before that time. It has been suggested, however, that a book, dating from early

Maccabean times, was later supplemented by splicing chapters 6–7 into the predictive survey in order to bring it up to date. The strongest argument for this thesis is that these two chapters seem to destroy the sequence of the survey. Yet it is possible to read the book as it stands as an orderly account and to understand chapters 7–9 as stereotypical depictions of the great evil at the end. These depictions draw on themes from the Maccabean crisis but are not meant to be descriptions of it. If so, then the entire book, which does not (in the surviving form of the text) claim to be revealed by an angel, can be read as an apocalypse from the first century BCE. It was written under the impress of events in Herod's time and immediately after; its purpose was to reassure the readers that God foreknew everything that would happen, that he is faithful to the covenant, and that he will have compassion on his people. No less an authority that Moses himself stands behind the message.

Wisdom Literature

In the Hebrew Bible books such as Proverbs, Job, Ecclesiastes, some psalms (e.g., 37), and several other texts are usually called wisdom literature. These works do not appeal to the covenant or Israel's sacred history; rather, they grapple in a more universal way with the meaning of life, with life's perplexities, and with how to live it properly. The sages normally accomplish their goal without appeal to a divine source of information or authority. Such literature continued to be written well after the wisdom works listed above were composed. Two of them are to be found among the deuterocanonical/apocryphal books: the Wisdom of Ben Sira, and the Wisdom of Solomon.

The Wisdom of Ben Sira (sometimes called Sirach or Ecclesiasticus; deuterocanonical/apocryphal)

The Wisdom of Ben Sira is the first book in Jewish literature to identify its actual author by name. At the end of his book the writer said: "Instruction in understanding and knowledge I have written in this book, Jesus son of Eleazar son of Sirach of Jerusalem, whose mind poured forth wisdom" (50:27). He apparently ran a school (he calls it his "house of instruction" [51:23]), and it is commonly thought that he was a scribe because he

115

praises the work of the scribe so highly in 38:24–39:11. Writing at some point between 200 and 170 BCE, he composed a work that reminds one of the book of Proverbs but which also differs markedly from the older book. Ben Sira (or Sirach, the Greek form of his name) wrote in Hebrew, but the Hebrew text of the book apparently was not preserved in most Jewish communities through the centuries. He had the good fortune, however, to have had a grandson capable of translating his book into the Greek language. The translator-grandson (who does not disclose his name) wrote a short prologue to introduce his translation (it is printed before the book in all modern translations) in which he said: ". . . my grandfather Jesus, after devoting himself especially to the reading of the law and the prophets and the other books of our fathers, and after acquiring considerable proficiency in them, was himself also led to write something pertaining to instruction and wisdom. . . ." The grandson reports that he came to Egypt in the thirty-eighth year of Euergetes; the king in question is Ptolemy VIII Euergetes II (170-164 BCE and 146-17) and thus the year of the grandson's arrival in Egypt was 132 BCE. It was sometime later that he made the translation. He claims: "I have applied my skill day and night to complete and publish the book for those living abroad who wished to gain learning and are disposed to live according to the law." The date for the grandfather's work is in large part an inference from the date of the grandson's activity. The Greek form of the book with the prologue is found in copies of the Greek Bible and thus made its way into the Bible of the Catholic Church. Although the book is mentioned fairly frequently in rabbinic literature, it did not attain canonical status in Judaism (or among Protestants).

More than half of the Hebrew version of Ben Sira has been rediscovered in the last century or so. Six partial copies, medieval in date, were found in the Cairo Geniza, and two small fragments of the text were identified in Qumran cave 2 (2Q18). At Masada, twenty-six fragments of a manuscript of the book dating from the first century BCE were discovered; the seven columns over which the text is spread preserve a substantial part of chapters 39:27–44:17. At Qumran Ben Sira 51:13-20b, 30b was found in the first Psalms scroll from cave 11 (11QPs^a col. 21.11-17; 22:1). This poem is an acrostic and had often been considered an addition to the book; it is now evident that it was a floating piece of poetry capable of surfacing in different contexts.

It is highly likely that Ben Sira wrote his book before the infamous decrees of Antiochus IV in 167 BCE, since he does not mention them. In his day the ways and wisdom of the Greeks had exercised their influence throughout the Near East for some time. Ben Sira's purpose seems to have been to convince his audience, presumably Jewish, that true wisdom was not to be sought in the books and teaching of the Greeks but in the writings and instruction of the Jewish tradition. There are at least two ways in which the book, however much it shares with earlier Israelite wisdom (especially Proverbs), is distinctive: Ben Sira identifies wisdom with the law of Moses, and he brings wisdom into connection with Israel's sacred history.

It is not easy to see what is the overall structure of the book, but the two major parts of it are introduced by poems that describe and praise wisdom. These poems are found in chapters 1–2 and 24. Another unit that clearly stands out from its context is chapters 44–50 which praise the heroes of Israel's past; it is preceded by a hymn on the works of God in the world (42:15–43:33). So in 42:15–50:23 we see God's glory in creation and then his might in history (compare the same sequence in Pss. 104–5).

The wisdom poems that introduce the halves of the book enunciate some of Ben Sira's principal teachings. In the first (chaps. 1–2) he declares that wisdom comes from the Lord and was created before everything (see Prov. 8), but he has poured her out on all, especially on those who love him. He highlights what he calls "the fear of the Lord" which is the beginning, fullness, crown, and root of wisdom. He follows these traditional thoughts with novel words: "If you desire wisdom, keep the commandments, and the Lord will lavish her upon you. For the fear of the Lord is wisdom and discipline, fidelity and humility are his delight" (1:26-27). The wise person, then, inwardly fears the Lord and outwardly obeys the commandments of God. Later he writes: "The whole of wisdom is fear of the Lord, and in all wisdom there is the fulfillment of the law" (19:20). He cautions his audience ("my child") that they should be prepared for testing but in all circumstances the one who fears God must trust in him.

There are other wisdom poems in the book (e.g., 6:18-37; 14:20–15:10; 16:24–17:24), but the poem in chapter 24 is especially noteworthy. The writer tells us that here she praises herself, and she does precisely this in verses 3-22 where she speaks in the first person. In verses 3-7 she presents herself in language reminiscent of Lady Wisdom in Proverbs 8. Though she "came forth from the mouth of the Most High, and covered the earth like a mist" (v. 3), she looked for a place to lodge. "Then the Creator of all things gave me a command, and my Creator chose the place for my tent. He said, 'Make your dwelling in Jacob, and in Israel receive your inheritance" (v. 8). There she grew and blossomed (vv. 13-17). The magnificent lady then invites all to come to her: "Those who eat of me will hunger for more, and those who drink of me will thirst for more. Whoever obeys me will not be put to shame, and those who work with me will not sin" (vv. 21-22). Then the author adds his comment: "All this is the book of the covenant of the Most High God, the law that Moses commanded us as an inheritance for the congregation of Jacob" (v. 23). He describes how wisdom overflows like the great rivers; her abundance no one has ever understood fully. Ben Sira, in verses 30-34, concludes the section by speaking of his own pedagogical labors as channeling her waters in an attempt to direct wisdom to all who seek her, now and in the future (see 51:13-30 where he describes his own study of wisdom).

While wisdom is praised enthusiastically in the book, Ben Sira and wisdom herself leave no doubt that God, who created wisdom, is greater still. His work in creation, accomplished by his word (42:15), is lauded in 42:15–43:33. Moreover, "[b]efore the universe was created, it was known to him, and so it is since its completion" (23:20; see 39:19-20). Everything is searched out by him and nothing is hidden from him (42:18-20). Near the end of the poem on creation we read: "We could say more but never say enough; let the final word be: 'He is the all'" (43:27). His greatness should inspire praise in people even though they cannot understand him or extol him sufficiently. This God shows both mercy and wrath (16:11) and is called upon to reveal himself to the nations so that they will know him (36:1-5). Ben Sira does teach a form of divine determinism, but in passages such as 15:11-12 he denies that God is to be blamed for the sin of humans and also asserts in 15:14 that God gave people free choice (see also 15:15-20).

The omnipotent and omniscient God of creation also manifests his glory in Israel's sacred history. The poet calls on the reader, at the beginning of his historical survey (44-50), to "sing the praises of famous men, our ancestors in their generations. The Lord apportioned to them great glory, his majesty from the beginning" (44:1-2). In the overview itself Enoch is the first hero mentioned (44:16 in some of the manuscripts) and he is named at the end of the part that covers the characters of the Hebrew Bible (49:14); chapter 50, which continues a number of themes from 44–49 (such as the emphasis on the priesthood and the cult), deals with a high priest named Simon, probably Simon I who lived in approximately 300 BCE. The entire section divides into two parts, each of which culminates in a similar doxology (45:25-26; 50:22-23) which follows an extended section on a priest or priests (Aaron/Phinehas and Simon). All of the great characters are included: Enoch, Noah, Abraham, Isaac, Jacob and his twelve sons, Moses, Aaron (a relatively lengthy section; 45:6-22), Phinehas, Joshua, Caleb, the judges (especially Samuel), Nathan, David (emphasizing his litur-gical contributions), Solomon, the northern kingdom and the prophets Elijah and Elisha, the southern kingdom, primarily Hezekiah, Isaiah, Josiah, Jeremiah, Ezekiel (who, Ben Sira reminds us, mentioned Job [49:8-9]), the twelve minor prophets, Zerubbabel, Jeshua, Nehemiah (Ezra is not mentioned). The section related to the Hebrew Bible terminates with men-tion of Enoch, Joseph, Shem, Seth, Enosh, and Adam (49:14-16). This long list allows one to infer which scriptural books Ben Sira knew as sources of information about the heroes of the past: the Pentateuch, Joshua, Judges, Samuel, Kings (with some information from Chronicles), Isaiah, Jeremiah, Ezekiel, the twelve prophets, Ezra, Nehemiah, the Psalms, Proverbs, and Job. His source for the high priest Simon is not known. The information from Ben Sira is one of the few early windows on the growth of what would later be called the Bible in Judaism. It is also of interest that the translator-grandson refers three times in his prologue to the law, the prophets, and the other books, three categories suggestive of the three divi-sions — law, prophets, writings — of the Hebrew Bible in its final form.

Ben Sira offers advice on practical subjects such as obligations towards parents (3:1-16), almsgiving and other duties to the poor (3:30–4:6), friendship (6:5-17), and many more. His teachings about women and chil-dren are at times jarring to modern sensitivities. He speaks of how terrible a woman's wickedness and wrath are (25:13-15); writes about a bad wife and the shameful effects she has on her husband; and encourages a man to leave his wife if she does not obey him (25:16-26). The joys of a good wife are viewed from the man's perspective (26:1-4, 13-18; see 36:26 31). Daughters, too, are presented as a grave concern to a man (26:10-12; 42:9-14). He states his point of view vigorously: "Better is the wickedness of a man than a woman who does good; it is woman who brings shame and disgrace" (42:14). Ben Sira also teaches that punishment is a normal part of paternal love and that a father who spoils his son will suffer for it later (30:1-13). By following such advice a social system dominated by males and male honor is maintained.

The Epistle of Enoch (1 Enoch 91–107 [108]; pseudepigraphal)

The fifth and last booklet in 1 Enoch is called the Epistle of Enoch. It is the literary home of the Apocalypse of Weeks (93:1-10; 91:11-17, which is treated above with other apocalypses) and of several other types of literary units. As a result of this variety it is difficult to classify chapters 91–107 under any single rubric, but they do share several features with the wisdom tradition and thus can be studied here. The Epistle may date to roughly the same time as the Apocalypse of Weeks, that is, not far from 170 BCE. At least there is no convincing reason for putting it at a later time. Parts of the Epistle, like most other booklets in 1 Enoch, have been preserved in the Aramaic fragments from Qumran cave 4.

The text presents itself, at least at the beginning, as an address given by Enoch to his sons as the spirit moves him to tell them all that will happen to them forever (91:1). After he exhorts them to pursue uprightness and to avoid sinful ways, he predicts the rise of great evil and divine judgment upon it. According to 92:1 the wisdom contained in Enoch's words is meant not only for his offspring but also for the righteous who will live in the latter generations. By this time Enoch is overwhelmingly familiar to the reader of his booklets as an inexhaustible source of wisdom and knowledge, whether about the past, present, and future or about the nature and workings of the universe. In light of his encyclopedic learning, it is curious that the paragraph immediately following the Apocalypse of Weeks (93:11-14) asks rhetorically whether there is anyone who can understand the length of heaven and the number of the stars. The expected answer is that there is not, even though Enoch is presented elsewhere as having such qualifications.

A large part of the Epistle deals with the division between the righteous and the sinners, especially the present plight of the righteous and the seeming triumph of the wicked, and the great reversal that will take place. Within 1 Enoch 94–105 much space is given to several series of woes pronounced on the sinners (94:6-10; 95:4-7; 96:4-8; 97:7-10; 98:8–99:2; 99:11-15; 100:7-9; 103:5). Some of these units designate as the objects of the woes the rich and powerful who oppress the righteous poor. God plans judgment on them; in fact the oppressed righteous will execute judgment on those who now mistreat them (95:3). Their deliverance will come from God (96:1-3), but the sinners will be shamed (97:1).

First Enoch 102:4–104:8 contains a debate about the fate of the righteous and the sinners, focusing on the question whether there will be a judgment. As happens in the Wisdom of Solomon (see below on Wisdom of Solomon 1–5), the sinners maintain that their sins have been unnoticed and that their fate at death will be the same as that of the righteous (102:6-8), but Enoch, from absolutely reliable sources, informs his readers that there will indeed be a judgment when the wicked receive punishment on the basis of the angels' record of their misdeeds (104:7-8). The righteous, however, even though they die, will rejoice. The Epistle does not teach a bodily resurrection but rather a joyful survival of the spirit. The righteous will be happy forever like the angels, and will become associates of the heavenly ones (103:3-4; 104:6). Thus Enoch's teachings serve as a source of wisdom and comfort for his beleaguered audience. They thought that their cries for help had not been heard, but, says Enoch, all has been recorded and God has promised to act decisively on their behalf. In this way Enoch offers the profoundest wisdom in an eschatological context.

First Enoch 106–7 is quite different from the preceding part of the Epistle and on a Qumran manuscript is in fact separated from the end of *1 Enoch* 105 by a blank line. Enoch, in the first person, tells an entertaining story about the birth of the remarkable child Noah and the concern his extraordinary features caused for his father Lamech. Lamech feared that he could not have fathered such a child and suspected that one of the Watchers and his wife were the parents of this prodigy. He sent his father Methuselah to the faraway place where his grandfather Enoch resided (during his sojourn with the angels) in order to learn from him the answer to the paternity issue and also what the birth of this child portended. Enoch of course knew the answer to both questions: Lamech was the father, and the remarkable traits of the child were signs that astonishing things would happen. He predicts the flood, the survival of Noah and his family, the renewal of evil after the flood, and finally the rise of a righteous generation. This story is closely paralleled in the Genesis Apocryphon from Qumran cave 1.

Chapter 108 may be an addition to the Epistle and is attested on no fragment from Qumran. It speaks of itself as another book of Enoch and contains his report to his son Methuselah of what he had seen about the fate of the sinners and the righteous, topics that dominate much of *1 Enoch*.

Baruch (or 1 Baruch; deuterocanonical/apocryphal)

The Book of Baruch is difficult to classify because it expresses its message(s) through several literary forms. Since a part near the middle of the book is devoted to wisdom, it is convenient to deal with the book in this section. It falls clearly into four distinct parts, unified by the theme of the

121

exile and what it entails for the people of God. It is not only difficult to classify the book; it is also difficult to date it. About the only clues come from the author's frequent practice of drawing upon books of the Hebrew Bible, which must therefore predate this writing. One of his deepest debts is to Daniel 9, which reached its final form in the 160s BCE. If he borrowed from the finished form of Daniel 9, then Baruch was written later, unless perhaps the writer shared a common source with Daniel. The oldest text available is in Greek, but the original, especially 1:1–3:8, may have been written in Hebrew.

The book receives its name from the character mentioned at the beginning, Baruch the scribe of the prophet Jeremiah (Jer. 32:12; 36:4; 43:3; 45:1). In later literature, he like Jeremiah was known as a famous figure of the exile, and a number of books claim him as their hero (2–3 Baruch). In Baruch he is mentioned only in the introductory section, where we learn that the composition is "the words of the book that Baruch son of Neriah son of Mahseiah son of Zedekiah son of Hasadiah son of Hilkiah wrote in Babylon, in the fifth year, on the seventh day of the month," at the time when the Chaldeans took Jerusalem and burned it with fire" (1:1-2). The historical information is confusing: it may be that this is a failed attempt to reproduce the information, found in 2 Kings and Jeremiah, that the Babylonians took Jerusalem in the fifth month (note that the text does not mention the month here; only in v. 8 do we learn that it is the month Sivan, that is, the third month). However that may be, the introduction situates the book near the time when Jerusalem was destroyed and exiles had been led away from the city. Those events supply the thematic setting of the book.

The four parts of Baruch are: 1:1-14, a historical introduction; 1:15–3:8, a confession of sin by the people remaining in Jerusalem and by the exiles; 3:9–4:4, on wisdom and the importance of finding her in order to avoid disasters such as the exile; and 4:5–5:9, in which Jerusalem bewails her lost children and is comforted with the news that they will return.

Baruch 1:1-14, as we have seen, situates the book at the time of Jerusalem's destruction. We learn that Baruch was in Babylon (something not mentioned in the Hebrew Bible). He is said to have read the contents of his book to the exiled King Jehoiachin (= Jeconiah) and the other Judeans who were in Babylon. The effect of the book was so strong that the exiles collected money to send to the high priest in Jerusalem, and Baruch somehow gathered the vessels taken from the temple to return them. The entire scene presupposes that there was an ongoing cult in Jerusalem, thus adding to the historical confusion in the book (the sequel assumes that there was a temple standing in Jerusalem). The money was to pay for offerings, and the Jerusalemites were urged to pray for Nebuchadnezzar and his "son" Belshazzar, and also for the exiles. The exiles urged them to read the scroll they were sending "to make your confession in the house of the Lord on the days of the festivals and at appointed seasons" (1:14). It is interesting that the date in the third month is very close to the time for the festival of weeks. Perhaps the scroll was to be read at that time.

The scroll contains the confession, written by Babylonian Jews, that the Jerusalemites are to make (1:15–2:5). In this section there are particularly strong parallels with Daniel 9. The confession acknowledges that God was in the right and that the people had broken the covenant and thus merited the punishment they had received, just as Moses had written in Deuteronomy 28. It is not entirely clear where the confession of the Jerusalemites ends and that of the exiles begins, but in 2:13-14 the exiles are speaking; perhaps their words began in 2:6, which parallels 1:15, the first verse of the Jerusalemite confession. The exiles acknowledge: "we have sinned, we have been ungodly, we have done wrong, O Lord our God, against all your ordinances. Let your anger turn away from us, for we are left, few in number, among the nations where you have scattered us. Hear, O Lord, our prayer and our supplication, and for your own sake deliver us, and grant us favor in the sight of those who have carried us into exile; so that all the earth may know that you are the Lord our God, for Israel and his descendants are called by your name" (2:12-15). Repentance is clearly required, and the exiles remind God that the contrite, not the dead, praise him. The exiles also appeal to Deuteronomy 28 (see 2:28-29 and compare Deut. 28:58, 62) which predicts sin but repentance in exile; at that point it promises that the Lord will return them to the land sworn to the ancestors and establish an eternal relation with them. In 3:1-8 the exiles cry out in repentance and lay much stress on the fact that they are suffering for what their ancestors have done. They ask God not to remember those sins but rather his power and name.

The short section on wisdom (3:9–4:4) is placed at this point. The paragraph is closely tied to the overall theme of exile. At the beginning Israel is called upon to hear the commands that give life and learn wisdom. They are to understand why they are in exile: "You have forsaken the fountain of wisdom. If you had walked in the way of God, you would be living in peace forever. Learn where there is wisdom, where there is strength, where there is understanding, so that you may at the same time discern where there is length of days, and life, where there is light for the eyes, and peace" (3:12-14). Much of the section is devoted to enumerating groups who have not succeeded in finding wisdom. In fact no one knows the way to her, but God has found her: "He found the whole way to knowledge, and gave her to his servant Jacob and to Israel whom he loved" (3:36). As in Ben Sira, Baruch identifies the law of Moses with wisdom (4:1). Those who hold fast to her will live; those who forsake her will die. This teaching provides the key in the present crisis as well. Consequently Israel is exhorted to "take her; walk toward the shining of her light" (v. 2).

The final section (4:5–5:9) revolves around Jerusalem. Israel grieved God and Jerusalem by its wickedness. In 4:9-16 Jerusalem speaks to her neighbors about her sadness because her children have been sent away. Their evil induced God to bring on a distant nation to defeat them. In 4:17-29 Jerusalem speaks to her exiled children and exhorts them to be courageous (vv. 21, 27, 30), to endure their present circumstances with patience (v. 25), and to cry to God who will save them. Finally, in 4:30–5:9 Jerusalem herself is encouraged with the promise that those who oppressed her children will suffer and that her children will return. The book ends with a section that draws on the highway-building language of Isaiah 40 to describe the route over which the exiles will return to mother Jerusalem.

One point that emerges clearly from the book is that for many Jews in the second temple period the exile did not simply end at the time of the first return described in Ezra 1. Exile was a state that continued. The situation of exile, whatever that meant for different individuals, became a rallying cry for preachers of repentance, who exhorted the people to return to the covenantal law so that the old relations between God and his people could be restored.

The Wisdom of Solomon
(deuterocanonical/apocryphal)

Solomon was the great wise man of Israel's past to whom several books in the Hebrew Bible were attributed (Proverbs, Song of Solomon, Ecclesiastes). His connection with wisdom continued into the period of Early Judaism as we can see from this work, which was undoubtedly written in Greek, perhaps nine centuries after the great king's death. The author uses the Greek translation of books such as Isaiah (see 2:12 = Isa. 3:10 Septuagint) when he quotes them; hence he could not have written before the

Greek translations of the relevant books were made. Some vocabulary items in the book which are not attested outside the Wisdom of Solomon until the first century CE suggest that it may not have been written until early in that century. Egypt is a likely possibility for the place where the author worked, but it is only a conjecture.

The book is a discourse through which the author exhorts the reader to pursue the way of wisdom. It falls into three principal parts. The first is 1:1–6:21, in which rulers are addressed and told about wisdom's gift of immortality. The author exhorts them to justice, which brings immortality (1:1-15); an evil way of life leads to death. He illustrates his point by describing a group of people who have, as he says, covenanted with death, by concluding that life is brief and there is no hereafter, so one should do as one wishes (1:16–2:24). They have, however, miscalculated because God has formed humans to be imperishable. They oppress needy, just individuals who oppose them and prove bothersome to them (2:10-20). This leads to a section in which the writer explains that the sufferings of the just are merely a trial. There is a clear difference between reality and appearances, because for the just "their hope is full of immortality" (3:4). Once the righteous die they will shine, judge the nations, understand truth, and remain with God in love; the wicked, however, are cursed.

The writer offers a short section (3:13–4:6) in which he argues that the sterility of a righteous person will become productive in the final analysis: the barren woman will be fruitful at the visitation (the eunuch is also mentioned), while the children of adulterers will never have honor or issue. Thus childlessness with virtue outranks the fertility of the wicked. It seems from this that the world of the spirit is superior to that of the body. Another way in which appearances can be deceiving is in the early death of a righteous person (4:7-20). According to Wisdom, honorable age is not measured by passing years but by understanding. Though he is not identified (no person is named in the Wisdom of Solomon), his example is Enoch, who was removed from the earth at an age far lower than that of his contemporaries. Yet his removal stemmed not from divine disfavor, but from the fact that he was perfected in a short time. Hence the quality, not the length of life, is the determining factor.

In Wisdom 5:1-23 the just are vindicated at the end. The ones who oppressed them finally sense their mistake — both with regard to the ones they oppressed and the fact that there is indeed a judgment at the end. The great reversal takes place at the final judgment, just as it does in the Similitudes of Enoch.

125

The final section of the first part of Wisdom of Solomon is an exhortation to rulers to seek wisdom, which may easily be found and which leads to immortality (unlike the ephemeral existence of the wicked). Rulers receive their authority from God, who examines what they do. Because they did not judge properly, God's judgment falls upon them. Rather, one should desire wisdom, show love for her by keeping her laws, and thus gain a kingdom.

The second part of the book (6:22–10:21) explains what wisdom is, the nature of the power she possesses, and Solomon's (not named of course) search for her. Kings are once again the audience. Solomon, in the first person, explains that he is only mortal and prefers wisdom above all. It is God who gives one the ability to value wisdom properly, and he gives accurate knowledge about the various aspects of the universe, including the calendar. Here we seem to have a form of the argument that what God has made demonstrates that he exists. The most famous verses in this section are 7:22-23 which list the twenty-one attributes of wisdom; the attributes are followed by 7:24–8:1 in which she is further explained:

> For wisdom is more mobile than any motion;
> because of her pureness she pervades and penetrates all things.
> For she is a breath of the power of God,
> and a pure emanation of the glory of the Almighty;
> therefore nothing defiled gains entrance into her.
> For she is a reflection of eternal light,
> a spotless mirror of the working of God,
> and an image of his goodness.
> Although she is but one, she can do all things,
> and while remaining in herself, she renews all things;
> in every generation she passes into holy souls
> and makes them friends of God and prophets;
> for God loves nothing so much as the person who lives with wisdom.
> She is more beautiful than the sun,
> and excels every constellation of the stars.
> Compared with the light she is found to be superior,
> for it is succeeded by the night,
> but against wisdom evil does not prevail.
> She reaches mightily from one end of the earth to the other,
> and she orders all things well.

In the sequel, the text carries on the theme of Solomon's search for wisdom, whom he wished to make his wife. She is here (8:6) called the one who fashions what exists; moreover, she knows about what happened long ago and what will come about (8:8). As no enterprise can succeed without her, the unnamed Solomon prays for wisdom (9:1-18; see his experience at Gibeon in 1 Kings 3:4-15). At the end of his prayer he mentions people who "were saved by wisdom" (9:18), a theme that is developed in chapters 11–19. The notion also controls 10:1-21 where there is a survey of wisdom's saving work in history, using such examples as Adam, Noah, and Abraham. The last part of the book's second section (10:15-21) deals with Moses and the exodus, and these become the focus in the third section (chaps. 11–19).

Chapters 11–19 offer a number of examples from the exodus and wilderness stories that illustrate the theme that Egypt received a measured punishment, through phenomena by which Israel profited (see 11:5). For instance, in 11:1-14 the poet deals with the plague in which the water of the Nile turned to blood; Israel, however, received water from the rock in the wilderness (see 11:14 for the idea of reversal). Or, in 17:1-18:4 the Egyptians experienced darkness and fear while Israel enjoyed light from the pillar of fire by night. So, as in chapters 2–5 where a reversal involving individuals was developed, here a reversal involving two nations is elaborated.

Inserted between the first two of these examples are two sections that examine different but related subjects. Wisdom 11:15-12:22 centers around the subject of divine mercy. God, despite his immense power, shows kindness to all. He corrects people little by little so that they learn to trust him. Since he was gracious even to the Canaanites, the worst people of all, he can be counted on to be merciful to his own people who in turn are exhorted to be kind. The second section (chaps. 13–15) handles idolatry, a subject that had arisen in the previous section. The writer distinguishes three kinds of idolatry. The first is the type practiced by nature worshipers (Stoics may be meant); for them he has some respect because they sincerely search for God through his creation. The second kind is the form practiced by those who manufacture idols; like the prophets Isaiah (44:9-20) and Jeremiah (10:1-16), he mocks them. The last and worst are the Egyptian animal worshipers who not only revere animals but choose the most loathsome kinds. The author also tries to explain the origin of idolatry and suggests several possibilities: e.g., a way to cope with the loss of a child, or honor accorded to the statue of rulers. He considers idolatry to be the heart and cause of all evil, an evil from which monotheistic Israel is immune.

Wisdom of Solomon, then, presents a remarkable picture of wisdom (which is not identified with the law of Moses) as an all-pervasive spirit, as the fashioner of all, and the one who has acted in Israel's history. She is to be sought most eagerly, because possessing her leads to immortality. Those who find wisdom know the way things are, and do not make the massive mistakes of the wicked who learn too late. In Wisdom of Solomon we find a writer in the wisdom tradition affirming belief in an afterlife.

Poetic Works

Some of the writings that have already been presented could be included under the rubric Poetic Works (e.g., Ben Sira and Wisdom), but there are other metrical compositions from the period of the second temple that do not belong in the wisdom category and certainly not in any of the others surveyed above. For convenience' sake they are placed in a classification of their own.

The Psalms of Solomon (pseudepigraphal)

According to the Bible, King Solomon was associated not only with wisdom but also with another sort of literature: "his songs numbered a thousand and five" (1 Kings 4:32b). Psalm 72, which carries the title "Of Solomon," may have served as a source or model for the *Psalms of Solomon*, which come from a time long after Solomon's death. It opens with a request: "Give the king your justice, O God, and your righteousness to a king's son. May he judge your people with righteousness, and your poor with justice. May the mountains yield prosperity for the people, and the hills, in righteousness. May he defend the cause of the poor of the people, give deliverance to the needy, and crush the oppressor" (Ps. 72:1-4). These subjects are themes in the Psalms of Solomon, as its author looks forward to a messianic ruler whose reign will be characterized by justice and who will rule all nations. The eighteen poems that circulated under Solomon's name are at least in part a response to Pompey's conquest of Jerusalem in 63 BCE and the events of that age. *Psalms of Solomon* 17 has received attention because it contains a lengthy description of a messiah who will come from the line of David. The earliest available form of the text of the *Psalms of Solomon* is in Greek and is found in the manuscripts of the Septuagint, but the poems may have been composed in Hebrew.

The date of the *Psalms of Solomon* cannot be determined precisely. The major clues come from Psalms 2, 8, and 17, which supply something of the historical setting against which at least these three poems were written. They speak of native leaders who were not legitimate rulers and whose time was characterized by massive corruption and evil. They are charged with violating the temple and cult. These appear to be the Hasmoneans. God raised up against them a foreign conqueror, who was welcomed to Jerusalem by some but who still had to take the city by force. He entered the temple but later met his death in Egypt, where his body was left unburied on the beach (see 2:26-27). The description fits Pompey's actions at Jerusalem and the way in which he met his end in 48 BCE. Psalm 2 (with 8 and 17) would then have been written after this event; perhaps the other poems were as well, but that is not certain. As nothing is said about the destruction of the temple, it is likely that the *Psalms of Solomon* were written before 70 CE. It has been claimed that the author of Baruch borrowed from the present work because *Psalms of Solomon* 11:2-5 and Baruch 5:5-8 are not only closely parallel but the version in the *Psalms of Solomon* is more cohesive and tightly arranged. Moreover, some scholars think that Baruch 5:5-8 is an addition to that book. However, the direction of borrowing is hardly obvious, and it is as likely that both draw upon a common tradition.

A number of the poems give expression to the feelings of oppression of the author and his group; they cry out to the Lord to save them, while acknowledging that he has been just to punish his people. Nevertheless, they confess that the Lord disciplines his own as a father would his own son; thus they must endure and continue to trust in the Lord who will certainly give eternal life to the righteous and destroy the wicked forever. Despite the present circumstances, there is an indissoluble bond between God and Israel.

A swift overview of the psalms will give an idea of their contents.

Psalm 1: The speaker may be Jerusalem bewailing her children's misdeeds. About one group the writer says: "Their lawless actions surpassed the gentiles before them; they completely profaned the sanctuary of the Lord" (1:8).

Psalm 2: This psalm, one of the three with the clearest historical references, talks of sinners who broke down walls without God's interfering with them. "Gentile foreigners went up to your place of sacrifice; they arrogantly trampled (it) with their sandals" (2:2). This came as punishment for the sins committed by some Jerusalemites who had defiled the sanctuary and committed sundry abominations (e.g., prostitution). The psalmist confesses that God's judgment was right but prays that he not delay repaying the overly zealous gentiles. It is likely, as noted above, that 2:26-27 describes Pompey's death. He did not understand that he was merely human and that God is the Lord. Rulers and others are called upon to acknowledge God, who has mercy on the righteous when they persistently call on him and who repays the sinners for what they have done.

Psalm 3: The psalmist contrasts the way of the righteous and the sinner. The righteous will enjoy eternal life, but sinners will experience everlasting destruction.

Psalm 4: The poet speaks against the deceitful, lustful, and hypocritical sort of person who attempts to impress others falsely. He prays that such people will be punished and their bodies left exposed at the end of their lives. Those who fear God innocently are blessed, and the Lord will save them from deceitful people.

Psalm 5: Here, as frequently, the psalmist praises the Lord God who cares for the poor and oppressed: "When we are persecuted, we call on you for help and you will not turn away from our prayer; for you are our God" (5:5). He also declares that moderate wealth is enough for the righteous (5:17).

Psalm 6: The happy person is one whose heart is ready to call on God; "when he remembers the name of the Lord, he will be saved" (6:1). The psalm depicts the way of life chosen by this sort of person.

Psalm 7: The poet expresses his confidence that God will protect Israel and not destroy her. "Discipline us as you wish, but do not turn (us) over to the gentiles" (7:3).

Psalm 8: The second of the psalms with recognizable historical allusions speaks of sounds of tumult and the sins of those in Jerusalem. The psalmist again declares that God is just in judging them for adultery, incest, stealing from the sanctuary, and defiling the sacrifices. "There was no sin they left undone in which they did not surpass the gentiles" (8:13). As a consequence of such evil, God brought an attacker from the ends of the earth. Though leaders allowed him in by opening Jerusalem's gates to him, he slaughtered many in Jerusalem. The poem offers praise to God who judges rightly and asks him to turn his mercy on his own.

Psalm 9: The exile showed God's righteousness, and no evildoer can hide from his knowledge. According to the psalmist, people can choose the way in which they walk for themselves. God cleanses people who confess their sins. Once more the poet asks for God's eternal mercy on his people.

Psalm 10: The psalm expresses one of the themes of the collection: "The Lord is good to those who endure discipline" (10:2). He is just in his judgments, and will be merciful to the poor of Israel.

Psalm 11: The poet prays that the Lord's mercy may rest upon Israel forever. Jerusalem sees her children assembled from all sides, as the mountains are flattened and the hills flee before them (cf. the parallel with Baruch 5:5-8). Jerusalem is told to don her glorious robes "for God has spoken well of Israel forevermore" (11:7).

Psalm 12: The poem contains a plea for deliverance from the wicked and a request for punishment upon them. It also asks that God protect the quiet person and save Israel eternally.

Psalm 13: The psalmist confesses that the Lord has protected him and others; God admonishes the righteous as a father does a beloved son. His mercy rests on the devout, on those who fear him. Sinners, however, are to be taken to destruction.

Psalm 14: The Lord is faithful to those who love him and endure his discipline; they will live forever. The poem contrasts their way and fate with those of sinners.

Psalm 15: God saved the psalmist when he was persecuted. Indeed, he is the hope and refuge of the poor. God's judging flame will not harm the righteous. Famine, sword, and death remain far from the righteous, but they pursue the wicked. God's mark is on the righteous for salvation and on sinners for destruction.

Psalm 16: The psalmist speaks of the experience of being far from the Lord and compares it to sleep. The Lord, however, came to his aid and saved him. For this he thanks the Lord and asks that he keep him from sin.

Psalm 17: The last of the psalms with clear historical allusions begins and ends by celebrating the Lord as Israel's eternal king. The psalmist recalls the promise to David but acknowledges that Israel fell into sin. As a consequence, sinners stood up against her and drove Israel out. God later overthrew them. But "a man alien to our race" (17:7) rose against Israel, treated her cruelly, and wasted the land. The devout had to flee to the wilderness. After describing how terrible the situation was, the psalmist calls upon God: "See, Lord, and raise up for them their king, the son of David, to rule over your servant Israel in the time known to you, O God" (17:21). This king will forcibly drive the sinners from Jerusalem and will gather the holy people whom he will rule righteously. He will distribute the people on the land according to their tribes and subject the gentile nations to his yoke. Those nations, rather than harming Israel, will come to Jerusalem with gifts and will see the Lord's glory. This king is called "the Lord Messiah" (17:32). The messiah is described in glowing terms — righteous, powerful, merciful, wise, free from sin — but the Lord is always his king, the one who raised him up.

Psalm 18: The Lord watches over all, including the poor, and disciplines his own like a firstborn son. "May God cleanse Israel for the day of mercy in blessing/for the appointed day when his Messiah will reign" (18:5). As in Psalm 17, he says that those who will be born in the days of the messiah will be blessed. He closes by blessing God as great, as the one who has set the luminaries in their unaltered courses.

The Prayer of Manasseh (included in the deuterocanonical books of Orthodox churches)

The Prayer of Manasseh is included among the Odes in some copies of the Greek Bible. The Odes are a collection of poems from the Bible and other sources. They are appended to the book of Psalms. The Prayer is a short, one-chapter work that develops an event hinted at in the Bible but not actually described there. The Manasseh of the title (who is never mentioned in the book itself) is King Manasseh, the greatest sinner among the kings of David's line. According to 2 Kings 21:1-18, he committed unprecedented evils in Jerusalem and was the cause for the destruction of Judah and Jerusalem. Second Chronicles 33 adds details to the biography of the king. In this later work Manasseh is indeed wicked and was imprisoned by the Assyrians who brought him to Babylon. "While he was in distress he entreated the favor of the Lord his God and humbled himself greatly before the Lord of his ancestors. He prayed to him, and God received his entreaty, heard his plea, and restored him again to Jerusalem and to his kingdom. Then Manasseh knew that the Lord indeed was God" (33:12-13). Second Chronicles 33:19 says that his prayer and other acts "are written in the records of the seers [or: of Hozai, according to the traditional vocalization of the Hebrew text]."

The fifteen verses of the Prayer of Manasseh are the attempt of a later writer to provide the words of Manasseh's prayer (see also the Qumran text 4Q381, fragment 33, lines 8-10, which are identified in the text as a

"Prayer of Manasseh, king of Judah, when the king of Assyria put him in prison"). The work belongs in a series of other Jewish compositions that record words of confession and penitence, with requests for mercy in times of distress (see Ezra 9; Neh. 9; the Song of Azariah, for examples). The suppliant begins by appealing to the Lord Almighty, the God of the ancestors and the creator, whose wrath is unbearable but whose mercy is "immeasurable and unsearchable" (v. 6). He reminds the deity that "you have promised repentance and forgiveness to those who have sinned against you, and in the multitude of your mercies you have appointed repentance for sinners, so that they may be saved" (v. 7). He then turns his attention to himself, noting that a spectacular sinner like himself needed repentance; his sins weighed him down terribly (vv. 9-10). He pleads for divine forgiveness and declares that when God, in his great mercy, saves him from his plight and so shows his goodness through him, he will praise him throughout his life.

The Prayer of Azariah and the Song of the Three Young Men (deuterocanonical/apocryphal)

One of the three additions to the book of Daniel in the Greek versions is called the Prayer of Azariah and the Song of the Three Young Men (they are also numbers 7 and 8 among the Odes appended to the Psalms in some Greek copies). The three young men in question are Daniel's friends Hananiah, Azariah, and Mishael (the text uses their Hebrew names). The two-part composition is inserted between Daniel 3:23 and 3:24 (which seem rather abrupt in the Aramaic text, as if something were missing). The addition has a two-verse prose introduction which precedes the twenty verses of the Prayer of Azariah; another prose section (vv. 23-28) then introduces the Song of the Three Young Men (vv. 29-68). These sixty-seven verses are numbered as Daniel 3:24-90 in Catholic versions of the Bible.

The Prayer of Azariah is a plea for deliverance in a time of crisis (the three are in Nebuchadnezzar's fiery furnace), although the crisis he envisages is far larger than the fate of the three. He blesses the God of the ancestors who is worthy of praise and who is just in judging Jerusalem and the three young men for their sins against the law. Despite this, Azariah prays: "For your name's sake do not give us up forever, and do not annul your covenant" (v. 11). He also bases his appeal on Abraham, Isaac, and Israel to whom the promises were made. Out of the lowly present circumstances of his people, he implores the deity: "Yet with a contrite heart and a humble spirit may we be accepted, as though it were burnt offerings of rams and bulls, or with tens of thousands of fat lambs" (vv. 16-17). He acknowledges that they seek and fear God, and prays for him to deliver them "in accordance with your marvelous works" (v. 20). Their enemies then would know that he was Lord of the entire world.

The second prose introduction (vv. 23-28) points out that though Nebuchadnezzar's men kept stoking the furnace to incredible temperatures, an angel of the Lord arrived, drove the flames from the furnace, "and made the inside of the furnace as though a moist wind were whistling through it" (v. 27). Their miraculous deliverance moved the young men to song as they "praised and glorified and blessed God in the furnace" (v. 28).

The song divides into two formally distinct parts. In verses 29-34 every verse begins with "Blessed are you" (except v. 30, which has "And blessed is your glorious, holy name") and the second line has a statement about praise and exalting God highly. The deity is pictured on his throne, high above all. This opening section of direct praise is followed by another (vv. 35-66a) in which different parts of the creation are summoned to praise the Lord. Verses 35-51 call upon the heavens and the entities associated with it to bless the Lord (angels, waters above heaven, powers, sun, moon, and stars, rain, dew, winds, etc.). The second parts of these lines urge them to "sing praise to him and highly exalt him forever." Then, in vv. 52-59 the earth and everything associated with it are ordered to join the cosmic choir (mountains, hills, all that grows in the ground, seas, rivers, springs, whales and other swimming creatures, wild animals, and cattle). Each of these lines, too, shares the refrain "sing praise to him and highly exalt him forever." After addressing the various parts of creation, the trio turn to all people and tell them to bless the Lord (vv. 60-66a): Israel, the priests of the Lord, the servants of the Lord, the spirits and souls of the righteous, the holy and humble in heart; finally they call upon themselves to bless him. Each of these lines shares the refrain of the preceding two sections. The final lines give the reason for the blessing and praise: "For he has rescued us from Hades and saved us from the power of death, and delivered us from the midst of the burning fiery furnace; from the midst of the fire he has delivered us" (v. 66b). A call to thank the one whose mercy endures forever ends the song. At this point one returns to Daniel 3:24, where Nebuchadnezzar is puzzled at seeing four men in the furnace, all unharmed. The addition explains who the fourth is: the angel sent to deliver the three (in Dan. 3:28 Nebuchadnezzar says that God had sent his angel to rescue them).

Mockery of Idols

The Hebrew Bible contains several sections in which writers gleefully detail the weakness of the idols worshiped by pagans and contrast their impotence with the almighty power of Israel's God (e.g., Isa. 44:9-20). This type of writing continued in the second temple period as the following two examples show.

The Letter of Jeremiah (deuterocanonical/apocryphal)

In the book of Jeremiah, the prophet writes a letter to the exiles in Babylon, urging them to settle down where they are and to pray for the welfare of their new city (see Jer. 29, which actually contains two letters from the prophet). At some unknown time in the early second temple period, someone wrote another letter in Jeremiah's name; this one was addressed "to those who were to be taken to Babylon as exiles by the king of Babylon, to give them the message that God had commanded him" (v. 1). It is reasonable to think that the Letter was composed in Hebrew, but the earliest text now available is in Greek. A small Greek fragment of it, dating from approximately 100 BCE, has been found in Qumran cave 7 (7Q2; a few words and letters from vv. 43-44 can be read on it). The short work is present in the witnesses to the Septuagint, at times as a separate book and at times as the sixth chapter of Baruch. For this reason, the NRSV presents the Letter of Jeremiah as an independent work yet places it directly after Baruch and numbers it chapter 6. It is possible that 2 Maccabees 2:2 refers to the Letter of Jeremiah when it says that the prophet instructed the people not "to be led astray in their thoughts on seeing the gold and silver statues and their adornment." However, the author of 2 Maccabees 2 also knew other Jeremiah traditions, so one cannot be sure his source was the Letter of Jeremiah.

Most of the one-chapter Letter is a relentless critique of idols, of those who worship them, and of the priests who minister before them. In writing the work, the author drew upon a well established anti-idol tradition in the Hebrew Bible (see, for example, Isa. 44:9-20), a tradition well attested in the book of Jeremiah as well (see 10:9, 11, 14-15 where idols are unfavorably contrasted with the Lord). The writer repeatedly demonstrates how helpless idols are, made by humans from wood overlaid with gold and silver, unable to help themselves, much less save others. He also

135

underscores priestly graft and corruption. The anti-idol polemic in verses 8-73 is divided into sections through the use of repeated phrases (see vv. 16, 23, 29, 40, 44, [49], 52, 56, 65, 69).

A work of this kind was meant to provide Jews with a perspective on the common sight of images in temples and in religious processions. The author does caricature the use of such idols, and one ought not to think that his understanding of them was shared by those who found it meaningful to worship through the medium of such images.

Bel and the Dragon (deuterocanonical/apocryphal)

The anti-idol story Bel and the Dragon, similar in theme to the Letter of Jeremiah, forms chapter 14 in the Greek versions of Daniel. It tells of more episodes in Daniel's heroic and unfailingly successful conflicts with the Babylonians, and for that reason could have been included in the section on Tales above. In part it is a story of contest, pitting Daniel against the Babylonians (as in Dan. 1, 2, 4, 5), and in part it is a story of religious persecution (like Dan. 3 and 6) in which his life is endangered because of his belief in the one living God.

The setting for the first episode (vv. 1-22) is the time of King Cyrus the Persian, when Daniel was "the most honored of all his friends" (v. 2). The story centers around the idol Bel (that is, Marduk, the creator god; Bel is the Babylonian pronunciation of the word Baal, meaning "lord," familiar from Canaanite religion). The Babylonians worshiped Bel, daily providing him with substantial quantities of food which disappeared each night. While the king worshiped the idol every day, Daniel worshiped his God. He was asked why he did so, and he explained that he worshiped the living God who created the universe and rules all, not man-made idols. The king countered that Bel was indeed a living god because he ate the food offered to him — an argument that made Daniel laugh. A contest ensued, with the issue being whether Bel was alive; the loser(s) of the contest (the priests of Bel or Daniel) faced a death penalty. The king himself set out Bel's food and then sealed the door to the idol's room with his own signet ring so that no one would enter it during the night and enjoy the food. It turns out that the priests and their families had a secret trapdoor through which they entered the room at night and ate what was offered to Bel while the temple was closed. Before the king sealed the room, Daniel took the clever precaution of having the floor sprinkled with ashes; only the king saw him do this. That night the priestly families entered in their normal fashion and had their usual feast. When the sealed doors were opened in the morning in the presence of the king and Daniel, the king thought his belief in Bel had been verified. He confessed: "You are great, O Bel, and in you there is no deceit at all" (v. 18). But a closer look at the footprints in the ashes revealed what had really happened. Once the priests had confessed to their duplicity, the king had them and their families executed. He gave Bel to Daniel who "destroyed it and its temple" (v. 22). Thus the exile, Daniel, conquered the god of the conqueror.

The second episode in the mockery of Babylonian gods (vv. 23-42) has two parts: the contest concerning the dragon (vv. 23-27) and Daniel's punishment and deliverance (vv. 28-42). The former has to do with "a great dragon, which the Babylonians revered" (v. 23). Here too the king argued that the dragon was a living god (at least he was visibly alive, unlike Bel) and ordered Daniel to worship it. Daniel refused and requested permission to kill the dragon without a sword. "Then Daniel took pitch, fat, and hair, and boiled them together and made cakes, which he fed to the dragon. The dragon ate them, and burst open. Then Daniel said, 'See what you have been worshiping!'" (v. 27). In both of these episodes the writer not only opposes idols but depicts their destruction.

The Babylonians, far from drawing the only logical conclusion from these events, accused the king of becoming a Jew by destroying Bel, the dragon, and the priests. When they threatened the monarch with death, he handed Daniel to them. For the second time in his remarkable career, Daniel was thrown into the lions' den, where he spent six days. The lions were deprived of their normal meals during this time but did not eat or even harm Daniel. An unlikely character, Habakkuk (identified in the Theodotionic version as the prophet Habakkuk; see Hab. 2:18-19 where there are anti-idol lines), now enters the scene. An angel ordered him to bring a stew he had made to Daniel to feed him in the lions' den (there are numerous references to food and feeding in this addition). In fact, when Habakkuk claimed ignorance about the lions' den, the angel picked him up by the hair and transported him from Judea to Babylon. He fed the stew to Daniel, after which the angel returned Habakkuk to Judea. Like King Darius in Daniel 6, Nebuchadnezzar came to the lions' den at the end of the appointed time and found Daniel sitting there unharmed. He, like Darius, acknowledged Daniel's God as the only one (v. 41). Daniel's accusers were then tossed to the famished lions who satisfied their hunger with them.

Philo and Josephus

Two Jewish writers of the second temple period stand out from all others because more of their writings have been preserved. Philo, the older of the two, lived in Alexandria, wrote in Greek, and composed many studies of the Pentateuch. Josephus, the younger of the pair, lived in Jerusalem and Rome, wrote in Aramaic (apparently) and in Greek, and provided us with lengthy histories of his own people. Indeed, for long stretches of second temple history, Josephus is our primary or often our only source of information. No short account of Philo and Josephus can do justice to their importance, but an attempt will be made to summarize their careers and their literary contributions.

Philo of Alexandria

Although many of Philo's writings have survived, little is known about his life. We do not even know when he was born or when he died. The few facts about his life come from occasional hints in his own books and a small number of external references (e.g., Josephus mentions him). His brother Alexander held the position of alabarch, apparently a high office that involved supervising the collection of revenues, and was so wealthy that King Agrippa I often borrowed money from him. A clear implication is that Philo belonged to an extremely prominent family in the large Jewish community of Alexandria. Philo's nephew Tiberius Julius Alexander, Alexander's son, abandoned his ancestral religion, became the Roman procurator in Judea in 46-48 CE, and played in important role for the Romans in their suppression of the Jewish revolt of 66-70 CE — another indication of the status enjoyed by people in Philo's family. Josephus considered him preeminent in every way and skilled in philosophy.

The one episode in Philo's life that is well documented is his participation in a failed delegation sent by the Alexandrian Jewish community to the emperor Gaius Caligula in 39-40 CE. Later Philo penned a work entitled *Embassy to Gaius* in which he deals (among other topics) with the circumstances of the mission, and Josephus also makes note of Philo's participation in it (*Ant.* 18.257-60). The delegates were commissioned to present the Jewish case regarding the pogrom that had broken out against them with the support of the governor Flaccus. Josephus, after noting what led up to the embassy, says: "Philo, who stood at the head of the delegation of the Jews, a man held in the highest honour, brother of Alexander the alabarch, and no novice in philosophy, was prepared to proceed with the defence against these accusations. But Gaius cut him short, told him to get out of his way, and, being exceedingly angry, made it clear that he would visit some outrage upon them. Philo, having thus been treated with contumely, left the room, saying to the Jews who had accompanied him that they should be of good courage, for Gaius's wrath was a matter of words, but in fact he was now enlisting God against himself" (*Ant.* 18.259-60). The last comment is interesting in that it is similar to Philo's assessment in his two works on the subject. At the time when he was dispatched to Caligula, Philo, the secretary of the group, says that he was an elderly man (*Embassy* 1.1, 28 [182]) — the only clue to the approximate date when he was born. On the basis of this statement, it is usually claimed that he was born ca. 20-10 BCE; perhaps he did not live long after his participation in the group (although he may refer to games that occurred in 47 CE). Philo does indicate that at some point he had gone on pilgrimage to Jerusalem (*Prov.* frg. 2, 64).

Philo wrote more works than those that survive, but the extant works, whether we have them in the original Greek or in translation (e.g., into Armenian), fill some twelve volumes in the Loeb edition. Christian scholars were instrumental in preserving his writings, many of which were collected by Origen in Caesarea; the church historian Eusebius gave a summary of his books in *Ecclesiastical History* 2.18.

It is common to classify Philo's literary works into those that are devoted to expounding the Pentateuch and those that are not. In the former category, his many writings on the books of Moses are divided into three large works. The first, *Questions*, contains questions and answers that give interpretations of the text; only parts of them on Genesis and Exodus are extant. A second and larger category is called the *Allegorical Laws*. Here Philo presents allegorical interpretations of passages from Genesis. True to his method, characters in the text are understood to represent states of the soul, and from them Philo draws moral lessons. The third work on the Mosaic law is called *Expositions*. In these Philo offers a more systematic study of the legislation and first organizes pentateuchal law under the rubrics of the ten commandments. He also presents studies of the special laws in each heading.

His second category of writings includes his important work on the *Life of Moses* and his treatises entitled *That Every Good Man Is Free* (in which he gives a substantial description of the Essenes) and *On the Con-*

templative Life (in which he speaks at length about the Therapeutae). Among his other works are his two compositions (which may be part of one work) on Flaccus, the governor of Egypt whose treatment of the Jews led to their sending the delegation to the emperor, and *The Embassy to Gaius*. In these last two works he not only treats the historical events but also conveys the point that attempting to force Jews, who were model citizens of the empire, to deny their religion by, for example, compelling them to set up statues of the emperor in their synagogues, would come at a high price for the Romans.

Philo's thought, which he never set forth systematically, involves an amalgam of teachings found in various Greek philosophical systems and in the scriptures. Scholars have long debated whether he can more aptly be described as a Hellenized Jew or a Judaized Hellene, but it is beyond doubt that he drew on both and did so extensively as he thought and wrote. Moreover, he was explicit about his debt to both traditions, as he cites frequently from classical sources (by name) and from the scriptures. It should also be kept in mind that much of what Philo had to say arises from exegesis of the Pentateuch and receives its order from that source, not from a systematic outline present in his mind. Naturally, as a citizen of Alexandria, his Bible was the Septuagint; whether Philo knew more than just a smattering of Hebrew is disputed. Philo considered the law of Moses to be absolutely authoritative and the repository of all wisdom, if one read it properly. In fact, the Greeks had drawn their wisdom from Moses. The proper way of reading the scriptures was through allegorical interpretation, yet Philo had a double view here as well. As one may see in his series of Questions and Answers, he, unlike some of his contemporaries, refused to give up a literal kind of interpretation and the implications that followed from it (such as celebrating festivals, observing the sabbath, and being circumcised). Nevertheless, an allegorical reading of the same texts led one to higher thoughts and abstractions, much as the soul was more elevated than the body.

For him God was beyond human comprehension and could be defined only by saying what he was not. This God, the one who exists, was, however, knowable through his powers, such as his creation and supervision of the world. An interesting concept for Philo is the Logos of God, the power in which all the others are summed up. In one sense the Logos is God's thought as he planned to create the world — a world that is divided into two parts: the intelligible world (Gen. 1) and the sensible world. The former resembles Plato's world of ideas or pure forms, while the latter is what is perceptible to the senses. The powers of God, such as the Logos, belong to the intelligible world but influence the sensible world. The influence of the Logos came especially through Moses and Aaron. Philo spoke of the Logos in other senses as a divine being separate from God himself, as the firstborn of God (like Lady Wisdom), and as the beginning. Since the Logos is the mental power of God in creating the universe, it remains in the universe as a natural law, governing the operation of the universe.

The Logos also manifested itself in the biblical patriarchs and became wisdom or virtue in the matriarchs — that is, through them a natural, unwritten law came to expression before the law was revealed to Moses. As he explains at the beginning of *On Abraham* (part of the *Expositions*):

> but, since it is necessary to carry out our examination of the law in regular sequence, let us postpone consideration of particular laws, which are, so to speak, copies, and examine first those which are more general and may be called the originals of the copies. These are such men as lived good and blameless lives, whose virtues stand permanently recorded in the most holy scriptures, not merely to sound their praises but for the instruction of the reader and as an inducement to him to aspire to the same; for in these men we have laws endowed with life and reason, and Moses extolled them for two reasons. First he wished to shew that the enacted ordinances are not inconsistent with nature; and secondly that those who wish to live in accordance with the laws as they stand have no difficult task, seeing that the first generations before any at all of the particular statutes was set in writing followed the unwritten law with perfect ease, so that one might properly say that the enacted laws are nothing else than memorials of the life of the ancients, preserving to a later generation their actual words and deeds. For they were not scholars or pupils of others, nor did they learn under teachers what was right to say or do: they listened to no voice or instruction but their own: they gladly accepted conformity with nature, holding that nature itself was, as indeed it is, the most venerable of statutes, and thus their whole life was one of happy obedience to law. (1.3-6)

His patriarchal models were two groups of three: Enosh, Enoch, and Noah; and Abraham, Isaac, and Jacob.

Moses enjoyed an extraordinary status in Philo's system. He was the supreme lawgiver, the ideal king, prophet, and priest, through whom the divine laws became incarnate. At the end of his earthly sojourn, Moses

141

divested himself of his body and returned to the immaterial realm, where he joined the luminaries in their praise and enjoyment of the divine being.

Philo's understanding of the creation, as we have seen, was a dualistic one, divided into intelligible and sensible worlds. His view of humans was similar: they consist of soul (higher, immortal) and body (lower, mortal). Evil in this system arises from matter. Israel, when it is obedient to the laws of Moses and avoids sensuous pleasures, is like the soul and pagans are like the body. The goal of all should be to deny the sensual and achieve a beatific vision of God.

Josephus

Josephus figured often in the historical survey above, since his writings are an invaluable fountain of information for Jewish life and history in the second temple period. He is unusual in several ways, one of which is that he wrote an autobiography (called *Life*), which he added as an appendix to his lengthy *Antiquities of the Jews.* Elsewhere in his voluminous writings he mentions other details about his life, with the result that we know a fair amount about him. He was a member of a prominent priestly family in Jerusalem and was born in the first year of the reign of the emperor Gaius Caligula (37-38 CE). He says that through his mother he was a descendant of the Hasmoneans (*Life* 2). As he recounts his early life, he leaves the reader with the impression that he was a prodigy: "While still a mere boy, about fourteen years old, I won universal applause for my love of letters; insomuch that the chief priests and the leading men of the city used constantly to come to me for precise information on some particular in our ordinances" (*Life* 9; cf. Luke 2:46-47). At age sixteen, he claims, he sampled the ways of life of each of the three Jewish groups, the Pharisees, the Sadducees, and the Essenes (he gives a lengthy description of the Essenes in *War* 2.119-66) and then spent three years with a desert ascetic named Bannus. After these experiences he returned to Jerusalem and decided to follow the way of the Pharisees. At age twenty-six he served as a member of a delegation dispatched to Rome to gain the release of some priests whom the procurator Felix had sent there as prisoners. So, at an early age Josephus saw the great capital city for himself and gained firsthand knowledge of the glory and power that was Rome. While there he was able to gain the assistance of

Poppaea, Nero's wife, for his cause (*Life* 16). Shortly after his return to Jerusalem, he found "revolutionary movements already on foot and widespread elation at the prospect of revolt from Rome" (*Life* 17).

The revolt against Rome was to have a profound effect on Josephus's life. Early in the war period, Josephus received an important assignment in Galilee. Exactly what that assignment was is difficult to determine because he presents two views on it — in fact, he presents two perspectives on his activities for the first six months of the revolt. Those views come to expression in his earliest book, entitled *War*, and in *Life* (on these see below). In the earlier work he pictures himself as the person appointed commander in Galilee from the beginning (*War* 2.568) while in the *Life* he claims he was more reluctant and that he was at first a member of a commission sent to Galilee to persuade extremists to put down their arms (*Life* 29). These two pictures are only one example of the problem of Josephus's two accounts of this crucial period in his life; as we will see, in the *Life* he defends himself against charges about his conduct in Galilee.

After preparing the Galilee militarily, Josephus led the fight in the north against the advancing Roman army under the command of Vespasian. The Romans defeated Josephus's forces and he himself was eventually captured by them. Josephus was brought before Vespasian and predicted that he would become emperor. Vespasian kept him in custody until he was indeed declared emperor by his troops in 69 CE in Egypt. At that point he released the prophetic Josephus, and the future historian returned to Judea with Titus, Vespasian's son, who now had the task of suppressing the revolt. At Titus's behest he would, from time to time, try to convince the defenders of Jerusalem to surrender, but to no avail; he was himself injured in the process (*War* 5.363-419).

After the war, Josephus received land from Titus and accompanied him to Rome. There Vespasian allowed him to live in his former residence, made him a Roman citizen, and gave him a pension (*Life* 422). While he was living in Rome and supported by the imperial family, he wrote *The Jewish War*, which is largely devoted to describing the revolt of 66-70 (-73). The conditions under which he compiled the work raise obvious and weighty questions about the objectivity of his reporting. Josephus continued to be favored by the second and third Flavian emperors Titus (79-81) and Domitian (81-96), but his later works were not sponsored by the emperor but by someone named Epaphroditus. We do not know when Josephus died, but perhaps ca. 100 CE is not far off.

Josephus's fascinating literary output consists of four works: the *Jew-*

ish War, the *Jewish Antiquities*, the *Life* which is appended to the *Antiquities*, and *Against Apion*.

1. The *Jewish War* (in seven books): It is not clear exactly when he finished the history of the Jewish war against Rome. It ends with the Masada story and an account of a Jewish revolt in North Africa and thus it could not have been written before 73 CE. He also says that he presented the books of his work to the emperors Vespasian and Titus (*Life* 361; *Against Apion* 50). As Vespasian died in 79, it could have been no later than that date, unless Josephus later revised an earlier form of the *Jewish War*.

The historian says he first wrote the work in the native language of his country (Aramaic?) for the Jews of Mesopotamia and later translated it into Greek (he had assistants to help him with the language; see *War* 1.3). For the *War* he could call upon several sources: his own experience (on both sides of the conflict), his notes, reports of people whom he interviewed, and the commentaries of Vespasian and Titus. *War* begins with a survey covering Jewish history from the time of the Maccabean revolt to the period before the war with Rome; but most of it, from the end of book 2 through to near the end of book 7, presents the Jewish revolt in great and painstaking detail. To this history he added several digressions (for example, on the three Jewish philosophies — the Pharisees, Sadducees, and Essenes — in 2.119-66) and composed a series of speeches by leading characters such as King Agrippa II who tried to dissuade the Jews from revolt (2.345-407), by Josephus himself during the siege of Jerusalem (5.363-419), and by Titus (3.472-84; 6.34-53, 328-50).

In general one can say that Josephus's history, written under Roman patronage, pictures the revolt as caused by radicals such as the Zealots and Sicarii, tyrannical leaders, and brigands. The Romans, especially Titus, were honorable in handling the situation, but they eventually did what the Jewish fanatics caused them to do: they destroyed the city, the temple, and a large part of the population. There is also a series of passages in which Josephus indicates the tragedy of the revolt came about ultimately through the plan of God himself.

2. The *Jewish Antiquities* (in twenty books): Josephus relates that he finished his lengthy history of the Jewish people in the thirteenth year of Domitian (81-96) when he himself was fifty-six years of age — that is, the year 93 or 94 (*Ant.* 20.267). In it he covers the history of his people from the very beginning (starting with Gen. 1) to the eve of the first revolt against the Romans. In the first ten books he paraphrases the scriptural story, using a Greek form of the Bible, as is evident from his use of 1 Esdras

and Esther in its longer Greek form. For the Persian and early Greek periods covered in book 11 and the first part of book 12, he had little information, but he does include some stories told in no other sources (e.g., the meeting of Alexander the Great with the high priest Jaddua, the Tobiad Romance) and other material, such as the *Letter of Aristeas*. The remainder of book 12 through book 14 follows the story from the rise of the Hasmoneans to the time of Antipater and his son Herod. Books 15–17 present a long account of the reigns of Herod and his son Archelaus, and books 18–20 take the history to the last Roman rulers in Judea before the revolt. Book 18 is the one that contains the famous and much discussed paragraph about Jesus (18.63-64). In those lines Josephus sounds as if he recognizes him as the messiah, but it is virtually certain that Christian scribes later touched up a shorter and more equivocal reference to Jesus.

The *Antiquities* represents an enormous investment of energy and took Josephus a long time to write. Research was needed to investigate the many sources he cites and to compile them into a coherent narrative. Without the extraordinary amount of information that he supplies in the *War* and the *Antiquities,* our knowledge of Jewish history and thought would be only a fraction of what it now is. One reason why he devoted so much labor to the task was to impress his readers, whether Jew or gentile, with the greatness of his people and with their illustrious and ancient past. To that end he also documents at length the respect shown to the Jews by foreign rulers. He declares that the lesson of his account is "that men who conform to the will of God, and do not venture to transgress laws that have been laid down, prosper in all things beyond belief, and for their reward are offered by God felicity; whereas, in proportion as they depart from the strict observance of these laws, things (else) practicable become impracticable, and whatever imaginary good thing they strive to do ends in irretrievable disasters" (*Ant.* 1.14).

3. The *Life:* As noted above, the *Life* is appended to the *Antiquities* in almost all of the manuscripts of Josephus's works. It was written primarily to give his version of what he did in Galilee at the very beginning of the revolt, concentrating on a period of a mere six months. A few details about his life precede and follow this account. He felt the need to defend his conduct because Justus of Tiberius had written a book about the revolt in which he claimed that Josephus and the Galileans had caused it. Josephus shifted the blame to Justus, while claiming that he himself had been a friend of the Romans.

Josephus's report about his activities in the *Life* does not tally well with his description of the same period in the *War*. In the *War* he pictures himself as the military leader in Galilee from the beginning (see *War* 2.568), while in the *Life* he says that he was sent with two other priests to Galilee to convince the radicals there to lay down their arms (*Life* 29). This is just one example of an entire series of discrepancies and serves as a reminder that Josephus's writing, although it focused on the past, was also influenced by the present.

4. *Against Apion* (in two books; it is called *On the Antiquity of the Jews* in some sources): Josephus's last surviving work (it mentions the *Antiquities* several times) is a defense of the Jews, their history, and their theocratic constitution. In it he responds to various charges against the Jews; for example, some asserted the Jews were not an ancient people since they were not mentioned by the early Greek sources. As part of his answer, Josephus contrasts the Greek histories with their inaccuracies and their greater concern for style than precision with the Jewish historiographic tradition which, in the biblical period, was guaranteed accuracy by the succession of prophets. He adds references to a number of ancient sources that do in fact mention the Jews. Josephus also opposed several writers who had written negative accounts of the exodus from Egypt. One of these was the Egyptian author Manetho who argued that Moses had led a band of lepers who, with help from descendants of the Hyksos, had plundered Egypt before being driven away by Pharaoh Amenophis (1.228-87).

The work receives its name from Josephus's dispute with Apion who had been sent by the Greeks of Alexandria to the emperor Caligula at the time when Philo was leading the delegation of Jews. Apion, too, had written most critically about the exodus, the temple cult, and other Jewish matters. Josephus refuted his claims in various ways, such as questioning his character and highlighting his inaccuracies.

Against Apion also includes a description of the Mosaic constitution, the theocracy in which a piety that had practical effects was central. This constitution was, in his view, far superior to anything the Greeks had invented, and produced the most beneficial results in human society.

Josephus's works, like those of Philo, were preserved by Christians, not by Jews. The reason is not difficult to identify. Justus of Tiberias was not the only one of his countrymen to question Josephus; in fact he mentions many other charges that were brought against him, a man who seemed to many to have betrayed his own people and to have profited greatly from his treason.

146

Great Archeological Discoveries

The last century or so has witnessed some spectacular rediscoveries of Jewish texts, both in the Holy Land and outside of it. These finds have added considerably to the already sizable body of literature that was available for the study of the second temple period. In the following paragraphs three of these discoveries will be described.

The Elephantine Papyri

The earliest Jewish texts outside the Hebrew Bible come from a surprising source: the island of Elephantine at the first cataract of the Nile River in Egypt. The island is located opposite the ancient mainland city of Syene (modern Aswan), near where the great modern dam was built. There a Jewish military colony served the Persian administration as guards at a fortress close to the Nubian border. We do not know when the group first moved there, but one of the texts says that their temple existed before the Persian king Cambyses (530-22 BCE) came to Egypt. If the claim is true, it means that the temple dates from late pharaonic times, perhaps from the twenty-sixth dynasty. We do know that there was a Jewish presence in Egypt immediately after Jerusalem was destroyed in 587/86 BCE because the prophet Jeremiah, who was compelled to go there, tells us about it and about the places where Jews lived. He does not mention Elephantine, but at least Jews were present in Egypt by the late 580s BCE. The Elephantine texts date from the fifth and early fourth century BCE.

The papyri from the Jewish military colony (composed of soldiers and their families) are written in Aramaic, the international language of the Persian empire. A few papyri from the region had come to light in earlier times, but the major discoveries were made early in the twentieth century by a German archeological expedition (three campaigns from 1906-1908), working on the west side of the mound, and a French expedition (four campaigns from 1906-1911), on the east side of the mound. The texts themselves, which show the Jews living among a variety of other peoples on the island and in the region, can be divided into four groups: the Jedaniah Archive, the Mibtahiah Archive, the Ananiah Archive, and Miscellaneous Contracts.

The first of these, the Jedaniah Archive (containing ten letters and one list), offers the most interesting material about the group and its history (see the historical section above). Jedaniah was the leader of the Jewish colony. In the so-called Passover Papyrus (Cowley 21) a Jew by the name of Hananiah writes to Jedaniah and the military group to report that in the fifth year of Darius (Darius II, who reigned over the Persian empire from 423-404 BCE) the king told his satrap in Egypt, Arsames, that the Jews were to keep the festival of unleavened bread. The complete name of the holiday is not preserved but its dates, 15-21 Nisan, are given and leaven is mentioned; perhaps, although the text is broken at the key point, passover is treated as well. Exactly what circumstances led to this royal order we do not know; it is not impossible that Jews had been prevented from celebrating the festival and that the king now was giving permission to observe it. We learn from another document (Cowley 38) that "Khnum [= the Egyptian god of the area] is against us from the time that Hananiah was in Egypt until now" (line 7). The text may be suggesting that Hananiah's arrival had set off controversy with the priests of the ram-god Khnum. Such ill feeling was to have serious consequences; some of the papyri indicate that the priests of Khnum later brought about the destruction of the Jewish temple on the island.

The incident is reported in two copies of the same document (Cowley 30 and 31), which shows both what had happened and details attempts by the Jewish leadership to rebuild the temple. It is a letter from Jedaniah and the priests in Elephantine (= Yeb in the texts) to Bigvai (or Bagohi) who is the governor of Judah; it is dated to 407 BCE (see lines 21, 30). Jedaniah and his colleagues tell Bagohi that in the fourteenth year of Darius (410 BCE) "when Arsames departed and went to the king, the priests of the god Khnub [= Khnum], who is in the fortress of Yeb, (were) in league with Waidrang who was governor here, saying: The temple of Ya'u the God, which is in the fortress of Yeb let them remove from there" (lines 4-6). Troops stationed in Syene carried out the destruction of the sanctuary and looted the valuables from it (lines 6-13; see also Cowley 27). It is at this point that the writers adduce the antiquity of their temple and the respect with which it had been treated: "Already in the days of the kings of Egypt our fathers had built that temple in the fortress of Yeb, and when Cambyses came into Egypt [525 BCE] he found that temple built, and the temples of the gods of Egypt all *of them* they overthrew, but no one did any harm to that temple" (lines 13-14). They note that their enemy Waidrang and his associates were executed and also mention the efforts they had made to gain the support of influential people so that they could obtain permission to rebuild the sanctuary: ". . . at the time when this evil was done to us, we sent a letter *to* your lordship and to Johanan the high priest and his colleagues the priests who are in Jerusalem, and to Ostanes the brother of 'Anani, and to the nobles of the Jews. They have not sent any letter to us" (lines 17-19). They encourage them to write to people they know in Egypt to support the project and suggest that they were ready to pay for their help (lines 28-29). Finally, the writers report about something "we have set forth in a letter in our name to Delaiah and Shelemiah the sons of Sanballat governor of Samaria" (line 29).

Cowley 32, a "Memorandum from Bigvai and Delaiah" (line 1), seems to contain a summary of the reply these two leaders from Jerusalem and Samaria gave to the earlier letter: "Let it be an instruction to you in Egypt to say to Arsames about the altar-house of the God of Heaven, which was built in the fortress of Yeb formerly, before Cambyses, which Waidrang, that reprobate, destroyed in the fourteenth year of Darius the king, to re-build it in its place as it was before, and they may offer the meal-offering and incense upon that altar as formerly was done" (lines 2-11). The suggestion is that only non-animal sacrifices be offered on the rebuilt altar, not animal sacrifices as had been the practice (see Cowley 30, lines 25-26). It is possible that animal sacrifices were considered offensive to Egyptians or it may be that there was some question about the propriety of offering such sacrifices in Egypt. Cowley 33 seems to contain a request from Jedaniah and four others who are named to rebuild the temple as before but without animal sacrifice; they also promise to pay certain sums if their request is granted. It is possible that one of the documents in the Ananiah Archive (Kraeling 12, lines 18-19) implies that the temple was rebuilt, since the party selling a house says the temple of Yahu is west of it; the text dates from 402 BCE.

The papyri in the other archives are less interesting from this standpoint but, as many of them are contracts, they do divulge much about life in the community. The eleven documents in the Mibtahiah Archive allow one to follow episodes in the life of a well-to-do family for three generations (471-410 BCE). Mibtahiah was apparently Jedaniah's aunt, and her several marriages and property dealings are recorded in the contracts. The thirteen documents of the Ananiah Archive fall between 456 and 402 BCE and are also legal in character. B. Porten's category of Miscellaneous Contracts contains six documents that span almost the entire fifth century BCE.

Another of the discoveries at Elephantine was a partial copy of the work called Ahiqar which has traditionally been placed by scholars in the category of Pseudepigrapha. The story had been known in a variety of ancient translations, but the Aramaic text from Elephantine is the earliest preserved version, although it is thought that the story may go back to a Mesopotamian original (Ahiqar's name has turned up in an Akkadian document as a royal advisor). The text as known from later versions centers around the life of a sage who was an advisor to the Assyrian kings Sennacherib and Esarhaddon. His adopted son Nadin turned against him and convinced the king to execute Ahiqar. The sage managed to avoid his death through a trick (substituting a slave for himself) and later, when his nephew was the king's advisor but was unable to handle a crisis that had arisen, the king expressed the wish that Ahiqar were still alive. He was then duly brought out, solved the problem, and saw to the execution of his nephew. Wise sayings were placed primarily at two locations in the story: at the point at which Ahiqar is instructing Nadin, and at the end where his punishment is treated. In the Aramaic form of the story there is a narrative (through the adoption of Nadin) where the fragmentary text breaks off; there is also a set of proverbial sayings. Perhaps this was the structure of Ahiqar in the Aramaic language at Elephantine. There is nothing Jewish about the story, but it was later apparently adapted by Jews, and in the Book of Tobit Ahiqar is Tobit's nephew (Tob. 1:21-22).

The Dead Sea Scrolls

The Dead Sea Scrolls have been called the greatest archeological discovery of the twentieth century, and for the world of the Bible that is an accurate assessment. Beginning with the chance discovery of cave 1 by bedouin shepherds in 1946 or 1947, the finds eventually included eleven caves with written materials, all located in the vicinity of some impressive remains of buildings at Khirbet Qumran, several miles south of Jericho on the northwestern shore of the Dead Sea. Some of the Qumran caves, including cave 4 which contained fragments of approximately 580 manuscripts, are located within a stone's throw of the Khirbet Qumran ruins. Archeologists soon established that the scrolls and fragments found in the caves were associated in some way with the buildings because the same sort of unusual pottery was found in both. We will first survey the manuscript finds, then the archeological data from the site of Qumran, and finally look at theories regarding the authorship of the texts and the history of the group involved.

(1) The Manuscripts and Fragments

Altogether more that 850 manuscripts have been identified among the fragmentary remains of texts found in the eleven caves. The caves richest in written material were 1, 4, and 11, with caves 1 (over seventy manuscripts) and 11 (thirty-one texts) being the only ones to house some complete or fairly complete manuscripts. Cave 4 contained the largest number of texts but almost all are in a rather poor state of preservation. Other caves contained fewer texts, with cave 9 holding only one small papyrus fragment and cave 10 a single jar fragment on which two letters were inscribed.

It is convenient to group the manuscripts from the caves into several large categories. As we have seen above in the survey of the Jewish literature of the second temple period, a number of the Qumran texts are copies of works that had been known before but only through later translations. The majority of the Qumran texts are, however, ones that were entirely new to researchers.

Biblical Texts In a sense all of the texts found at Qumran are related to the Bible, whether they are copies of biblical books or related in some other way. The Qumran literature is biblically saturated; the authors knew the ancient writings of Israel and reflected their content, style, and lessons in their own writings. For the period with which we are dealing we must recognize that the word *biblical* is anachronistic, since there was, as far as one can tell, no fixed canon of scripture for the men of Qumran. What is meant by saying that there are biblical scrolls and biblically related works at Qumran is that there are copies of books that were later incorporated into the Hebrew Bible, and other writings influenced by those books. Several categories under the "biblical" rubric should be distinguished.

First, just over two hundred manuscripts, almost all of them very fragmentary, have been identified as *copies of biblical books* (that is, books that later became parts of the Hebrew Bible). The most famous of these is the great Isaiah scroll found in cave 1, the only complete manuscript of a biblical book. It dates from about 100-75 BCE.

The statistics about the biblical manuscripts are worth noting. The book most frequently attested is Psalms (thirty-six copies), followed by Deuteronomy (twenty-nine) and Isaiah (twenty-one). The only others found in more than ten copies are Exodus (seventeen), Genesis (fifteen), and Leviticus (thirteen). Quite a number of biblical books are poorly represented: 1–2 Samuel, Job, Song of Solomon, Ruth, and Lamentations

151

(four each); Judges, 1–2 Kings, and Ecclesiastes (three each); Joshua and Proverbs (two each); Ezra and 1–2 Chronicles (one each); and Nehemiah and Esther (none). That is, Psalms and most books of the Pentateuch are very well represented, while the historical books and the wisdom writings are not. Though there is an element of chance involved in the discovery and identification of fragmentary texts, the numbers do indicate which books were available in multiple copies, and presumably used extensively.

The greatest benefit coming from all these manuscripts is that they provide us with the oldest copies of books in the Hebrew Bible, copies that are roughly one thousand years older than the ones available before the scroll discoveries. The value of being able to move back one thousand years in the transmission history of a book, especially for a period when everything had to be handcopied, is considerable. Not surprisingly, the biblical scrolls from Qumran have already made a significant contribution to study of the wording of the scriptural text, as one can see by checking recent translations of the Hebrew Bible such as the NRSV. In many cases the scrolls preserve the Hebrew text exactly as it was known before, and thus they demonstrate how carefully Jewish scribes copied the sacred texts over the centuries. In some other cases, however, the results have been different. For one, the scrolls at times demonstrate that where the traditional copy of the Hebrew text (the Masoretic Text) and the Greek translation differ, the variation in the Greek version was due to the translator's having a different Hebrew text before him. This involves not only single words and phrases but even entire books. For a minor example, Exodus 1:5 in the Masoretic Text says that seventy descendants accompanied Jacob into Egypt; the Greek has seventy-five (as does Acts 7:14). The first Exodus manuscript from Qumran cave 4 also reads seventy-five. For a case involving an entire book, Jeremiah is a good example. The Greek translation of Jeremiah is about one eighth shorter than the traditional Hebrew text; at Qumran Hebrew copies of both the longer and shorter versions have been identified. Second, in at least one instance a scroll preserves a reading, quite possibly an original one, found in no other biblical manuscript. The first Samuel manuscript from cave 4 places an extra paragraph between our 1 Samuel 10 and 1 Samuel 11. The paragraph, which many believe to be original, gives fuller details about King Nahash's policy of gouging out the right eyes of those he reduced to servitude. It may be that look-alike phrases in a Hebrew text before and after this paragraph led a scribe to omit it accidentally with the result that it disappeared from the textual tradition, only to be rediscovered at Qumran (the paragraph can be found in the NRSV at the end of 1 Samuel 10).

A second category includes *excerpts and translations of biblical books.* These texts are closely related to the Bible or are copies of select biblical passages. Tefillin and mezuzot are small containers holding parchments bearing quotations of a few passages from Exodus and Deuteronomy. Tefillin were tied to a person's head or left arm, while mezuzot were attached to the doorpost of a house. At least twenty-eight of the former were found at Qumran, and eight mezuzot. The scriptural excerpts, copied in tiny letters, also attest some variations from the traditional Hebrew text.

Targum is the term used for an Aramaic translation of a book in the Hebrew Bible. A few of these have turned up at Qumran: small samples of Leviticus and Job in cave 4, and a well preserved scroll with the Aramaic of Job from cave 11. In addition, there are copies of Greek translations of biblical books in cave 4: two of Leviticus, one of Numbers, and one of Deuteronomy. There are also two small fragments of a Greek Exodus manuscript from cave 7.

One of the more interesting finds is a series of seventeen works that are verse-by-verse *commentaries on biblical books.* As these commentaries first cite a biblical passage and then offer comment on it, they serve as further witnesses to the wording of the biblical text. They also display an interesting way of interpreting biblical prophecies (including some psalms): the commentator regularly interprets the ancient prophecies as referring to his own time (which he believed to be the time of the end). Since the commentators relate prophecies to their community and circumstances, they provide extremely valuable references to the history of the group.

Distinct from these continuous commentaries are the thematic commentaries, that is, works which cite a number of biblical passages relevant to a particular topic or theme. An example is the Melchizedek text from cave 11 which assembles scriptural passages about jubilees and sabbatical years and also psalms that the author sees as related to Melchizedek (who is pictured as an angelic judge of the end time). Another work, 4QTestimonia, compiles a series of texts on a topic but gives them almost no commentary: The writer quotes biblical passages about a prophet, king, and priest, and adds a prophecy about Jericho from another work, possibly the *Psalms of Joshua* (4Q378-79?). The last passage does contain a brief comment on Joshua 6:26.

There seems to be at least one other type of commentary. Some texts deal with passages from a single book but treat only a selection of passages, not the complete text. Good examples are found for the book of Genesis (for example, 4Q252 = Commentary on Genesis A).

A fourth category consists of *paraphrases of or quotations from biblical books.* A lengthy work preserved in five copies from cave 4 is called Reworked Pentateuch. In most places it simply reproduces the continuous biblical text, but in a few passages it offers additional explanatory or supplementary material. For example, it supplies a song for Miriam in Exodus 15.

A final category consists of *copies of deuterocanonical/apocryphal and pseudepigraphal books.* We do not know exactly which books were considered authoritative at Qumran. Nor do we know in what sense they were considered authoritative. The status of some books especially in these two categories is not clear. Some of them seem to have been held in high esteem there; about others there is no evidence. Among the deuterocanonical/apocryphal books represented at Qumran are the Wisdom of Jesus ben Sira (two small fragments from cave 2 and substantial parts of the acrostic poem in chap. 51 which is in the cave 11 Psalms scroll), Tobit (present in five copies; four in Aramaic and one in Hebrew), and the *Letter of Jeremiah* (in Greek). To this list we should add Psalm 151 which is included among the many psalms in the large Psalms scroll from cave 11. Among the pseudepigraphal books are *1 Enoch* (four of the five component booklets are represented on eleven manuscripts) and *Jubilees* (fourteen or fifteen copies). A work called the *Book of Giants* (represented in as many as eight copies) develops the story about the enormous offspring of the marriages of angels with women in *1 Enoch,* and may also be an Enochic work. Some additional texts seem to be related in different ways to the pseudepigraph entitled the *Testaments of the Twelve Patriarchs:* Aramaic Levi and a *Testament of Naphtali* from cave 4 may have been sources of individual parts of these works. There are fairly strong reasons for thinking that at Qumran the writings of Enoch and the *Book of Jubilees* were considered authoritative. If that was the case, then they should be placed in the above category entitled "copies of biblical books."

Non-biblical Texts   While they are influenced by the biblical text, the works included in this section are less closely related to the Bible than those just mentioned. Many types of texts fall under this broad rubric, some of which were clearly written for the needs of the small Qumran community or the larger group (the Essenes) to which it seems to have belonged. Others betray no specific connection with Qumran, and seem to be writings that the group shared with larger parts of the Judean population. Here several general categories will be described, and works likely to be sectarian will be noted.

The first category is *legal texts*. A number of Qumran writings focus on the law of Moses, and either offer interpretations of it, or apply it to the situation of the group, or both. The group obligated itself to continuous study of and obedience to the law of Moses as they understood it. Their views about the law seem to have been the primary factor distinguishing them from other Jews of the time.

The *Temple Scroll* (three or four copies), the longest of all the Qumran texts, is another version of Exodus 25–40, Leviticus, Numbers, and parts of Deuteronomy. It attaches instructions for building a huge and spectacular temple complex to the place where Exodus speaks about constructing the tabernacle. Its detailed description of the temple includes information on what is done in each area of it. A fairly lengthy section is devoted to the festivals celebrated there, and the final part of the work is a paraphrase of parts of Deuteronomy. The text tends to treat topics in full at the point where they are first mentioned in the Bible; this entails adducing related passages from elsewhere in the Pentateuch. The work presents itself as a first-person revelation by God to Moses and may well be sectarian.

Another writing, 4QMMT (*Some of the Works of the Law;* six copies), begins with a section about the correct calendar (almost certainly a 364-day solar year, as in *1 Enoch* and *Jubilees*), follows with a segment which lists twenty-two laws concerning which the writers disagree with those to whom the composition is addressed, and closes with a friendly exhortation to heed examples from kings of the past and to accept the teachings communicated in 4QMMT. The text appears to have been written at an early point in the break between the authors and their opponent(s) when opinions and positions had not hardened to the point of inflexibility.

Many other legal texts could be mentioned here, but two categories in particular, both of which were fundamental to communal life, should be noted. The first type is a set of texts called rules. The *Rule of the Community* may be called a constitution for the Qumran group. It describes the annual ceremony for entry of new members into the covenant, explains their dualistic theology, gives rules governing communal life (e.g., for the multi-year process of entry, for meetings, organization, penalties for infractions, etc.), explains the purpose of the group and of their move to the wilderness (in obedience to Isa. 40:3), and, in some forms, concludes with a section on the leader and a long poem by him. There are ten copies from cave 4, one from cave 1 (almost completely preserved), and one from cave 5. Some of the copies from cave 4 show that the text changed over time as it was used.

Another of these rule texts is called the *Damascus Document*. One longer manuscript and a much shorter copy of it were known before the Qumran discoveries; they had been found in a storage room (a genizah) of a synagogue in Cairo in 1896. Eight copies of it were found in Qumran cave 4, one in cave 5, and one in cave 6. The *Damascus Document* consists of two parts: an admonition or exhortation which urges "my children" to obedience and cites examples of disobedience; and a section of laws (e.g., sabbath laws and laws about a community and its life). It seems that the *Damascus Document* was meant for a wider group than just the Qumran community, one that was less cut off from normal society. So, for example, whereas those who joined the Qumran group placed all of their wealth in the community coffers, the members of the community behind the *Damascus Document* were required to contribute only two days' wages per month.

The second set of legal texts are calendrical in nature. They do not give a list of all dates in a year as modern calendars do, but limit themselves to highlighting certain dates (especially for sabbaths and festivals) and periods. The Qumran community accepted a solar calendar of 364 days by which the festivals were dated; they also accepted a 354-day lunar calendar and synchronized it with the solar arrangement. In this respect it agreed with the Astronomical Book of Enoch but not with *Jubilees,* which rejects a lunar calendar. Besides dates in the solar and lunar calendars, these texts also coordinate the biblical list of twenty-four priestly divisions (1 Chron. 24:7-18); that is, they used the priestly list as a way to identify weeks. We know that the priestly divisions took turns officiating at the temple, with one group serving for one week, after which time it was replaced by the next one on the list. Hence, a date could be expressed as being day one, two, three, etc. in the week of whatever priestly course would have been on duty then. Since there were only twenty-four divisions, each served at least twice in a 364-day solar year and four of them would serve three times. This meant that after six years the rotation would return to its starting point, with the first division serving in the first week of the year. These six-year units became categories for designating larger units of time. The fact that such lists were kept shows the community's ongoing interest in the life of the temple, despite their separation from it. Some evidence in the texts from Qumran suggests that the group's disinctive solar calendar was a cause of friction with other Jews and was a factor in their decision to separate from them.

Second, a large number of texts which we could call *new pseudepigra-*

pha, are difficult to classify but resemble the Pseudepigrapha in that they evince a similar growth of traditions around biblical characters. The *Genesis Apocryphon* is a lengthy work, written in Aramaic, that retells scriptural stories about Noah and Abraham, heavily supplemented from other sources. A number of the additions in the Noah section find parallels in *Jubilees* (e.g., the many specific geographical details about the division of the earth among Noah's descendants). Other texts contain material concerning Levi, the ancestor of the priests, Moses, Joshua, Joseph, Jeremiah, Ezekiel, Daniel, and others, such as Qahat and Amram, the grandfather and father of Moses. The *Genesis Apocryphon* may have been produced by the Qumran community, but it is not always easy to determine whether books in this category are sectarian.

A third category consists of *poetic works.* One of the first Qumran texts to be found, the *Thanksgiving Hymns* scroll (Hodayot, in Hebrew) from cave 1, offers clear evidence that works resembling the biblical psalms were written by and for the group at Qumran. Six additional copies of the collection were found in cave 4. Scholars have divided these poems into two categories: those of one strong leader, possibly the Teacher of Righteousness himself, and those of the community, that is, poems of an individual but not expressing the same strong sense of personal calling to leadership present in the first category. God is heartily praised for his almighty power in creation and for choosing and saving the psalmist from the dangers and terrors of evildoers and wicked ways. There are also poems that do not belong to the Hodayot collection but resemble them nevertheless. Some other substantial poetic works such as the so-called *Non-Canonical Psalms* have also been found (4Q380-81).

Quite a number of texts fall into the fourth category, *liturgical works.* These texts are related to worship in one way or another. The Qumran community did not participate in the temple's sacrificial cult but did offer their own forms of worship. A set of texts provide festival prayers and daily prayers and reveal an early stage in the growth of fixed prayers for specific occasions. This is the appropriate context for mentioning the *Songs of the Sabbath Sacrifice* (eight copies from cave 4, one from cave 11, and one from Masada) which gives the text of songs for the thirteen sabbaths in a quarter of a year. The text speaks in detail about the angelic worship of God in heaven, and expresses the Qumranic notion of communion between those involved in earthly and heavenly worship. The text seems to be a forerunner of the hekhalot tradition in Judaism which focuses on the cult in the heavenly sanctuaries.

157

A series of texts from the Qumran caves are classified as *wisdom texts* because they resemble Proverbs, Job, or Ecclesiastes. Like their biblical predecessors, they include instructions about prudent living, about dealing with poverty or wealth, and about avoiding the seductress; but some Qumran texts also exhort their audience to consider the "mystery of what is/what is to become" (the translation is uncertain). The phrase seems to designate the structure of reality, the way things are as created by God, but also what will happen in his plan. This mystery underscores the importance of creation in wisdom literature and indicates how the wisdom tradition had developed an interest in eschatology, that is, in the time when God will judge the wicked and reward the righteous.

The final category consists of *eschatological texts*. A number of the texts already mentioned have eschatological teachings in them (e.g., the commentaries), but some devote more space to the topic than others. For example, the *War Scroll* (one copy in cave 1 and six from cave 4) deals with the final war, and may offer more than one scenario for it. It predicts battles by the sons of light against Israel's traditional enemies over a forty-year period but also a sequence in which the sons of light in concert with the angels will defeat Israel's enemies and their angelic supporters three times, will lose to them three times, and will prove victorious in the seventh and decisive encounter when God himself intervenes on their side. There are also copies of a New Jerusalem text which gives a detailed guided tour of the future Jerusalem.

Several of the Qumran texts mention messianic figures. At times there is reference to just one messiah (e.g., 4Q521), while in others (e.g., the *Rule of the Community*) two are anticipated (called the messiahs of Aaron and Israel). Not much is said about what the messiahs will do, but the lay messiah (the branch of David or the messiah of Israel) will fight the enemy (the Kittim) and kill their leader (4Q285). The idea of reviving the dead in the future is noted in at least one text (4Q521), but whether that meant belief in a resurrection or some other form of future existence is debated. It is clear that the Qumranites anticipated the arrival of the judgment in the near future and were preparing for it in their wilderness dwelling.

(2) Archeological Evidence

Once it was established that the pottery found in the Qumran caves and at the building site were the same, it became likely that the people who were associated with the buildings were also those who used the caves. The five seasons of archeology at Qumran, led by Roland de Vaux, a Dominican priest and director of the École Biblique in Jerusalem, provided enough data for de Vaux to formulate a theory about the occupational history of the site. Though there was evidence of occupation at Qumran in the seventh century BCE (it is often thought to have been the City of Salt mentioned in Josh. 15:62), the sectarian phases came much later. De Vaux posited two phases for the time when the Qumran community occupied the site:

- Phase Ia: A short period involving a modest population; no pottery or coins were found in the loci belonging to it. De Vaux suggested that phase Ia began during the reign of John Hyrcanus (134-104 BCE) or possibly Simon (142-134 BCE) and was soon superseded by a new stage in the development of the site.
- Phase Ib: The buildings were expanded considerably and the famous system for supplying water to the site was completed. The new construction brought the site to the size that tourists see today when they visit Qumran. The nature of the rooms led the excavators to believe that the buildings were not residential; de Vaux thought the buildings constituted a communal center where a group met for meals and other occasions. The members of the community probably lived in various kinds of shelters in the vicinity and probably did not reside in the buildings. This phase extended from some point in the reign of Hyrcanus until 31 BCE. Amid the ruins there is evidence of a fire and damage caused by an earthquake. As Josephus indicates that an earthquake struck the area in 31 BCE, de Vaux concluded that this was the event that brought phase Ib to a close. He also argued that the earthquake and fire were simultaneous, although the evidence is not conclusive.
- Phase II: De Vaux thought that the site was left in ruins from 31 BCE until some time after the end of Herod the Great's reign (he ruled from 37-4 BCE). At that point members of apparently the same group returned to the site and rebuilt it almost to its former dimensions. This phase continued until the site was destroyed by the Romans when they were suppressing the first Jewish revolt, probably in the year 68 CE when Roman troops were in the area of Jericho. Further support for the date comes from the fact that eighty-three coins dated to the second year of the revolt were discovered at Qumran but only five from the third year. Again there is evidence of fire, and some Roman arrowheads have been found at the site.

There are several cemeteries at Khirbet Qumran. The largest includes some 1,100 neatly arranged tombs; the few that have been opened contained skeletons of males, aligned north-south with the head to the south. Possessions were not buried with the corpse. A grave that was not in the ordered part of the large cemetery contained a female skeleton, and some in other, smaller cemeteries also held the bones of females and children. These finds in the cemeteries have been part of the longstanding debate about whether the inhabitants of the Qumran area were all males or whether there were some females as well (see below).

De Vaux's reading of the archeological evidence has generally been accepted, but in more recent times a few modifications have been introduced. For one, the tenuous phase Ia is regarded as dubious by some; it may never have existed. If so, the settlement at Qumran was constructed no earlier than ca. 100 BCE. It is too soon to say that there was no phase Ia, since coins from the reign of John Hyrcanus have been located and some structures may precede phase Ib. A second part of de Vaux's reconstruction that has come under attack is the occupational gap of some thirty years that he assumed for the reign of Herod, after the buildings were destroyed by earthquake and fire. It may be that the site was rebuilt soon after it was destroyed. At least the evidence of coins does not suggest any gap in occupation.

(3) The Qumran Community and Its History

Virtually every issue connected with the Dead Sea Scrolls has been embroiled in controversy at one time or another. One such problem is the identity of the group responsible for the scrolls, whether they wrote them or simply copied and cared for them. Not every scholar would agree that there even was a local community associated with the scrolls in the caves. That is, a few students of the scrolls have maintained that there was no group living at the site other than soldiers stationed at what they regard as fortress Qumran; during the first revolt against Rome the scrolls were placed in the caves for safekeeping by people from Jerusalem (and perhaps elsewhere). However, no archeologist who has studied the ruins in detail has labeled the fully developed Qumran complex a fortress, since its contours and features match those of no known military installation. Moreover, the outer walls are too thin for a fortress, and the water supply of the alleged fortress would be exposed to anyone outside the walls. As a result, most have concluded that the people associated with the buildings were also those who were responsible for the scrolls in the caves. It should be recalled that the same kind of pottery was found in both the ruins and in the caves.

Since the very first days of scrolls study, the people at Qumran have been most frequently identified as a branch of the Essenes, one of the three Jewish groups (with the Pharisees and Sadducees) mentioned and described by Josephus and other ancient sources. Two kinds of arguments have been advanced in support of this hypothesis. The first is the evidence provided by the Roman geographer Pliny the Elder, who died in 79 CE. He described the area of the Dead Sea in his book *Natural History*. After speaking about Jericho and various places in Judea, he deals with the Jordan River and then with the Dead Sea:

> To the west [of the Dead Sea] the Essenes have put the necessary distance between themselves and the insalubrious shore. They are a people unique of its kind and admirable beyond all others in the whole world, without women and renouncing love entirely, without money, and having for company only the palm trees. Owing to the throng of newcomers, this people is daily re-born in equal number; indeed, those whom, wearied by the fluctuations of fortune, life leads to adopt their customs, stream in in great numbers. Thus, unbelievable though this may seem, for thousands of centuries a race has existed which is eternal yet into which no one is born: so fruitful for them is the repentance which others feel for their past lives! Below the Essenes was the town of Engada. . . . (G. Vermes and M. D. Goodman, eds., *The Essenes According to the Classical Sources* [Sheffield: Sheffield Academic Press, 1989], 33)

After the reference to Engedi, Pliny mentions Masada, showing that in his description he was moving from north to south along the west side of the Dead Sea. He places a group of Essenes north of Engedi, and there is no archeological evidence for such a site other than at Qumran. Hence, the Roman geographer was probably describing the Qumran community and calling them Essenes.

A second line of argumentation arises from the ancient descriptions of the Essenes found in the writings of Josephus, Philo of Alexandria, and others. There is an extended series of parallels between what they report about Essene practices and beliefs and what we find in the sectarian texts from Qumran. The full range of parallels have often been studied and need not be repeated here; rather a few examples will make the point clear enough. First, Josephus says that the Essenes adhered to a view of fate that distinguished them from the other groups: whereas the Sadducees attributed no human actions to the workings of fate (which seems to mean "divine predetermination" in the context) and the Pharisees credited some human actions to fate but not others, the Essenes attributed all human actions to its workings (*Ant.* 13.171-73). The sectarian Qumran texts give clear evidence of their authors' belief that God had determined before human history exactly what would happen; in fact, it is a fundamental belief in such texts (see, for example, 1QS 3:15-16, 21-23, Hodayot 1:7-8). Second, Josephus says that upon joining an Essene group, the new member merged his wealth with that of the community, and with this practice they managed to meet the needs of each member and also overcome the divisions between rich and poor in their society (*War* 2.122). This is precisely what is mandated in the Qumran *Rule of the Community* as it describes the process of entry into the group (1QS 6:18-23). A related phenomenon is also attested in the Damascus Document (CD 14:12-16). It is surely remarkable that Josephus records something seemingly so insignificant as the Essene prohibition of spitting during group meetings (*War* 2.147) and that the same law is mentioned in the *Rule of the Community* (7:13).

It would not be accurate to claim that the data from the sectarian scrolls and from the ancient descriptions of the Essenes coincide perfectly. For example, Josephus never mentions that the Essenes had their own special solar calendar of 364 days, while it is attested in an entire series of texts from Qumran. But the extent of the overlap is impressive evidence, and the picture presented in the scrolls agrees with that for no other group. It has been shown that on some points of legal interpretation the Qumran texts side with positions that in the Mishnah are attributed to the Sadducees, but this is not the same as saying they were Sadducees. Both the Essenes and the Sadducees interpreted the law of Moses in a very strict way (unlike the Pharisees, relatively speaking) and as a result agreed on a number of points. Yet when one examines the beliefs of the two groups (such as their views of fate), the teachings of the scrolls stand in diametric opposition to Sadducean doctrines, thus showing that the group from Qumran could hardly be Sadducees, if all of the sources for the Sadducees are in fact describing the same group.

A related point is worth stressing. The sectarian writings from Qumran offer a consistent picture that accords well with ancient descriptions of the Essenes, as we have seen. In the face of such evidence, it is highly unlikely that the scrolls represent the views of a broad spectrum of

Jewish society at the time, as they probably would if they were hidden there by the residents of Jerusalem. For example, there is nothing in the scrolls that is distinctively Pharisaic, which would be most surprising if the Pharisees were as prominent in society as Josephus claims they were.

Given that it is most likely, with our limited amount of evidence, that the people of Qumran were a small branch of the larger Essene movement, we should next turn to the questions of why they settled on the northwest side of the Dead Sea, and what happened while they resided in that area. Identifying the men of Qumran as Essenes rests on a considerable body of evidence, but the history of the group is far less certain. The following sketch includes the available evidence yet is necessarily hypothetical in places.

The first column of the *Damascus Document* speaks about the rise of a group some 390 years after God gave the people and temple into the hand of Nebuchadnezzar. The number apparently derives from Ezekiel 4:5 and may convey some symbolic meaning in the *Damascus Document*; however, one ought not rule out the possibility that it is literal. The new group or movement consisted of people who realized their guilt and sought God sincerely. After they passed another twenty years of uncertainty, God raised up for them a Righteous Teacher to guide them in the proper way. A Teacher of Righteousness (presumably the same one) is also mentioned in some of the Qumran commentaries as a leader of the group. He is called a priest, and it is claimed that God had revealed to him the meaning of the mysterious words uttered by the ancient prophets. That is, he was an inspired interpreter of prophetic revelations, and he is also credited with building up a community at God's behest. The numbers of years mentioned in the *Damascus Document*, if accurate, would place the rise of the Teacher in the 170s BCE.

The Teacher of Righteousness had an opponent dubbed the Wicked Priest in the scrolls. His name is never given, but it is likely that the title Wicked Priest (*hakkohen harasha'* in Hebrew) is a wordplay on the title *hakkohen haro'sh*, one form of the title high priest, and that consequently the Wicked Priest was the high priest of the time. If so, the fact that the Wicked Priest took the trouble to deal with the Teacher of Righteousness suggests that the Teacher enjoyed some status. According to the Commentary on Habakkuk, the Wicked Priest pursued the Teacher to his place of exile (it is not named) and tried to "swallow up" him and his followers on their Day of Atonement (1QpHab 11:4-8). This passage first suggested to scholars that the Wicked Priest and the Teacher of Righteousness employed different calendars to date the holidays, since the high priest could hardly have chased dissidents on the sacred Day of Atonement when the solemn temple ritual demanded his presence and on a day when travel was forbidden. The episode suggests that the Wicked Priest thought the Teacher and his followers posed a certain danger and that he was aware of the different calendar that they used. One of the Psalms commentaries says that the Teacher sent a "law" to the Wicked Priest (4QpPs^a 4:8-9), a work that may be the one known as *Some of the Works of the Torah* which, as we have seen, spells out twenty-two legal points of dispute between the two parties and has at least one statement about the 364-day calendar at the beginning of the preserved section.

The identity of the Wicked Priest is unknown, but many believe he may have been Jonathan, the first Maccabean high priest (152-142 BCE), or Simon, his brother and successor (142-134 BCE; some scholars maintain that there was a series of wicked priests which included these two and others as well). If he was Jonathan or Simon, the disputes between the Teacher and the Wicked Priest would have occurred in the middle third of the second century BCE. However, the Qumran structures may not have been built until some time later, perhaps not until 100 BCE. Hence the Teacher and his followers would have withdrawn to another place (or places) before moving to Qumran. Where such a place might have been, we do not know, but one possibility is Damascus; the *Damascus Document* refers several times to the new covenant in the land of Damascus.

The eventual choice of Qumran as the home of the group seems to have been made in response to biblical prophecies about the wilderness. The *Rule of the Community,* in a passage that speaks about the group's separation from the impious, cites Isaiah 40:3 as the warrant for their settling in the wilderness (1QS 8:12-14):

> And when these become members of the Community in Israel according to all these rules, they shall separate from the habitation of unjust men and shall go into the wilderness to prepare there the way of Him; as it is written, *Prepare in the wilderness the way of . . . , make straight in the desert a path for our God.* (Translation by Vermes)

Not only did the community move to the wilderness in a literal sense, but they also chose their particular wilderness with some care. They seem to have selected the site of Qumran under the influence of Ezekiel 47, which predicts that in the restored Israel of the future there would be a stream running from the temple to the Dead Sea. It would become wider as it went and on its banks would grow fruit trees that would yield a crop every month. Moreover, the waters of this stream would freshen those of the Dead Sea. Ezekiel's stream was to reach the Dead Sea not far from Engedi, a place a short distance to the south of Qumran. So, the Essenes at Qumran lived in a place that would (soon, they believed) see Ezekiel's miraculous stream change the character of their wilderness (cf. Isa. 35).

We do not know exactly what caused the separation of the people of Qumran from their fellow Jews, but opposition to the powerful claims made by and for the Teacher of Righteousness probably played a part. A plausible case can also be made that disputes about interpretations of biblical laws figured prominently, especially in the aftermath of the period when the so-called Hellenizing high priests ruled (175–59 BCE) and in the early days of the Maccabean high priests. It may be that the Teacher and his group argued for their approach but eventually realized that not only were they not going to be successful but that opposition to the new military high priests was hopeless. Physical separation seemed the only path to take.

The archeological evidence implies that the Qumran group, with perhaps a short gap in occupation late in Herod's reign, continued to live around the site for about 170 years, perhaps more. The fact that they remained there and did not reintegrate themselves into society indicates that their opposition to current conditions did not weaken. It is likely that they had a negative view of the Hasmonean rulers, although there is some uncertainty about how consistent that opposition was, since 4Q448 seems to speak positively of King Jonathan (probably Alexander Jannaeus). However that text is to be understood, the Qumran settlement endured until it was destroyed accidentally in Herod's reign, only to be rebuilt along the same lines as before. The similarity of the buildings before and after this destruction probably means that the same group occupied it. Nothing about the conditions in Jerusalem after Herod's reign would have been seen as an improvement by these traditionalists, and so they remained at Qumran awaiting a new day.

Qumran was reduced to ruins, probably during the first revolt against Rome. Coins from the first years of the revolt have been found, but only a few for that third year and none after it. Also, Josephus reports that Roman troops were operating in the region of Jericho during 68 (the third year of the revolt), and some Roman arrowheads have been found at Qumran. The buildings were burned down and presumably many members of the community perished defending the site. One wonders whether the covenanters saw in the revolt the beginning of the war of the sons of light against the sons of darkness that would bring this world to an end and usher in a new age. It did indeed usher in a new age, but the Qumran community was not to be a part of it.

The small community (no more that one hundred to two hundred men) may have exercised some influence on their contemporaries. As we have seen, there are passages in rabbinic literature that echo debates on points disputed by the Qumran community, and early Christianity exhibits some parallels with material found in the scrolls. For example, the book of Acts indicates that the first Christians in Jerusalem had all things in common (2:44; 4:32), just as the people of Qumran did. But their greatest gift to posterity was to be their library which they presumably hid in the caves as the Romans approached and which was not to be found again until the twentieth century.

Masada

While the Dead Sea Scrolls may be the most famous archeological discovery of the twentieth century, Masada has aroused more powerful emotions, whether of pride or of horror. For some it is a symbol of Jewish resolve, of resistance to the end, of a preference for death over slavery and abuse; for others it is a misguided tragedy of massive proportions. Masada is a controversial story of ancient times that has had modern repercussions. We will look first at the story of Masada in more detail than was done in the historical survey; then we will examine the finds from Masada, both written and material.

(1) The Story

For what happened at Masada long ago we are dependent on the narrative of Josephus who dealt with the episode at some length in the *Jewish War*. Masada (= fortress, stronghold, in Hebrew) lies on the west side of the Dead Sea, about fifteen miles south of Engedi. Visitors to the site know it as a most impressive rock formation that rises dramatically from the desert floor. On its west side it towers some six hundred feet above the surrounding land and on the east it reaches more than eight hundred feet above the desert. Josephus wrote that the spectacular rock was first fortified by Jonathan the high priest (*War* 7.285), who could be either Jonathan, the second Maccabee, or Alexander Jannaeus (Jonathan was his Hebrew name). This Jonathan apparently gave the place its name. The supreme architect of the site was, however, Herod the Great, who built extensively on the summit and around Masada. Early in his career (42 BCE) he had captured the stronghold and later (40 BCE) left his family there while he went to Rome where the senate gave him the kingship of Judea. When he returned, he found his family besieged by Antigonus, the last Hasmonean king. Herod broke the siege and rescued his family.

The king recognized the possibilities of the natural fortress, whether for national or personal safety, as he feared attack from Cleopatra in Egypt and from his own subjects (*War* 7.300). Josephus reports that he enclosed the summit (an area of some twenty-three acres) in a casemate wall which contained thirty seven towers, each fifty cubits high (= about seventy-five feet), with rooms and buildings along the inside. The soil on Masada was rich enough to permit farming, thus insuring food for the residents even if they were prevented from leaving. According to Josephus, Herod built a palace on the west side of Masada and had workmen carve out vast reservoirs lower down on the rock formation so that water from flash floods could be caught in them and brought to the surface by laborers (7.286-93). Herod also stockpiled food and weapons there (7.295-99). After his death and the removal of his son Archelaus, the Romans apparently took over control of Masada (from 6-66 CE).

The episode that has etched Masada in Jewish memory occurred several decades later. In the summer of 66 CE a group whom Josephus quite consistently labels *Sicarii* (revolutionaries who carried short daggers called *sicae* in Latin) captured the site very early in the revolt against Rome. Josephus felt nothing but disgust for these people: "And now some of the most ardent promoters of hostilities banded together and made an assault on a fortress called Masada; and having gained possession of it by stratagem, they slew the Roman guards and put a garrison of their own in their place" (*War* 2.408). He also notes that Menahem, a son of Judas the Galilean who had violently opposed Roman rule earlier in the century, went with his friends to Masada, broke into Herod's cache of weapons, and with them armed himself and his friends and took over leadership of the revolt in Jerusalem (2.433-34). Menahem was soon murdered, but some of his followers, including a relative named Eleazar son of Jairus, escaped to Masada (2.446-48). Yet another rebel leader, Simon bar Giora, also used Masada as a base for raids on Idumea (see 2.652-54).

167

Elsewhere Josephus gives indications of what the residents of Masada did during the revolt against Rome. As a graphic illustration he tells the story of the raid on Engedi. He says that the Sicarii of Masada normally confined themselves to local sallies to gain supplies (*War* 4.400), but during a lull in the Roman military campaign and at the time of the festival of tabernacles when many Jewish residents would make pilgrimage to Jerusalem (which was apparently still possible), the Sicarii attacked Engedi. "Those of the inhabitants who were capable of resistance were, before they could seize their arms and assemble, dispersed and driven out of the town; those unable to fly, women and children, numbering upwards of seven hundred, were massacred. They then rifled the houses, seized the ripest of the crops, and carried off their spoil to Masada" (4.403-4). This they did to fellow Jews. Josephus mentions John bar Giora who, after being expelled from Jerusalem, went to Masada. The people there eventually permitted him "to accompany them on their raids upon the surrounding district" (4.506; see also 508 and 516).

In *War* 7.252 the historian begins to tell the story that has made Masada famous or notorious, the dramatic events that took place there at the very end of the revolt against Rome. They occurred several years after Jerusalem was demolished: the date usually proposed is the year 73, although some have argued for 74. In 73 Flavius Silva had become governor in Judea when only Masada remained as a rebel holdout; so, he marched there with his troops. Josephus takes the trouble to remind readers again that the Sicarii at Masada, led by Eleazar, had not only used violence against non-Jews but also against other Jews who happened not to agree with their radical stance (7.252-58). In fact, he breaks off his narrative to summarize the atrocities committed by these and others whom he regarded as extremists, people who, he says, masked their barbarity behind their "professed zeal for virtue" (7.270; see 254-74).

Returning to his story, the historian describes Silva's maneuvers to secure the area around Masada: he stationed garrisons in key places and built a wall around the site to prevent escape. He also set up his camp at the most convenient point for a siege, "where the rocks of the fortress abutted on the adjacent mountain" (7.277), that is, on the west where a spur runs part of the way up the side of the rock. Jewish prisoners were used to transport supplies. Having told of these preparations, Josephus pauses to describe Masada (7.280-303). The siege itself involved building an embankment on the spur; there the Romans constructed a stone platform on which they set up their siege engines. At that place they also installed a ninety-foot-high tower from which they could shoot at the defenders on Masada high above. A battering ram was dragged up the spur and used to hammer the casemate wall around the summit. They succeeded in breaching it, but the Sicarii built another wall inside the first, using packed earth wedged between wood beams. Such a structure was better able to absorb the blows of the battering ram. With his major weapon rendered ineffective, Silva ordered that the troops throw burning torches at the wall which was partly made of wood. The tactic was effective, but the wind blew the ensuing flames toward the Romans, threatening their own war machinery. The wind, however, suddenly and inexplicably started blowing in the opposite direction — as if by divine providence, Josephus remarks (7.318). The wall burned down, yet the Romans strangely deferred their charge into Masada until the morning.

The overnight delay provided an opportunity for Eleazar, the Sicarii leader, to deliver his two famous speeches in which he urged collective suicide on the defenders of Masada. They were faced with a terrible choice: abuse, slavery, or death (or a combination of these) at Roman hands; or death by their own hands. As his audience Eleazar gathered a group of the bravest men. In his first address (7.323-36) he held before their eyes the prospect of a noble death (7.326) but also acknowledged the guilt of the group for their part in the revolt and for their failure to recognize God's purpose in the events of the last years. Indeed he confessed that it was God himself who had deprived them of all hope (he had in mind most immediately the change in direction of the wind that day): "all this betokens wrath at the many wrongs which we madly dared to inflict upon our countrymen. The penalty for these crimes let us not pay to our bitterest foe, the Romans, but to God through the act of our own hands. It will be more tolerable than the other" (7.332-33). Thus the historian has Eleazar convict himself and his fellows of guilt in the revolt. Under the circumstances now they "preferred death to slavery" (7.336).

His first speech failed to carry the day, and, in order not to lose the few he had convinced, Eleazar began a second address, this one on the immortality of the soul (7.341-88). He claimed that death liberated the soul so that it could go to its eternal home free of troubles (7.344). Using an analogy and the example of Indian philosophers eager to depart from the body, he maintained that the deity had brought events to such an end that they had to die. He also cited numerous examples in which non-Jewish neighbors had slaughtered Jews and in which people who fell into Roman hands suffered hideous fates. Reminding the men again of what awaited their wives, children, and themselves, he declared: "No, while these hands are free and grasp the sword, let them render an honorable service. Unenslaved by the foe let us die, as free men with our children and wives let us quit this life together! This our laws enjoin, this our wives and children implore of us. The need for this is of God's sending, the reverse of this is the Romans' desire, and their fear is lest a single one of us should die before capture. Haste we then to leave them, instead of their hoped-for enjoyment at securing us, amazement at our death and admiration of our fortitude" (7.385-88).

The historian, who of course composed the speeches himself, tells us that this second time Eleazar convinced his audience; they eagerly went about their grisly tasks after tearful farewells to their families. Each man is supposed to have executed his wife and children; the men were then killed by ten men chosen by lot, and finally the ten drew lots and thus chose one man to kill the other nine. He in turn ended the entire process by taking his own life (7.389-401). Only two women and five children who had hidden survived the carnage, while 960 died (7.401). One of the women was the one who told the Romans the next day what had happened (7.404). Josephus does say that the Roman troops, upon entering Masada, admired the resolve and contempt for death shown by those who perished there (7.406). After appointing a garrison to man the site, the rest of the Romans left Masada (7.407).

(2) Archeological Evidence

The Structures While there had been a number of visitors to Masada in the nineteenth and early twentieth centuries and some more in-depth studies were made in the 1950s, the most thorough excavations of Masada were the two seasons directed by Yigael Yadin from 1963-65. Yadin was famous as an Israeli general and archeologist who had written fundamental studies of some of the Dead Sea Scrolls, had made important finds in the Nahal Hever, and had led large-scale expeditions at the northern site of Hazor. The Masada excavations involved a study of the surface and surrounding areas of Masada, including the water system, the Roman camps, and the ramp on the west side.

Atop Masada the excavations uncovered evidence of occupation in the Hasmonean period, the Herodian period, and the time of the First Revolt against Rome. It has proved difficult to identify structures from Hasmonean times when, according to Josephus, the site was made into a fortress, but there seem to be some. It may be that the small palaces at the midpoint of the summit come from that period, including a part of the western palace, which was to be expanded in Herod's time. A few other structures have also been attributed to the Hasmonean age. But Herod was the great builder of Masada. During his reign, the spectacular three-tiered palace was constructed on the northern tip of the mountain, taking advantage of the stair-like levels on that end. In the palace complex was also a bath house with tepid, cold, and hot rooms, and a number of large storage rooms on several sides of it. Herod also expanded the western palace and had the casemate wall built around the summit; it included many towers and rooms and contained gates on the east and west. Herod was also responsible for the system for catching and storing water in enormous cisterns. There were twelve of these on the northwest side of Masada. Four larger ones caught water from periodic floods in the wadi on the north side, and eight smaller ones at a higher level tapped the water from another wadi farther south. Much of Josephus's description of the site has, therefore, been borne out by the archeologists.

The phase when Masada was occupied by the Sicarii was very short (only seven or eight years) and thus would not normally be recognizable in the archeological record. But there is evidence that Herodian structures were modified. For example, rooms in the casemate wall and in the palaces were used as dwellings, some ritual baths (miqva'ot) were made, and a synagogue was fashioned from what may have been a stable in the northern part of the casemate wall. A number of the ostraca found very likely belonged to the Sicarii (see below).

In the Byzantine period a church was built on Masada.

Coins A large number of coins were found on Masada. Some were from the Ptolemaic and Seleucid periods, others from the Hasmonean high priestly kings. Naturally some Herodian coins, coins from the times of the Roman governors, and coins minted by the Jewish kings Agrippa I and II were present as well. But the most interesting coins come from the period of the revolt against Rome. There are various coins from years one through four but also some rare examples from year five, Jerusalem's final year. There are, in addition, Roman coins, including the Iudaea capta coins, coins from non-Jewish cities, and even a few from the Byzantine period.

Written Material Archeologists found a large number of written items on Masada, most of which are nonliterary, while a small number of literary texts were also located.

The literary texts are all fragmentary, but several are of considerable importance. The first six (Mas1–1f) are pieces from copies of books in the Hebrew Bible: two of Leviticus, one each of Deuteronomy and Ezekiel, and two of Psalms. Some of the biblical texts were found under the synagogue. Another fragment, Mas1h (Mas1g has been cancelled), contains a sizable portion of the Hebrew text of the Wisdom of Jesus ben Sira (chaps. 39:27–44:17); the scroll dates from the first century BCE. Another text is a fragment that has been identified as coming from *Jubilees* but which actually bears only a slight resemblance to a small part of it (Mas1j). One of the more interesting finds was a copy of *Songs of the Sabbath Sacrifice* (Mas1k), a text that is attested in nine copies at Qumran (4Q400–407, 11Q17); it has been viewed by some as evidence that at least one resident of Qumran fled to Masada around the time when Qumran was destroyed. The fact that *Songs of the Sabbath Sacrifice* is probably a sectarian text that presupposes the 364-day calendar adds strength to this suggestion. The remaining fragments are texts named apocryphal Joshua, apocryphal Genesis, a Qumran-type fragment, two pieces in paleo-Hebrew, and one unclassified fragment in Aramaic.

The nonliterary written items total 951. They have been divided into thirteen categories, although not all are exclusive. Numbers 1-301 are tags with letters, that is, ostraca with just one or a couple of letters; their purpose may have been to indicate the contents of vessels, possibly for secular use. Numbers 302-80 are tags bearing specific names (especially Yehohanan); these (and the first 301) may have been used as tokens in the food rationing system of the Sicarii. Each of another group of tags bears a single name (381-419); they were perhaps lots for determining which priests carried out which duties. Lists of names (420-28) is the fourth category; the names are followed by numbers, and in some cases amounts of money seem to be what is indicated by them. The fifth category, called "lots" by Yadin, consists of small ostraca, all written by the same scribe and each bearing a name (or a nickname). Yadin thought these were the lots used to select the ten men who were to kill the others. However, there are more than ten of them, and one has the name of Ben Yair (that is, Eleazar ben Yair, the leader) on it. Josephus does not say that he was one of those chosen by lot. A few inscriptions designate priestly shares (441-61); they are recognizable by phrases such as "tithe of the priest" or "for holy things" or "kosher for the purity of holy things." One jar has the name of a high priest on it. Numbers 462-515 have the names of owners inscribed on stone jars, while another group (516-53) indicate what were the contents of containers. There are three letters (554-56) on sherds, apparently dealing with issues about payments. Numbers 557-84 convey instructions about the bread supply: they mention the day and month, and contain an order that the bearer is entitled to a certain number of loaves of bread. The persons involved seem to have represented groups because the number of loaves can be large (e.g., 1,020). Amounts or capacities of jars and monetary totals are indicated in numbers 585-605. The last two categories are writing exercises and scribbles (606-41; persons learning to write practiced by writing the alphabet and names), and varia (642-701; 702-20 belong in the same category) which are of uncertain reading and identification.

The remaining items are somewhat different. Numbers 721-38 are papyri with Latin writing on them (including a snippet of Virgil, *Aeneid* 4.9). Numbers 739-47 are papyri with Greek texts, 748-49 are bilingual; 750-71 are Latin ostraca and 772-94 are Greek ostraca. There is also a large number of tituli picti, i.e., inscriptions on jars (795-927), some Latin, some Greek, some bilingual, others of uncertain language. Finally, 928-45 are graffiti, and 946-51 are amphora stamps in Latin.

CHAPTER 3

Synthesis: Leaders, Groups, and Institutions

The purpose of this chapter is to summarize the evidence for leaders, groups, and institutions in the period of the second temple. The topics treated here have figured at one point or another in the earlier chapters, but the organization and coverage of those chapters were not conducive to more systematic treatment of them. A fundamental problem that arises in trying to assimilate the evidence has to do with the nature of our sources. In addition to those surveyed in the literature section, there are also extensive rabbinic sources, such as the Mishnah (compiled about 200 CE) and the Talmuds (the Palestinian Talmud is perhaps from the fifth century and the larger Babylonian Talmud possibly from the sixth), which often deal with the second temple period. So, for example, an entire tractate of the Mishnah is devoted to the sanhedrin and others to the various festivals. Some scholars incorporate this later evidence into their picture of the second temple and no doubt there is ancient material in these later sources. The problem comes in trying to determine what is early and what is late. The survey below is limited almost entirely to the sources that come from the second temple period; there are only occasional references to the rabbinic texts.

RULERS AND LEADERS

Throughout the second temple period, the Jewish people, whether in the land or in the diaspora, were under the control of foreign nations. First it was the Persians, then the Greeks (the Ptolemies and the Seleucids), then the Romans. For some periods we have fairly extensive evidence, but for others little can be gleaned from the sources about how the Jewish people governed themselves in the matters permitted to them by their overlords. Although the Jewish people were ruled through different governmental means during the eras of the empires, one constant factor in their self-government was the powerful position of the priests, especially the high priest and his closest associates.

The Priests

According to the Bible, the priests were the sons of Aaron, and they alone were permitted to serve at the altar in the temple (e.g., Exod. 28–29; Num. 18:1-20). Other personnel in the temple complex — the Levites and their specialized subgroups such as singers and gatekeepers — were subordinate to the descendants of Moses' brother (Num. 16; 18:21-32). The priests were compensated for their work by receiving stipulated parts of many types of sacrifices, contributions, and a tenth of the tithes given to the Levites. Among the priests there were several levels of authority, and at the top of the entire class was the high priest himself.

High Priest

Our sources yield a complete list of the names of the high priests who served during the time when the second temple stood. Nehemiah 12 tells us who the first six were, beginning with the Joshua/Jeshua mentioned in Ezra and the prophecies of Haggai and Zechariah and continuing through the Jaddua who, Josephus says, met Alexander the Great. Josephus repeats these names and adds all the others through the last one to hold office before the Romans destroyed the temple in 70 CE. It seems likely that for large stretches of the second temple era the high priest was the supreme official in Judaism; it is not certain that there was always a civil governor alongside him.

The high priesthood was a hereditary office that was, according to the Bible, passed down in the line of Zadok, the leading priest in David's time. The first high priest after the exile — Joshua or Jeshua — was the son of Jozadak who was in turn the son of the last high priest in the first temple (see 1 Chron. 6:14-15; 2 Kings 25:18). As far as we know, the high priesthood was passed from father to son in his family for more than three centuries, with just one exception in the third century when an heir was too young to assume the office and two older males in the family became high priest before the young man, Onias II, took over. This practice lasted until the Seleucid king Antiochus IV appointed Jason, the brother of Onias III, high priest in his brother's place in 175 BCE.

For the first centuries of the second temple the sources say little about what the high priests actually did, but several of them attribute diplomatic roles to these high-ranking officials. So, for example, one of the Elephantine papyri mentions that the residents of Yeb wrote to the high priest Johanan as part of their effort to gain support for rebuilding their temple. Josephus presents Jaddua as the one who met and spoke with Alexander the Great, and the *Letter of Aristeas* pictures the high priest Eleazar as corresponding with Ptolemy II. Of these sources, only the papyrus from Elephantine has a very high degree of historical probability behind it. Nevertheless, the Tobiad Romance also speaks of the high priest (Onias II) as the one in charge of paying certain funds to the Ptolemaic treasury.

According to the sources, the high priests were:

In the Persian period
   Joshua (among the first returnees from exile)
   Joiakim
   Eliashib (contemporary of Nehemiah)
   Joiada
   Johanan (mentioned in one of the Elephantine papyri written in
      408 BCE)
   Jaddua (contemporary of Alexander the Great)
In the Hellenistic period
   Onias I
   Simon I (perhaps the Simon of Sirach 50)
   Manasseh (served when Simon's son Onias was too young)
   Eleazar (also served when Onias was too young; see the *Letter of
      Aristeas*)
   Onias II (of the Tobiad Romance)

Simon II (at the time of the Seleucid takeover of Judea)
Onias III (removed from office by Antiochus IV)
Jason (appointed by Antiochus IV in 175 BCE)
Menelaus (high priest during the decrees of Antiochus IV)
Alcimus

Once the Maccabees became high priests, not only political but also military powers became associated with the occupant of the office, since Jonathan and Simon were commanders of armies. The Hasmonean high priesthood, which became hereditary with the accession of Simon, extended from the time when Jonathan assumed office (152 BCE) until 35 BCE when Herod had the last of them, Aristobulus III, murdered. It should be recalled that there was a seven-year period (159-152 BCE) when no high priest served — or at least no source mentions one as serving. This appears to have been the only time when the office may have been vacant.

Maccabean/Hasmonean high priests
Jonathan (152-142 BCE)
Simon (142-134 BCE)
John Hyrcanus I (134-104 BCE)
Aristobulus I (104-103 BCE; the first to call himself a king)
Alexander Jannaeus (103-76 BCE)
Hyrcanus II (76-67, 63-40 BCE) and his brother Aristobulus II
   (67-63 BCE)
Antigonus (40-37 BCE, son of Aristobulus II)
Aristobulus III (35 BCE, grandson of Hyrcanus II)

The last named high priest was appointed by King Herod. Once he had eliminated the last of the Hasmonean high priests in 35 BCE, Herod did away with the hereditary principle and took to installing new high priests more frequently. Josephus says that he appointed men who were not from eminent families (*Ant.* 20.10) and that he, his son Archelaus, and the Roman officials who followed them appointed some twenty-eight men to the office before the destruction of the temple in 70 CE. The remaining ones were:

In Herod's time
Ananel (from Babylon, appointed before Aristobulus III; he may
   have served twice)

Jesus son of Phiabi

Simon son of Boethus (Herod's father-in-law; from an Alexandrian family)

Matthias son of Theophilus

Joseph son of Ellem

Joazar son of Boethus

In Archelaus's time

Eleazar son of Boethus

Jesus son of See

Roman appointees

Ananus (or Annas) son of Sethi (6-15 CE; see Luke 3:2; John 18:13-24; Acts 4:6)

Ishmael son of Phiabi

Eleazar son of Ananus (Annas)

Simon son of Camithus

Joseph Caiaphas (18-36 CE; the high priest during Jesus' trials; see *Ant.* 18.35; Matt 26:3, 57; Luke 3:2; John 11:49; 18:13-14, 24, 28; Acts 4:6; he was Ananus's son-in-law)

Jonathan son of Ananus (Annas)

Theophilus son of Ananus (Annas)

Appointees of the Jewish king Agrippa I (41-44)

Simon Cantheras son of Boethus

Matthias son of Ananus (Annas)

Elionaeus son of Cantheras

Appointees of Herod of Chalcis (King Agrippa's brother, 44-48)

Joseph son of Camei

Ananias son of Nedebaeus

Appointees of the Jewish king Agrippa II (50-66)

Ishmael son of Phiabi

Joseph Cabi son of Simon the high priest

Ananus son of Ananus (Annas)

Jesus son of Damnaeus

Jesus son of Gamaliel

Matthias son of Theophilus

Appointee of the people during the First Revolt

Phanni son of Samuel

A look through the list reveals that some names recur; the family of Phiabi produced three high priests, that of Boethus four, the family of

Ananus (Annas) eight, Cantheras two, and Simon two. As a result, nineteen of the twenty-eight high priests were from just five families.

One of the attested functions for the high priests was their important cultic role on the Day of Atonement when they entered the holy of holies and offered stipulated sacrifices (Lev. 16). The high priests could participate in any sacrifice at the great altar before the temple, but Josephus says that they did not always accompany the priests on such occasions "but on the seventh days and new moons, and on any national festival or annual assemblage of all the people" (*War* 5.230). Another role assumed by the high priest was as leader of the sanhedrin (on which see below). We do not have many accounts of the sanhedrin in action, but we do have Josephus's story about the session that attempted to judge the youthful Herod after he had executed some individuals without trial. Herod managed to avoid prosecution by a show of force (*Ant.* 14.165-79). Perhaps the most famous meeting has to do with the trial of Jesus (see Mark 14:53-65 with parallels), while the book of Acts also mentions actions by the sanhedrin involving the first followers of Jesus (e.g., 5:17, 21; 22:30; 23:5). In these instances the high priest presided over the sanhedrin.

A feature of the high priesthood noted in the sources is the splendid clothing worn by the occupants of the office on festal occasions. They are described at length in Exodus 28. They include the ephod (apparently an apron of sorts; it contained two stones on which were written the names of the twelve sons of Israel), the breastpiece (attached to the ephod and containing four rows of three stones each, again containing the names of the sons of Israel), the robe with bells at the lower hem, and a rosette on which was engraved "holy to the Lord," to be attached to a turban. Those vestments seem to be under consideration in Zechariah 3, and are celebrated in Sirach 45:6-13 and chapter 50, where the high priest Simon "put on his glorious robe and clothed himself in perfect splendor" (50:11). Josephus too (see *War* 5.231-36) describes the high priestly garments as does Philo who found cosmic symbolism in them (*Life of Moses* 2.109-26).

During the period when the Romans assumed control of Judea, the governor took over these symbolic clothes and permitted the high priest to have them only during festivals. As Josephus explains, the robe worn by the high priest when he sacrificed was at all other times kept in the citadel located to the northwest of the temple complex. Herod himself kept custody of the robe, and after him the Roman rulers placed it under their control until the reign of Tiberius (14-37 CE). At that time custody of the robe was given as a favor to the people by Vitellius, governor of Syria; Jewish control of it continued until the death of Agrippa I in 44 CE. When Roman authorities then tried to reclaim the high priestly garment, the Jewish people sent a delegation to the emperor and apparently gained their wishes. At this point in his narrative, Josephus details how it had been handled at an earlier time (and in doing so mentions some temple officials):

> Formerly it was under the seal of the high priest and the treasurers (of the temple), and one day before a festival the treasurers would go to the commander of the Roman garrison and, after inspecting their own seal, would take the robe. Then, when the festival was over, they would bring it back to the same place, and after showing the commander of the garrison a seal corresponding (to the first one), would again deposit the robe. (*Ant.* 15.408)

The garment was thought to convey such a powerful impression that the authorities worried about the political and social effect it might have.

Leading Priests

Several sources refer to priests who held higher positions than did the ordinary ones. There is evidence for this already in 2 Kings 25:18, which says that the Babylonians deported the chief priest Seraiah and "the second priest Zephaniah, and the three guardians of the threshold." For the second temple period Josephus refers to some priestly officers of the temple, and the Gospels and Acts contain references to such individuals and also to a much discussed group termed "the chief priests" (the word used is the plural of the Greek term for high priest). A number of temple officials are mentioned or described in rabbinic literature, but there are not very many helpful passages from the second temple era.

The "chief priests" were obviously leading men among the priests and are mentioned often in connection with the sanhedrin (see below), but exactly who they were is difficult to say. It is possible that they were priests drawn from the small number of families from which the high priests came, and, in Roman times, at least some of them were probably former high priests (see, e.g., *War* 2.243; 6.114).

There was an official who was called the captain of the temple (*sagan, strategos*). For example, Acts 4:1 says that "the priests, the captain of the temple, and the Sadducees" came to Peter and John who were preaching in the

181

temple complex and placed them under arrest. In the next chapter "the captain of the temple and the chief priests" were puzzled that the apostles were not in prison where they had been confined (5:24; see v. 26; see also *Ant.* 20.131, 208). From these passages it is evident that the captain of the temple had police powers to handle disturbances that arose in the temple area. There are also passages in which more than one leader of the temple police is mentioned. Luke, as he describes Judas's betrayal of Jesus, says that he went to "the chief priests and officers of the temple police," groups that were involved in the subsequent arrest of Jesus in the garden (Luke 22:4, 52).

There were others who held offices at the sanctuary. So, for example, there was a treasurer (*Ant.* 15.408; 18.93; *War* 6.390), and the later sources indicate that there were leaders of each of the twenty-four shifts of ordinary priests (see below).

Ordinary Priests

Although we do not know how many ordinary priests there were at any time during the second temple period, it is likely that their number was substantial and that there were far more of them than could serve in the temple at one time. First Chronicles 24:1-17 sets forth the solution for the large number of priests: they were divided into twenty-four watches or shifts and these rotated service at the temple. According to the sources, a priestly watch served for one week and then was relieved of its duties by the next one in the list. Once they had worked through the list of twenty-four shifts, the rotation began again. A result was that each of the twenty-four groups served at least twice during a year — a total of forty-eight weeks — and that a few groups also served a third time at the end of the year. A number of calendrical texts from Qumran use the names of the twenty-four groups as designations of weeks and provide tables listing which groups would be serving at any particular festival in their 364-day calendar. Six-year cycles were worked out in these texts. In a year of 364 days (= fifty-two weeks) four groups would serve three times; hence, after six years, the cycle would revert to its starting point, that is, with the first group serving during the first week of the year.

There are a few references to these groups in the second temple sources. For example, the Maccabees came from the watch of Joiarib (1 Macc. 2:1), and John the Baptist's father Zechariah came from the order of Abijah (Luke 1:5).

It seems reasonable to expect that among the priests there would be interest in the large corpus of priestly law found in the Pentateuch. Not only would they be concerned about learning what Leviticus and Numbers, for example, stipulated about their responsibilities in sacrifice, medicine, purity, and the like; they would also be concerned to apply the legal principles of the Torah to new situations as they arose. This is not to say that only priests would have been involved in study and amplification of scriptural law (the mainly non-priestly Pharisees were to become experts in the subject), but it stands to reason that there would be special emphasis on such matters among the priests.

Civil Rulers

There are several references to civil rulers in the early part of the second temple era. In the Bible, first Sheshbazzar (Ezra 5:14) and then Zerubbabel (Hag. 1:1) are called governors, and, while it is only a possibility that Sheshbazzar was from the family of David, it is certain that Zerubbabel was (1 Chron. 3:18-19; Shenazzar may be the same person as Sheshbazzar). The fact that Zerubbabel is paired with the high priest Joshua (in Ezra and Haggai) shows that the two held office at the same time and thus had different duties. After Zerubbabel (last mentioned in about 520 BCE) no governor is named in the Bible until Nehemiah, who came to Jerusalem in that capacity in 444 BCE and continued in office until at least 432 BCE (see Neh. 5:14). In Nehemiah 5:15 he charges that "the former governors who were before me laid heavy burdens on the people" (cf. Mal. 1:8). It may be that the names of at least some of these governors have now surfaced on bullae, seals, and jar impressions: Elnathan (who may have married Zerubbabel's daughter Shelomith; see 1 Chron. 3:19), Yeho'ezer, and 'Ahzai, although the dating of the materials is not certain. Later, the governor Bagohi is mentioned in one of the Elephantine papyri (number 30), while a governor named Yehezqiyah figures on coins from the end of the Persian and beginning of the Hellenistic ages. Whether there were governors in office between Bagohi and Yehezqiyah is not known, but it seems a reasonable inference.

Our sparse evidence regarding civil rulers in the early centuries contrasts with the fuller evidence for later times. As we have seen, with the rise of the Maccabees Jewish self-government took on a new form. The famous brothers exercised military, priestly, and civil authority, and, beginning with

Aristobulus I (104-103 BCE), took the title of king as well. The family retained the royal title through the reigns of Alexander Jannaeus (103-76 BCE) and the queen Alexandra (76-67 BCE), but with the arrival of the Romans the Hasmonean monarchy came to an end. A series of Roman officials ruled Jewish territory until Herod became king in 37 BCE. He and his descendants governed all or parts of that region for decades, but in Judea itself, with the ouster of Archelaus in 6 CE, the form of government changed once more. First a series of Roman prefects held office (from 6-41 CE), and, following the brief reign of Agrippa I (41-44 CE), they were succeeded by procurators who governed the area until the outbreak of the revolt in 66 CE.

Sanhedrin/Council

While there may have been a ruling council of prominent men in Jerusalem in the early centuries of the second temple period (see, for example, Jth. 4:8; 11:14; 15:8), the first explicit mention of one is in a decree of the Seleucid king Antiochus III (223-187 BCE) preserved by Josephus in *Antiquities* 12.138. There the king is quoted as saying that when he arrived at Jerusalem the senate (Greek *gerousia*) came out to meet him. References to what appears to be the same body become more frequent in the early Maccabean period when one is attested for the times of Judas (2 Macc. 1:10; 4:44, preceding the rise of Judas; 11:27), Jonathan (1 Macc. 12:6), and Simon (1 Macc. 13:36; 14:20, 28 mentioning a group of elders which may be the same as the council).

References to a *sanhedrin* first surface in Roman times. Scholarly views about a Jewish sanhedrin vary quite widely because the sources suggest differing pictures. The term *sanhedrin* is a general one and can be used for councils of diverse kinds, whether local or national. So, for example, the Roman Gabinius, shortly after Pompey's conquest of Jerusalem in 63 BCE, set up five councils and divided the Jewish nation into five parts centered in Jerusalem, Gadara, Amathus, Jericho, and Sepphoris (*Ant.* 14.91). The one in Jerusalem, however, seems to have been especially important. If one follows the Greek texts (Josephus, Philo, the Gospels, Acts), the sanhedrin was a political and judicial body that was headed by the high priest and dealt with the cases of individuals charged with important crimes (e.g., Herod, Jesus). If one follows the later rabbinic sources, the sanhedrin was a group of scholars who gathered to deal with religious issues and were headed by the two leading Pharisees at the time. One solution has been to posit two sanhedrins, one religious and the other political, although no source mentions such an arrangement.

However that issue is to be decided, there was a sanhedrin in Jerusalem that tried cases and that was composed of several kinds of members. When the sanhedrin is mentioned, the high priest is present and seems to be in charge. For example, Hyrcanus II was persuaded to summon the sanhedrin that attempted to try the future king Herod (*Ant.* 14.165-79), and Caiaphas was in charge when Jesus was brought before the council (see, for example, Matt. 26:57, 59; Mark 14.53, 55; 15:1; Luke 22:66; John 11:47-50; *council* in the NRSV is a translation of the word *sunedrion*). Later, a high priest named Ananus convened a sanhedrin that tried James, Jesus' brother (*Ant.* 20.200). Naturally, the Roman government exercised some authority over the sanhedrin; Josephus in this same passage cites the view of Ananus's opponents that it was not lawful to assemble a session of the sanhedrin without the governor's consent. Also, the Jewish king Agrippa II summoned the sanhedrin to decide whether the singers among the Levites would be allowed to wear linen garments as the priests did (*Ant.* 20.216-18). Earlier Herod had killed the members of the sanhedrin who had summoned him to stand trial (*Ant.* 14.175).

According to the later Mishnah, the sanhedrin consisted of seventy-one members (Sanhedrin 1.6). Groups who are mentioned in connection with the sanhedrin are the chief priests (e.g., Matt. 26:57-59; Mark 14:53-55), scribes, Pharisees, Sadducees, and elders. In other words, the sanhedrin consisted of very important people, clerical and lay, who had great powers to try individuals for varied offenses. In a memorable case, the apostle Paul appeared before the sanhedrin, had a harsh exchange with the high priest, and exploited the contradictory opinions of the Pharisees and Sadducees regarding life after death to his own advantage (Acts 22:30–23:10; cf. Acts 4:6; 5:17, 21; 6:12–7:60).

There is a long-standing debate about whether the sanhedrin had the authority to execute those whose crimes warranted such a penalty. One reason why the issue has arisen is that John 18:31 quotes those charging Jesus with criminal behavior as saying "[w]e are not permitted to put anyone to death"; elsewhere, though, one gets the impression that capital punishment was a power wielded by the sanhedrin (e.g., when Herod was tried, the sanhedrin seemed inclined to execute him [*Ant.* 14.177]). It may be that the Roman authorities did permit the sanhedrin to execute those guilty of violating the relevant Jewish laws; it is also not clear that John 18:31 is speaking about a meeting of the sanhedrin.

GROUPS

Other sorts of influence were excercised by different groups who are named in the sources.

Early Second Temple Period

As we have seen several times, our sources for the early centuries of the second temple period are especially meager. As a result, the various factions that may have existed among the Jewish people are not well known. While this is true of Judea, it is even more the case for the diaspora. Nevertheless, scholars have attempted to tease from the texts evidence for groups and differing viewpoints during the early second temple period.

It has been maintained, for instance, that in the early restored community described in the Bible there were advocates of a priestly, hierarchical, static point of view, and that they were opposed by visionaries who looked for a mightier intervention of God in human affairs than embodied in the restoration — the rather modest return from exile and rebuilding of the temple and Jerusalem. There certainly were divergent opinions about relations with other peoples, as the books of Ezra and Nehemiah show: those two leaders vigorously opposed assimilation, but the common people intermarried with neighboring ethnic groups and interacted with them in other ways. We do know that while some attached great authority to the Mosaic books, others used them but appealed to wider traditions. Examples of the latter approach are the authors of the early Enoch texts who seem to have based themselves on sources beyond what Genesis had to say about the seventh man from Adam. Also, even within priestly circles not all appear to have agreed. The Zadokites retained control of the Jerusalem temple, but the author of Aramaic Levi may have belonged to a group that opposed the ruling priests and attached their teachings to the pre-Aaronic figure Levi.

In Hellenistic times, especially in the late third and early second centuries BCE, there were factions in Judea who were pro-Ptolemaic (many of the Tobiads, for example) and others who were pro-Seleucid (perhaps Onias II, the high priest of the Tobiad Romance; the brothers of Hyrcanus in the same story?).

When the Hasmoneans gained their victories over Seleucid forces, they became a great force in Judean society, and their influence grew even greater when they acquired the high priesthood. Not all applauded their rise in power, as we can tell from sources such as 1 Maccabees 14 and probably the Qumran sectarian literature. The Qumran community arose in the early Maccabean period, it seems, although the move to Qumran may have happened somewhat later. The small group that lived around the community center was apparently a band of dissidents who could trace their views to earlier sources such as the Enoch literature and the *Book of Jubilees.*

Late Hellenistic and Roman Times

Josephus first mentions three major Jewish parties — the Pharisees, Sadducees, and Essenes — within his narrative about Jonathan's reign as high priest and military leader (152-142 BCE). In other places in his writings he mentions individual members of these groups, but in two places especially he provides more informative descriptions of what made each one distinctive. Judging by the length of his descriptions, he found the Essenes to be the most interesting — or perhaps his sources were more plentiful for them.

Pharisees

Josephus describes Pharisaic views in two sections of his writings: *War* 2.162-63, 166, and *Antiquities* 18.12-15. Besides these, he mentions Pharisees at a number of points in his narratives. One prominent feature of this group or movement was that they were "the most accurate interpreters of the laws" (*War* 2.162; see *Ant.* 17,41; *Life* 191; Acts 22:3, cf. 23:6). The traditional interpretation of the law developed by the Pharisees is perhaps the most outstanding way in which they were distinguished from other groups. As the historian explains elsewhere, "the Pharisees had passed on to the people certain regulations handed down by former generations and not recorded in the Laws of Moses" (*Ant.* 13.297; cf. 13.408). Mark 7:5, which refers to scribes and Pharisees, describes it as "the tradition of the elders" (cf. Matt. 15:2). What seems to be intended by these phrases is the tradition, passed along orally, of how to interpret and apply the law of Moses in daily life. Although, says Josephus, there were some six thousand Pharisees (*Ant.* 17.42), he attributes to this small part of the population a considerable influence over the masses and even over authorities (*Ant.* 18.15; 13.288, 298). It may be that the name "Pharisee" means "one who is separate," with the separation being from impurity. Issues of purity and impurity were important ones to the Pharisees, and they held themselves to much higher standards than did most Jewish people. Although there were some Pharisaic priests, it appears that many of them were not from the line of Aaron.

Josephus mentions several other beliefs of the Pharisees, beliefs in which they held positions different from those of the other parties, especially the Sadducees. They believed that both fate and human decision were involved in human actions and that there was an afterlife in which the righteous would experience resurrection and the wicked eternal punishment (*War* 2.162-63; *Ant.* 18.12-14, where he notes their simplified lifestyle). Acts 23:8 adds that they believed there were angels and spirits.

In his narrative references to Pharisees, Josephus indicates that they were influential during the reign of John Hyrcanus (134-104 BCE). He, however, broke with them after a Pharisee by the name of Eleazar urged him, if he wanted to be righteous, to relinquish the high priesthood and retain just the civil rule of the nation. When he became convinced by a Sadducean friend that Eleazar spoke not only for himself but for the Pharisees in general, Hyrcanus decided "to abrogate the regulations which they had established for the people, and punish those who observed them" (*Ant.* 13.296; see all of 13.291-98). As a result, the Pharisees seem to have lost whatever official power they had possessed earlier in Hyrcanus's reign. When Alexander Jannaeus ruled (103-76 BCE), he treated them (and others) harshly; Pharisees were included among those crucified by Jannaeus for their opposition to him. On his deathbed he urged his successor and wife Alexandra "to yield a certain amount of power to the Pharisees, for if they praised her in return for this sign of regard, they would dispose the nation favorably toward her" (13.400; see 13.379-83 with 13.398-404). Alexandra honored her dying husband's request, and the Pharisees, who had never lost their popular influence, regained official power as well. Their regulations were restored (13.405-9: "while she had the title of sovereign, the Pharisees had the power" [13.409]). After her reign, the Pharisees are mentioned relatively rarely: during Herod's kingship, although he treated some favorably, others he executed for opposing him (see *Ant.* 15.370; 17.41-46); and some were involved in prominent positions during the first revolt (e.g., *Life* 197). We do know that some Pharisees were members of the sanhedrin (see, for example, Acts 23).

It should be recalled that the epithet "those who seek smooth things" which occurs in some of the Dead Sea Scrolls (e.g., the Commentary on Nahum) has been considered a reflection of the critical attitude held by the Qumran Essenes toward the Pharisees. For the Essenes, they were not seekers of "laws" (halakhot) but of the easy way (halaqot). This bit of inter-party rivalry is a helpful reminder that, however legally pedantic the Pharisees may seem in Christian tradition, at least some of their contemporaries regarded them as overly moderate (see also *Ant.* 13.294 for their leniency in punishments). It is usually thought that, with some changes, the Pharisaic standpoint and approach survived the destruction of 70 CE in the form of rabbinic Judaism, and that the early rabbinic texts such as the Mishnah incorporate many Pharisaic teachings.

Sadducees

The word may be derived from the name Zadok, probably the Zadok who was a leading priest in the time of David and Solomon. Confining ourselves to second temple sources, Josephus again supplies the principal information, but his testimony can be supplemented from some New Testament passages and perhaps from the Qumran scrolls which, according to some scholars, contain a Sadducean form of law.

The Sadducees included high-ranking individuals, some of whom were leading priests. For example, in *Antiquities* 13.298 Josephus describes them as "having the confidence of the wealthy alone but no following among the populace, while the Pharisees have the support of the masses." He makes a similar point in *Antiquities* 18.17: "There are but few men to whom this doctrine has been made known, but these are men of the highest standing. They accomplish practically nothing, however. For whenever they assume some office, though they submit unwillingly and perforce, yet submit they do to the formulas of the Pharisees, since otherwise the masses would not tolerate them." Whatever these statements mean and whatever bias in Josephus they may reflect (he claims he became a Pharisee), they do suggest a different social status for members of the two parties. There are also passages which connect certain high priests with the Sadducean group. Josephus mentions the high priest Ananus who assembled the sanhedrin to condemn Jesus' brother James: he "was rash in his temper and unusually daring. He followed the school of the Sadducees, who are indeed more heartless than any of the other Jews . . . when they sit in judgement" (*Ant.* 20.199). Another case is found in Acts 5:17 which mentions the high priest "and all who were with him (that is, the sect of the Sadducees)." It would be hasty to conclude from this that all high priests were Sadducees, but some were.

One characteristic of the Sadducees is that they are supposed to have accepted only the written law as authoritative and that, as a result, they rejected the traditions of the elders espoused by the Pharisees. As Josephus puts it, after mentioning the Pharisaic position: "for which reason they [the Pharisaic regulations] are rejected by the Sadducean group, who hold that only those regulations should be considered valid which were written down (in Scripture [this parenthetical addition is from the translator]) and that those which had been handed down by former generations need not be observed" (*Ant.* 13.297; cf. 18.16: "They own no observance of any sort apart from the laws"). Exactly what this means is disputed. Some have concluded that the Sadducees accepted only the law of Moses as scripture, but that does not seem to be what Josephus is saying. Rather, he reports that in legal matters the Sadducees rejected the unwritten regulations of the Pharisees. He does not mention their views of the other parts of scripture, and there is no evidence that the Pharisees and Sadducees differed regarding which books were scriptural.

The Qumran texts may have something to contribute to explaining the situation. It has been shown that a text such as the Halakhic Letter (4MMT) expresses some legal stands that are identified in the Mishnah as Sadducean (Yadayim 4.6-7). Also, in many (but not all) cases the legal rulings of the sectarian texts can be characterized as stricter or more severe than the corresponding Pharisaic/rabbinic ones. In this way, too, they could be said to be Sadducean in character. What appears to be the case is that the Sadducees and the Qumran sectarians adhered to a conservative, strict approach to interpreting and applying the law of Moses, an approach that may well have been one maintained and transmitted in priestly circles. These circles seem not to have had the oral tradition which characterized the Pharisees, but they clearly had traditions, some of them written (as in the Qumran texts).

The sources report that the Sadducees and Pharisees differed on several teachings. One text that puts the matter briefly but clearly is Acts 23, the story of Paul's appearance before the sanhedrin, which was composed of Pharisees and Sadducees: "The Sadducees say that there is no resurrection, or angel, or spirit; but the Pharisees acknowledge all three" (v. 8). Paul, who was a Pharisee, then exploited the difference and produced confusion in the sanhedrin (cf. *Ant.* 18.16; *War* 2.165). The claim about the

Sadducean denial of angels or spirits is peculiar, since such beings are mentioned in the law of Moses and elsewhere in scripture; perhaps the Sadducees denied only the developed sorts of angelologies that some of their contemporaries had fashioned (e.g., the Essenes). Besides these views, Josephus also says that the Sadducees espoused free will: "They maintain that man has the free choice of good or evil, and that it rests with each man's will whether he follows the one or the other" (*War* 2.165).

As we have seen, Josephus relates that the Pharisees were influential early in John Hyrcanus's reign but that he broke with them when he followed the advice of a Sadducean friend. Presumably this would have entailed a more dominant position for Sadducees in Hyrcanus's administration. If it did, they lost their influence in Alexandra's reign when she is supposed to have left the control of the nation largely in Pharisaic hands. Whatever their status may have been at different times, some members of the Sadducees held seats on the sanhedrin (e.g., Acts 23).

Essenes

Of the three Jewish groups whom he distinguishes, Josephus writes by far the most about the Essenes. His most extended section about them is in *War* 2.119-61, with shorter ones in *Antiquities* 13.171-72 and 18.18-22. He also refers to a few Essenes in his narratives (e.g., *Ant.* 15.371-79 on the Essene Manaemus who predicted that Herod would become king). Philo, too, deals with them (*Every Good Man Is Free* 75-91), and Pliny the Elder, the Roman naturalist, describes what appears to be the Qumran community in *Natural History* 5.73. Oddly, the New Testament never mentions the Essenes under any recognizable name.

There has been a long dispute about the meaning of "Essenes," with the most likely proposal being that it signifies "those who do" (the law). They were apparently not as large a group as the Pharisees; Josephus and Philo say that there were more than four thousand of them (*Ant.* 18.21; *Every Good Man Is Free* 75) who could be found throughout the towns of Israel (*War* 2.124). Their way of life certainly caught the attention of those who described them. As Josephus puts it, they formed close-knit communities, avoided luxury, marriage (though not out of principle), and riches, and exercised remarkable self-control in every way. He gives a lengthy account of their communal life and notes in it the practice of giving up one's property to the community upon joining. The Essenes cared for their own (whether members of the local group or visitors) out of the community purse and thus did away with the social distinctions brought about by wealth. He describes their daily regimen of prayer, work, bathing, a meal, work, and another meal. They were also true to their word and were greatly interested in the writings of the ancients.

The Essene admission process, which lasted several years, also receives the historian's attention. He mentions the different stages in it and the great oath at the end of it. Their judicial practices and communal meetings are noted, and their strict observance of the sabbath (stricter than all others) is highlighted. Josephus records the four levels in Essene groups and also their sufferings during the war against Rome. He speaks of their belief that souls are immortal, and their accuracy in prediction. He also notes that there was an order of Essenes who married. To this summary of the long section in *War* 2 we may add from the *Antiquities* that the Essenes attributed all human actions to fate, performed their own sacrificial rites, worked at agricultural pursuits, and did not own slaves.

If the Qumran community was, as seems highly likely, a branch of the Essenes, then its sectarian writings show us the legal posture of the group, its extensive and learned interpretation of scripture, its emphasis on praise and prayer, and its views of other Jewish parties. The very close relationship between the practices and views of the Essenes as given in the ancient sources and what is found in the Qumran Rule of the Community and other sectarian texts, coupled with Pliny's location of Essenes on the shore of the Dead Sea, has led a large number of scholars to the conclusion that they were a part of the Essene party.

Others

We have such information from Josephus and it is at times supplemented by other sources. Presumably there were more than three groups or points of view in Judea and Galilee in the late second temple period (and, of course, in the far-flung diaspora), and within the three that Josephus emphasizes there were, one would think, differences of opinion at any one time and various changes as time went by. One other group that the historian does mention is the so-called fourth philosophy. He devotes a section to it directly after his short account of the other three "philosophies" (*Ant.* 18.23-25). Someone named Judas the Galilean became its head. "This school agrees in all other respects with the opinions of the Pharisees, except that they have a passion for liberty that is almost unconquerable, since they are convinced that God alone is their leader and master. They think little of submitting to death in unusual forms and permitting vengeance to fall on kinsmen and friends if only they may avoid calling any man master" (*Ant.* 18.23). He mentions them in connection with the census taken by Quirinius after Archelaus was ousted from office in 6 CE. In *War* 2.118 Josephus credits Judas with stirring up a revolt and criticizing his contemporaries "for consenting to pay tribute to the Romans and tolerating mortal masters, after having God for their lord. This man was a sophist who founded a sect of his own, having nothing in common with the others." This last comment is curious, in light of Josephus's later statement in *Antiquities* about their extensive agreements with the Pharisees. According to *Antiquities* 18.4, Judas sought and received the assistance of Saddok, a Pharisee, in calling the people to oppose the census as a form of slavery. In a personal appraisal of them and what they started, Josephus claims that they sowed the seeds of the rebellion that was to lead more than sixty years later to the events of 70 CE (*Ant.* 18.6-10). There is a genealogical connection between Judas and two leaders of the first revolt of 66-70: Menahem (*War* 2.433; he took Masada in 66 and led the revolt in Jerusalem for a time) and Eleazar ben Jair (*War* 7.253; the leader of the Masada group); but Josephus does not refer to the rebels under Judas as Zealots or Sicarii. Whatever the origins of these latter two groups, at least Josephus does not call them by the same name as the fourth philosophy.

Mention should also be made of the Therapeutae described by Philo in *On the Contemplative Life.* He depicts them as a group of men and women who had withdrawn to the area around the Mareotic Lake, where they lived their lives in ways that often remind one of Essene practices. There were other groups, such as the Samaritans; they had their own long history, including some major conflicts with the residents of Judea. They were centered about Mt. Gerizim, north of Jerusalem, had their own scriptures (including the Torah), and practiced their own rites.

WORSHIP

During the nearly six centuries of the period, worship was centered in the Jerusalem temple, but other locations for study, prayer, and praise also came into being.

The Temple

The time when the second temple stood defines the extent of the period we are studying, and in fundamental ways this building complex in Jerusalem was the center of Judaism both for those living in the land and in the diaspora.

The Temple Structure

We have little information about the actual structure of the second temple before Herod drastically changed the building (after 20 BCE). According to the decree of King Cyrus preserved in the book of Ezra, the Lord's house "was to be rebuilt, the place where sacrifices are offered and burnt offerings are brought; its height shall be sixty cubits and its width sixty cubits, with three courses of hewn stones and one of timber; let the cost be paid from the royal treasury" (6:3-4). These dimensions are surprising because those of Solomon's temple are reported to have been "sixty cubits long, twenty cubits wide, and thirty cubits high" (1 Kings 6:2); the height of the second temple would have been twice that of the first and the width three times larger — highly unlikely in the opinion of many commentators. Perhaps these were only outer limits placed by the king on how much he was willing to finance. Apart from the Ezra passage, we have virtually no descriptions of the second temple, from its completion in 516/15 BCE to Herod's rebuilding. Josephus does quote a description of it from Hecateus of Abdera (a Greek writer who lived at the time of Alexander the Great and Ptolemy I). He wrote that a wall enclosing the temple area measured some five hundred feet long and was about one hundred fifty feet wide, with two entrances. He mentions the square altar which was about thirty feet on each side and fifteen feet high. He says there was a large building next to it containing an altar and a lampstand, both of which were kept lit perpetually. He also notes the absence of any image in the temple (*Against Apion* 1.198-99). Another source is the *Letter of Aristeas*, which presents what seems to be a rather idealized picture of the temple, its contents, and its rituals. "On the top of the hill the Temple had been constructed, towering above all. There were three enclosing walls, over seventy cubits in size, the width being proportionate and the length of the equipment of the house likewise; everything was built with a magnificence and expense which excelled in every respect" (84). He also mentions that the "house faces east"

(88), and he was greatly impressed with the water supply through underground reservoirs (89-91). Aristeas claims to have been able to see all from the nearby citadel that was fortified with several towers; it served as a defensive structure for the temple (100-104). In his glowing description of the high priest Simon and his service in the temple, Ben Sira reports that he "repaired the house, and in his time fortified the temple. He laid the foundations for the high double walls, the high retaining walls for the temple enclosure. In his days a water cistern was dug, a reservoir like the sea in circumference" (50:1-2). His description, which resembles that of Aristeas (note the enclosure walls and the water supply) indicates that the temple had to undergo repairs and was a fortified structure. Simon's reconstructive work is often related to the damage caused in the war, during which the Seleucid king Antiochus III won control of Palestine from the Ptolemaic kingdom (around 200 BCE). Antiochus wrote a letter, quoted by Josephus, in which he refers to repairs that may be needed after the recent wars (*Ant.* 12.141). It is possible, however, that Ben Sira's Simon was Simon I, who lived some one hundred years earlier.

Several texts say that the temple was enriched by magnificent gifts, usually from foreign monarchs. We have seen that Cyrus's decree included an order that the cost of the temple be paid from the royal treasury, and Darius I executed that decree (Ezra 6:8). Also, Artaxerxes I in 458 BCE greatly beautified the temple with the lavish gifts that he and his advisors sent by the hand of Ezra (Ezra 7:11-24). Later, in Hellenistic times, Ptolemy II is reported to have dispatched astonishing presents to the sanctuary in Jerusalem (*Letter of Aristeas* 33, 42, 51-82). Antiochus III made contributions to the sanctuary, cultus, and priests in consequence of the assistance and warm welcome he had received from the inhabitants of Jerusalem in his latest war with the Ptolemies (*Ant.* 12.138-44). He is also credited with issuing a decree that no foreigner was to enter the temple precincts (*Ant.* 12.145). After the Seleucids took control of the land, Seleucus IV (187-175 BCE) is credited with defraying the costs of the cult as other kings had done in the past (2 Macc. 3:2-3).

Besides the damage inflicted on the temple in the time of Antiochus III, the building needed major repairs after it was desecrated during the reign of Antiochus IV. In 169 BCE the king "entered the sanctuary and took the golden altar, the lampstand for the light and all its utensils. He took also the table for the bread of the Presence, the cups for drink offerings, the bowls, the golden censers, the curtain, the crowns, and the gold decoration on the front of the temple; he stripped it all off. He took the sil-

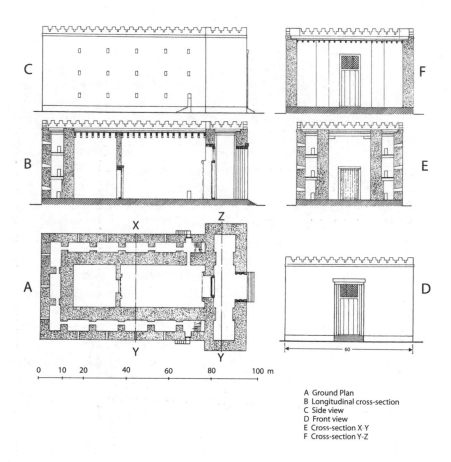

A Ground Plan
B Longitudinal cross-section
C Side view
D Front view
E Cross-section X-Y
F Cross-section Y-Z

The Temple of Zerubbabel, reconstructed (T. A. Busink)

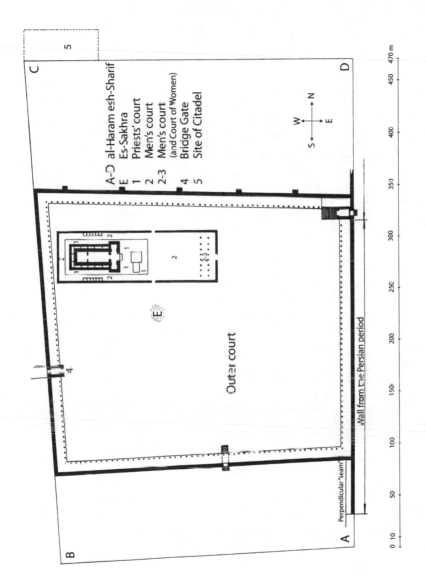

The Pre-Herodian temple (T. A. Busink)

A-D al-Haram esh-Sharif
E   Es-Sakhra
1   Priests' court
2   Men's court
2-3 Men's court
     (and Court of Women)
4   Bridge Gate
5   Site of Citadel

Outer court

Wall from the Persian period

Perpendicular "seam"

0 10   50   100   150   200   250   300   350   400   450   470 m

197

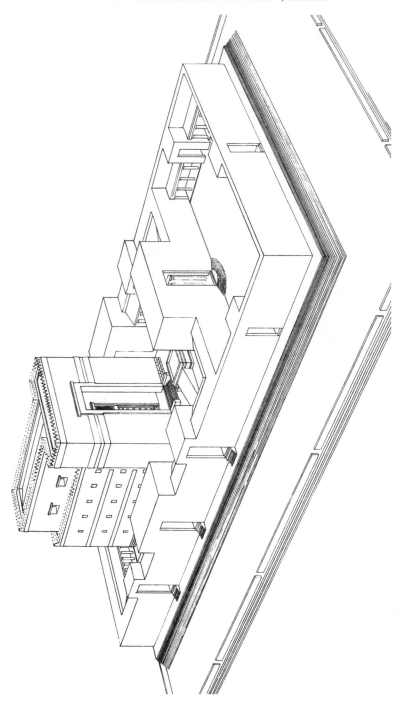

Plan of the Inner Sanctuary of the Herodian temple (reconstruction by T. A. Busink)

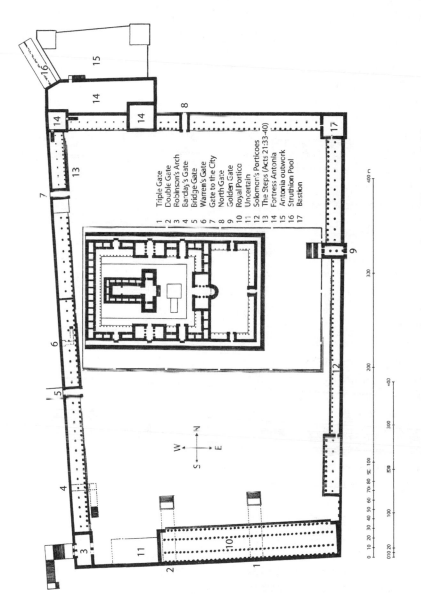

1 Triple Gate
2 Double Gate
3 Robinson's Arch
4 Barday's Gate
5 Bridge Gate
6 Warren's Gate
7 Gate to the City
8 North Gate
9 Golden Gate
10 Royal Portico
11 Uncertain
12 Solomon's Porticoes
13 The Steps (Acts 21:33-40)
14 Fortress Antonia
15 Antonia outwork
16 Struthion Pool
17 Bastion

Plan of the Herodian temple (reconstruction by T. A. Busink)

199

ver and the gold, and the costly vessels; he took also the hidden treasures that he found" (1 Macc. 1:21-23; see v. 39). A few years later, when the Maccabean forces were able to reach the temple mount before reconsecrating the temple itself, they found a distressing sight: "the sanctuary desolate, the altar profaned, and the gates burned. In the courts they saw bushes sprung up as in a thicket, or as on one of the mountains. They saw also the chambers of the priests in ruins" (4:38). Judas and his men went about their work on the temple and surrounding area. They constructed a new altar for burnt offerings because the old one had been defiled by pagan sacrifices. "They also rebuilt the sanctuary and the interior of the temple, and consecrated the courts. They made new holy vessels, and brought the lampstand, the altar of incense, and the table into the temple" (4:48-49). It sounds from these lines as if the renovations were extensive. In 159 BCE the high priest Alcimus "gave orders to tear down the wall of the inner court of the sanctuary. He tore down the work of the prophets!" (1 Macc. 9:54) Apparently this attempt to obliterate the distinction between the inner and outer courts was not carried through to completion (v. 55). The Maccabean high priest Simon "strengthened the fortifications of the temple hill alongside the citadel, and he and his men lived there" (1 Macc. 13:52); he also "made the sanctuary glorious" (14:15). Alexander Jannaeus, after being pelted with citrons by pilgrims to the temple for the festival of tabernacles, built a wooden wall around the altar and the temple itself to keep the people from having such free access to him as he officiated at sacrifice (*Ant.* 13.372-73). The temple once more sustained damage when Pompey laid siege to it: his war engines catapulted large stones against it and flattened some of the surrounding defensive towers. Although a number of priests are said to have died as they carried out their sacrificial duties in the temple, Pompey entered the temple, even the holy of holies, but permitted no further harm to it and ordered that the temple be cleansed and the cult be resumed (*Ant.* 14.58-73). When Herod took Jerusalem after being named king, some cloisters in the temple were burned but no other destruction is mentioned (14.476).

The references here to the courts of the temple and the chambers of the priests remind one that the temple complex consisted of more than the relatively simple building that was the temple proper. It, like Solomon's temple, apparently included three sections: the porch (fifteen feet by thirty feet), the holy place (sixty by thirty), and the holy of holies (thirty by thirty). But much more was needed to have an operating national cult: places had to be provided for priests' residences while on duty, places were needed for the animals and equipment for sacrifices (see Neh. 13:4-9), and, of course, places were required for the many people who came to the temple for sacrifices, other religious rites, and for the pilgrimage festivals. The references given above indicate the presence of priests' chambers and of at least two courts within the large temple enclosure, but they do not give us precise numbers and dimensions. As early as Nehemiah 8:16 we read of courts of the temple but not of how many there were or what their dimensions might have been. Hecateus says nothing about multiple courts.

We have more detailed information about the temple of Herod. In *Antiquities* 15.380 Josephus begins to tell how the king rebuilt the Jerusalem temple. He dates the inception of the process to Herod's eighteenth year (= 20 BCE) and says that the building, the most magnificent of Herod's many architectural feats, was meant by the monarch as an eternal memorial to himself and perhaps to project himself in the image of David and Solomon. He prepared the populace for his bold plan by means of a public speech in which he claimed to have advanced the nation beyond any level they had before attained. Although his oratorical effort did not entirely allay concerns, he promised that he would not tear down the old structure until all the materials were ready for the new one. The ancient sanctuary was then torn down to the foundations (which were removed), new foundations were laid, and a temple 150 feet in length was constructed in its place. A massive amount of work went into reinforcing the temple mount through walls which rose to great heights and which were made of enormous stones; by placing them at the proper points and filling in low-lying areas, the surface of the temple area was expanded. Part of one of these walls today is known as the Western Wall (formerly the Wailing Wall), the only part of Herod's temple that can still be seen. The king himself saw to the building of the surrounding structures and enclosures — the only ones with which he could be directly involved since he was not a priest. Finishing this large project took his men eight years (*Ant.* 15.420). The relatively small sanctuary at the center of the large temple complex was constructed by specially trained priests who completed their work in eighteen months (15.421). Some work continued on the complex for many years after this (cf. John 2:20, in which the people say it has been under construction for forty-six years), and in the reign of Nero an attempt was made to increase the height of the sanctuary by thirty feet, but the outbreak of the First Revolt prevented completion of the plan.

In *Antiquities* 15.380-420 and in *War* 5.184-226, Josephus describes the temple compound in considerable detail. He was, we should recall, a priest and was personally familiar with the structure. These facts make his description a valuable one, even though it disagrees in some details with the temple description in the later Mishnaic tractate Middot. He speaks about three courts or enclosures. The outermost one had many white marble columns and porticoes in double rows around it; the whole area was paved with variegated stones. The middle enclosure or court, which one reached by going up fourteen steps, was surrounded by a stone wall (about four and one-half feet wide) which contained at regular intervals inscriptions warning foreigners against entering beyond this point on pain of death (archeologists have found examples of them). On the north and south sides it had three gates each, while on the east (the direction the temple itself faced) was a simple large gate through which Jews in a state of purification and their wives were permitted to enter. There was a special women's court on the east side of the area. The inner part of the area was set apart for ritually pure men alone. The innermost enclosure only priests could enter, and inside it stood the sanctuary itself (its facade was 150 by 150 feet in height and breadth). It was reached by another twelve steps; in front of it stood the altar of burnt offerings (see *Ant.* 15.419-20; it was seventy-five by seventy-five feet and twenty-two feet six inches high [*War* 5.225]). The ground floor (there was another above it, some sixty feet high) of the temple was ninety feet long, ninety feet high, and thirty feet wide. Lengthwise, it was divided into two: the holy place took sixty feet, and the holy of holies the other thirty. The holy place contained the lampstand with seven lamps, the table for the bread of the presence, and the altar of incense. Of the holy of holies Josephus said: "In this stood nothing at all" (*War* 5.219). Around the sanctuary proper were three-storied structures containing rooms of various kinds.

The entire temple, once made glorious by the wealth and skill of Herod, must have been an impressive sight. Josephus says about it:

> The exterior of the building wanted nothing that could astound either mind or eye. For, being covered on all sides with massive plates of gold, the sun was no sooner up than it radiated so fiery a flash that persons straining to look at it were compelled to avert their eyes, as from the solar rays. To approaching strangers it appeared from a distance like a snow-clad mountain; for all that was not overlaid with gold was of purest white. From its summit protruded sharp golden spikes to prevent birds from settling upon and polluting the roof. Some of the stones in the building were

forty-five cubits in length [sixty-seven feet six inches], five in height [seven feet six inches] and six in breadth [nine feet]. (*War* 5.222-24)

Herod's temple perished in the carnage of 70 CE.

For the sake of completeness we should recall that four other temples are attested for the second temple period: the one at Elephantine, the temple of Onias in Leontopolis (Egypt), the Tobiad sanctuary at Araq el-Emir in the Transjordan, and the Samaritan temple on Mt. Gerizim. None of these, however, attained the prominence of the Jerusalem temple or lasted as long.

The Sacrificial System

The temple was a place where sacrifices were offered and where other ceremonies related to the sacrificial system took place. The priestly legislation in the Bible (for example, Lev. 1–7) defines a variety of offerings that would be required for specific occasions — whether for faults committed or for celebration and thanksgiving. An appealing feature of the sacrificial legislation is that it made provisions for the financial status of the one bringing an offering: if one was poor, less was required (see, for example, Lev. 5:7-13). The altar was the site of two mandatory daily sacrifices. Exod. 29:38-42 stipulates that each day one lamb was to be offered in the morning and one in the evening (twilight, according to Num. 28:4, 8) of every day. In addition to the various forms of sacrifices for specific circumstances, there were also detailed instructions about the offerings to be brought during each sabbath (Num. 28:9-10), each new moon (Num. 28:11-15), and each festival (Num. 28–29). Sacrifices involved animals in some cases and dry goods in others; often both were stipulated along with libations. The materials necessary for the sacrifice required that there be places for animals, equipment for handling them, and means to wash away the blood and refuse that resulted. According to biblical legislation, only the priests were allowed to officiate at the altar (e.g., Exod. 28; Num. 18).

Great expenses were involved in operating the temple and its sacrificial system. Gifts were made to it from time to time, but a regular means for raising the necessary funds was the annual half-shekel tax levied on all adult Jews. Exodus 30:11-16 imposed such a tax in the wilderness period (cf. 38:26), while in the time of Ezra and Nehemiah the people pledged to "charge ourselves yearly one-third of a shekel for the service of the house of our God: for the rows of bread, the regular grain offering, the regular burnt offering, the sabbaths, the new moons, the appointed festivals, the sacred donations, and the sin offerings to make atonement for Israel, and for all the work of the house of our God" (Neh. 10:32-33). The Exodus passage may have later been understood as entailing a yearly payment (cf. 2 Chron. 24:4-10), not a one-time assessment (as it was understood at Qumran; see 4Q159 fragment 1 lines 6-7). At any rate, one-half shekel became an annual tax for all Jewish males of twenty years and above. There is a reference to the collection of the tax in Matthew 17:24-27. After 70 CE, all Jews throughout the empire were ordered to pay the annual tax "into the Capitol as formerly contributed by them to the temple at Jerusalem" (*War* 7.218), that is, for the temple of Jupiter Capitolinus.

Festivals

One of the important functions served by the temple was as the center for celebration of festivals. The Hebrew Bible gives instructions for the annual celebration and remembrance of important occasions in Israel's history, along with a few other occasions to be marked with annual observances. The major sources of information about most of the holidays are Leviticus 23 and Numbers 28–29 (see also Deut. 16).

(1) Passover

The passover from Egypt was to be remembered every year on the fourteenth day of the first month. Much of the biblical legislation for the celebration can be found in Exodus 12 where it is attached directly to the story about the departure from Egypt, the the event it celebrates. A one-year-old lamb or goat without blemish was to be selected for each household on the tenth day of the month; it was to be kept until the fourteenth, when it was to be slaughtered and its blood sprinkled on the doorpost of a dwelling so that the Lord would see it and pass over that house when he came through Egypt at night. Exodus 12 also gives instructions about the foods to be eaten and the way in which they were to be consumed.

(2) The Festival of Unleavened Bread

Beginning on the day after passover was a related seven-day holiday that also commemorated the exodus from Egypt. Its first and last days were to be marked by assemblies. Exodus 12 explains about both passover and un-leavened bread: "In the first month, from the evening of the fourteenth day until the evening of the twenty-first day, you shall eat unleavened bread. For seven days no leaven shall be found in your houses; for whoever eats what is leavened shall be cut off from the congregation of Israel" (vv. 18-19). The prohibition of leaven is explained by the speed with which the Is-raelites were forced to leave Egypt: "They baked unleavened cakes of the dough that they had brought out of Egypt; it was not leavened, because they were driven out of Egypt and could not wait, nor had they prepared any provisions for themselves" (12:39).

This holiday is the first of three pilgrimage festivals. The name derives from the fact that it was one of the three occasions when "all your males shall appear before the Lord God" (Exod. 23:17; see vv. 14-15). In the age of the second temple, appearing before the Lord meant traveling to the temple. It is not said that passover is such a pilgrimage festival (although in Deut. 16:2 that is the requirement), but large numbers of people flocked to the temple in Jerusalem for passover and for the festival of unleavened bread. Offerings for the days of unleavened bread are mentioned in Leviti-cus 23:8, and Numbers 28:19-25 gives more details.

After a section about the festival of unleavened bread, Leviticus also mentions that a ceremony called the waving of the barley omer (an omer is a dry measure) followed (Lev. 23:9-14). The occasion is not dated other than to say that the first of the barley harvest was presented "on the day af-ter the sabbath" (Lev. 23:11), but the time of the omer waving is important because it served as the starting point for the count of days that led to the festival of weeks (see below).

(3) Second Passover

Anyone who had become unclean through touching a corpse or was away at the time of passover was permitted to make up for missing the holiday by celebrating it on 2/14 (Num. 9:9-12).

(4) The Festival of Weeks

The second pilgrimage festival received its name from the fact that, to calcu-late its date, one was to start with the date on which the barley omer was waved and "count off seven weeks; they shall be complete. You shall count until the day after the seventh sabbath, fifty days; then you shall present an offering of new grain to the Lord" (Lev. 23:15-16). The fact that the omer ceremony was not dated in a clear way led to uncertainty about when the festival of weeks was to occur; as a result Jewish groups differed on the matter, with some celebrating it early in the third month and others, such as the author of *Jubilees* and the Qumran community, placing it on 3/15 in their calendar. They dated the omer ceremony to 1/26 which was the day after the first sabbath following the festival of unleavened bread. That is, they understood Leviticus 23:11-16 literally as referring to a weekly sabbath after the festival of unleavened bread. Others read Leviticus 23:11 to mean that the omer ritual took place the day after the first day of unleavened bread (1/16, understanding sabbath to mean "festival" as it sometimes does in the Bible).

The festival of weeks was associated by the author of *Jubilees* and the Qumran community with the covenant made with Noah and renewed with Abraham, Isaac, Jacob, and the nation at Sinai: all of these ceremonies occurred in the third month (see Exod. 19:1). In the Greek-speaking world, the festival of weeks became known as pentecost after the fact that it fell on the fiftieth day after the omer waving. Acts 2 presents a well-known picture of Jews from the entire diaspora as well as from Judea coming to Jerusalem for the pilgrimage festival.

(5) The First of the Seventh Month

In rabbinic times 7/1 became known as Rosh Hashanah, that is, the beginning of the year, new year's day. It is never given this name in biblical or second temple sources, but it is clear that, of all the firsts of the months, the first of the seventh month had a special status even in the Hebrew Bible. It was to be a day for a sacred convocation and complete rest (Lev. 23:23-25). Numbers 29:1-6 details the sacrifices to be brought on this date and calls it "a day for you to blow the trumpets" (v. 1; see Lev. 23:24).

(6) The Day of Atonement

Leviticus 16 and other passages date the day of atonement to 7/10. It is not a holiday in the sense of a time for celebrating but is a solemn day: "In the seventh month, on the tenth day of the month, you shall deny yourselves [or: fast], and shall do no work, neither the citizen nor the alien who resides among you. For on this day atonement shall be made for you, to cleanse you; from all your sins you shall be clean before the Lord. It is a sabbath of complete rest to you . . ." (Lev. 16:29-31). The chapter describes the offerings and ceremonies of the day, the only day in the year on which the high priest was allowed to enter the holy of holies. Atonement is made not only for the people but also for the sanctuary. The ritual of the two goats is a familiar part of the day: lots are cast over two goats, with one chosen for the Lord, the other for the enigmatic Azazel. The one for the Lord is offered as a sin offering, while the one for Azazel has all the sins of Israel for the year symbolically placed on it before it is driven away into the wilderness (vv. 21-22).

(7) The Festival of Tabernacles (or Booths)

Exactly one-half year after the festival of unleavened bread, the Israelites were to celebrate the festival of tabernacles at the end of their harvest season. At an early time it seems to have been a most important occasion (Solomon's temple was dedicated during this festival, 1 Kings 8:2, 65-66), and it did not lose its significance as time progressed. One of the more detailed descriptions of tabernacles in second temple sources is found in the Gospel of John 7–8, where Jesus' actions and his words spoken during the holiday are described. There two rituals associated with the festival are connected with addresses that Jesus gave. The first was the daily ritual of drawing water from the pool of Siloam and bringing it into the temple complex; the rite on the last day of the festival was the setting for his reference to himself as the living water (7:37-39). The second was the lighting of the court with large torches, the backdrop for his light of the world speech (8:12-59). At some point already in the period of the Hebrew Bible an eighth day was added to the holiday (see Lev. 23:36).

(8) Hanukkah

As we have seen, Hanukkah is the festival instituted by the Maccabean forces to celebrate the rededication of the temple and altar, after it had been polluted by an alien cult. The first Jews to celebrate it decreed that it should last eight days beginning on 9/25 (1 Macc. 4:52-59). The length of the holiday may be patterned after the festival of tabernacles, as 2 Maccabees calls Hanukkah "the festival of booths in the month of Chislev" (2 Macc. 1:9). Josephus speaks of it as a festival of light (*Ant.* 12.325; see 2 Macc. 1:8). Hanukkah is not mentioned in the Hebrew Bible (perhaps because of its late date) and also fails to appear in the Qumran calendars (perhaps because of its Maccabean associations).

(9) Purim

The festival of Purim (= lots) is explained in the book of Esther as the holiday celebrating the deliverance of the Jews from Haman's plan to exterminate them, and their victory over their opponents. It is celebrated in the twelfth month, on the fourteenth day (see also 2 Macc. 15:36, where it is called "Mordecai's day"). It too makes no appearance in the Qumran texts, just as no copy of Esther has been found in the caves. A reason for its absence from Qumran may be that Purim would fall on a sabbath in the 364-day calendar.

While these nine festivals were celebrated by the Jewish people generally, the Qumran group did not recognize Hanukkah and Purim but added two firstfruits festivals (the festivals of wine on 5/3 and of oil on 6/22). Moreover, because they followed a 364-day calendar, they would have celebrated their holidays almost always at different times than did the rest of the nation. The sources do occasionally mention other holidays, such as the day on which the takeover of the Jerusalem citadel occurred in Simon's time (1 Macc. 13:52; the date was 2/23) or the day of Nicanor (2 Macc. 15:36; on 12/13, the day before Purim); it was not celebrated after 70 CE. Also, the Jews of Alexandria celebrated a day in honor of the translation of the Pentateuch into Greek (Philo, *Life of Moses* 2.41-43), and 3 Maccabees claims that the deliverance from persecution described in the book was also the occasion for a holiday (6:30-36; see Josephus, *Against Apion* 2.55).

Other Forms of Worship

It should not be thought that the temple in Jerusalem was a magnificent place for offering sacrifices and nothing more. It was indeed that, but the sources mention the presence of additional features of the temple services (and of other places where worship was conducted).

(1) Music

The Bible gives ample indication that music was a significant part of worship while the second temple stood. Numbers 10:10 speaks of trumpets that were to be blown when burnt offerings were made and during festivals. Several of our sources trace the origins of liturgical music to David, the sweet singer of Israel. First and Second Chronicles, which are postexilic rewritings of earlier works such as 1–2 Kings and have additions reflecting second temple times and perhaps ideals, indicate that the great king appointed levitical singers and instrumentalists, some four thousand in number, who "shall offer praises to the Lord with the instruments that I have made for praise" (1 Chron. 23:5). They were to "stand every morning, thanking and praising the Lord, and likewise at evening, and whenever burnt offerings are offered to the Lord on sabbaths, new moons, and appointed festivals" (23:30-31). The three major groups of these musical Levites were the sons of Asaph, Heman, and Jeduthun "who should prophesy with lyres, harps, and cymbals" (25:1; cf. vv. 6-7). At Solomon's dedication of the temple, in the Chronicler's version, the levitical singers participated with their instruments and the priests blew their trumpets. We even learn some of their words of praise: "For he is good, for his steadfast love endures forever" (2 Chron. 5:12-13). These words, perhaps quoting Psalm 136:1, are a reminder that a number of biblical psalms are associated with these singers: the name of Asaph appears in the titles of Psalms 50, 73–83, Heman in 88, and Jeduthun in 77. Also, the Korahites, a levitical group (1 Chron. 6:22), have their name attached to Psalms 42, 44–49, 84–85, 87–88. There are other indications that many of the psalms were used in worship: Psalms 113–18 (the Hallel Psalms; see Matt. 26:30 and parallels) were sung at passover, and the Songs of Ascents (Pss. 120–34) were presumably intoned as pilgrims came to Jerusalem for the three great festivals. The title of Psalm 92 identifies it as a song for the sabbath day.

The books of Chronicles, Ezra, and Nehemiah contain many references to the levitical musicians and their work (e.g., 2 Chron 7:6; 8:14; 15:14; 20:19; 23:13, 18; 30:21; 34:12; 35:15; Ezra 2:41, 70; 3:10-11; 7:7; Neh. 7:44, 73; 11:17, 22-23; 12:8, 27-29, 36, 42). An especially descriptive passage is in 2 Chronicles 29:25-30 where King Hezekiah:

> stationed the Levites in the house of the Lord with cymbals, harps, and lyres. . . . The Levites stood with the instruments of David, and the priests with the trumpets. Then Hezekiah commanded that the burnt offering be offered on the altar. When the burnt offering began, the song to the Lord began also, and the trumpets, accompanied by the instruments of King David of Israel. The whole assembly worshiped, the singers sang, and the trumpeters sounded; all this continued until the burnt offering was finished. When the offering was finished, the king and all who were present with him bowed down and worshiped. King Hezekiah and the officials commanded the Levites to sing praises to the Lord with the words of Da-

vid and of the seer Asaph. They sang praises with gladness, and they bowed down and worshiped.

Ben Sira, too, traces the musical aspects of worship back to David: "He placed singers before the altar, to make sweet melody with their voices [some copies add: and daily they sing his praises]. He gave beauty to the festivals, and arranged their times throughout the year, while they praised God's holy name, and the sanctuary resounded from early morning" (47:9-10). The same writer, after picturing the sacrifices offered by the high priest Simon assisted by the priests, adds: "Then the sons of Aaron shouted; they blew their trumpets of hammered metal; they sounded a mighty fanfare as a reminder before the Most High" (50:16). Once the people had prostrated themselves, "the singers praised him with their voices in sweet and full-toned melody" (v. 18).

This picture of music with sacrifice is supplemented by some of the Qumran texts. One is the composition called "Songs of the Sabbath Sacrifice" in which there are songs for the thirteen sabbaths in a quarter of a year. An intriguing text from cave 11 also ties music to David and to the sacrificial system. "YHWH gave him an intelligent and brilliant spirit, and he wrote 3,600 psalms and 364 songs to sing before the altar for the daily perpetual sacrifice, for all the days of the year; and 52 songs for the Sabbath offerings; and 30 songs for the New Moons, for Feast-days and for the Day of Atonement" (11QPs^a 27.4-8).

The sources make reference to music that accompanied special occasions, such as the rededication of the temple by Judas Maccabeus and his men (1 Macc. 4:54 [see 2 Macc. 10:7]; 1 Macc. 13:51; cf. also Jth. 15:14–16:17).

(2) Prayer

Prayers, of course, were offered long before the second temple period, but in our sources we find an especially large number of them in varied forms and contexts. It is no surprise that individuals uttered prayers in times of crisis and that these often contain words of confession (e.g., Neh. 1:4-11, when he heard of the terrible conditions in Jerusalem; the Prayer of Azariah; the Prayer of Manasseh). Judith prayed before she set her plan in motion to save her people (9:2-14), and Tobit (3:2-6), Sarah (3:11-15), and Tobias (8:5-8) offered prayers (see also Addition C of Greek Esther for the prayers of Mordecai and Esther; Susanna 42–43; 1 Macc. 4:30-33; 3 Macc.

2:1-20; 6:1-15). Some of the prayers offer surveys of biblical history and use biblical examples (e.g., Ezra in Neh. 9:6-37; Daniel in Dan. 9:3-19).

One of the unsolved questions relating to prayers is whether there were fixed prayers for set times during the second temple period. Naturally, the temple was the focus of worship, and one might expect fixed prayers to arise in connection with rituals performed there. Second Chronicles 7, reflecting Solomon's dedicatory prayer in 1 Kings 8, contains numerous references to praying toward the temple (6:24, 26, 29, 32, 34-35, 39); Isaiah 56:7 calls the temple "a house of prayer," and Daniel prayed toward the temple three times each day (6:10; in Acts 3:1 Peter and John went "to the temple at the hour of prayer, at three o'clock in the afternoon"). In Luke 1:10 the people pray at the temple at the time of the incense offering. The Qumran texts have provided a rich source of new information regarding the development of Jewish liturgy since there are many prayer texts among the scrolls and they are often connected with fixed occasions: for example, 4Q503 gives evening and morning blessings for the days of a month; 4Q504-6 provide liturgies for the weekdays, and prayers for the festivals are present in 1Q34, 1Q34bis, 4Q507-9. It could be argued that these texts belonged to a small sectarian group and that they do not therefore represent practices followed by other Jews. Yet, these texts often have nothing specifically sectarian about them and thus may reflect wider practice. If so, they indicate the development of fixed prayers in the time of the second temple. It is interesting that the Qumran community saw its prayers as (temporary) substitutes for sacrifice: "They shall atone for guilty rebellion and for the sins of unfaithfulness, that they may obtain loving-kindness for the Land without the flesh of holocausts and the fat of sacrifice. And prayer rightly offered shall be as an acceptable fragrance of righteousness, and perfection of way as a delectable free-will offering" (1QS 9.4-5)

The Synagogue

Consideration of worship forms that did not involve sacrifice of animals or other goods leads naturally to the study of the synagogue, an institution where non-sacrificial worship took place. At some point in our period, synagogues came into being and served the needs of Jewish people in the diaspora who lived at some distance from the temple. Yet we know that there were synagogues in the land as well, even in Jerusalem. Some sources use the Greek word *proseuche,* meaning "prayer, place of prayer," to designate Jewish places of worship. If these were synagogues, we have references to them beginning in the third century BCE in Egypt (the same word is used in Acts 16:13, 16). Readers of the New Testament know that it contains numerous references to synagogues, both in the land (e.g., Nazareth) and elsewhere (many in Acts).

A few sources give us some idea of what happened at the synagogues. In *The Special Laws* 2.62 Philo says:

> So each seventh day there stand wide open in every city thousands of schools of good sense, temperance, courage, justice and the other virtues in which the scholars sit in order quietly with ears alert and with full attention, so much do they thirst for the draught which the teacher's words supply, while one of special experience rises and sets forth what is best and sure to be profitable and will make the whole of life grow to something better.

He emphasizes the instructional aspect of the service and seems to be referring to the reading of scripture (the teacher's words) and its exposition. Josephus offers a similar picture:

> For ignorance he left no pretext. He appointed the Law to be the most excellent and necessary form of instruction, ordaining, not that it should be heard once for all or twice or even on several occasions, but that every week men should desert their other occupations and assemble to listen to the Law and to obtain a thorough and accurate knowledge of it, a practice which all other legislators seem to have neglected. (*Against Apion* 2.175)

In Luke 4:16-28 Jesus goes to the Nazareth synagogue on the sabbath as he customarily did. "He stood up to read, and the scroll of the prophet Isaiah was given to him" (vv. 16-17). Hence, not only the law but also a prophetic portion figured in the service. After completing the lection from Isaiah, "he rolled up the scroll, gave it back to the attendant, and sat down" (v. 20) before he expounded the passage (v. 21; cf. Matt. 4:23, etc.). In Acts, the apostle Paul is regularly pictured as going to the local synagogue upon arriving at a city. When he and his companions came to Antioch in Pisidia, they followed their practice (13:14-49). "And on the sabbath day they went into the synagogue and sat down. After the reading of the law and the prophets, the officials of the synagogue sent them a message, saying, 'Brothers, if you have any word of exhortation for the people, say it'" (vv. 14-15). Paul offered such a message and was invited back the next week. The Mishnah (Megillah 4.3) says that prayer was a regular part of the synagogue service.

Only a few of the many synagogues in the land during our period have been excavated. As we have seen, there was one on Masada. Others have been found at Herodium and at Gamla in the Golan.

SCRIPTURES

Many of the literary works that were surveyed in Chapter 2 make reference to earlier Israelite/Jewish literature and do so in such a way that they attribute great authority to it. It is very likely that there was not a *Bible* in the second temple period — that is, an accepted, defined, and *closed* corpus of supremely authoritative texts — but there is no doubt that there were some books widely held to contain divine teaching. The Torah of Moses, to which Ezra and Nehemiah often refer, is the most obvious example, but much prophetic literature would also have to be included. Indeed, one characteristic of later prophecy in the Hebrew Bible is its use of earlier prophetic texts.

At some point, apparently after the destruction of Jerusalem in 70 CE, a Jewish canon of scripture was defined. It contained three sections: the Torah, the prophets, and the writings. The Torah consisted of the five books of Moses (Genesis through Deuteronomy), the prophets included the historical books Joshua, Judges, 1-2 Samuel, 1-2 Kings, Isaiah, Jeremiah, Ezekiel, and the twelve minor prophets (Hosea through Malachi), and the writings involved the remaining books (Psalms, Proverbs, Job, Ruth, Esther, Ecclesiastes, Lamentations, Song of Songs, Daniel, Ezra, Nehemiah, and 1-2 Chronicles). There is evidence from before the formalizing of the canon that the scriptures were divided into sections; what is lacking is evidence that all the categories were closed and thus contained a fixed set of books.

Groups of Authoritative Writings

As noted above, Ezra and Nehemiah allude to the Torah or law of Moses as dictating the way in which the people were to live. Hence, to cite one example, the people lived in booths during the seventh month and celebrated a festival as commanded in the law (Neh. 8:13-18). And Ezra, in a well-known scene, read the law to the people assembled at the Water Gate (Neh. 8:1-12). The confessional prayer offered in Nehemiah 9 shows awareness of the biblical history from creation, through the patriarchs, the Egyptian sojourn, the wilderness trek, the conquest, the period of the judges and of Israel's history in the land, and finally of exile and return.

Most of our meager evidence about developments toward a canon of scriptural books comes from later sources, as we might expect. A helpful case is the Prologue to the Greek translation of the Wisdom of Ben Sira. In it the author's grandson, writing late in the second century BCE, three times makes mention of categories of traditional literature. He opens the Prologue by writing: "Many great teachings have been given to us through the Law, and the Prophets and the others that followed them, and for these we should praise Israel for instruction and wisdom." A few lines later he commends the author: "So my grandfather Jesus, who had devoted himself especially to the reading of the Law and the Prophets and the other books of our ancestors, and had acquired considerable proficiency in them, was himself also led to write something pertaining to instruction and wisdom. . . ." In the third passage, he apologizes to the reader for possibly having translated some phrases improperly: "For what was originally expressed in Hebrew does not have exactly the same sense when translated into another language. Not only this book, but even the Law itself, the Prophecies, and the rest of the books differ not a little when read in the original."

There are a few other passages from different writers and periods in which we encounter a similar threefold division of the traditional books considered of greatest value. Philo, for instance, in speaking of the Therapeutae mentions that they study "laws and oracles delivered through the mouths of prophets, and psalms and anything else which fosters and perfects knowledge and piety" (*On the Contemplative Life* 25); and the author of Luke quotes the risen Jesus as saying: "These are my words that I spoke to you while I was still with you — that everything written about me in the law of Moses, the prophets, and the psalms might be fulfilled" (Luke 24:44). In this case "the psalms" means, of course, in the first instance the book of that name, but it may also stand for the third division of scripture in which Psalms is the first book. One Qumran text (4QMMT) may even distinguish four categories, although only three are relatively certain: the book of Moses, the books of the prophets, David, and possibly some annals (C 10-11). In all cases of threefold division, the third is given a general (or, for Luke's "psalms," a potentially general) term. In fact, it is more common to find references to two sections of the sacred and authoritative writings: the law and the prophets. Note, for instance, Matthew 7:12: "In everything do to others as you would have them do to you; for this is the law and the prophets." The intention is to refer to the entire scriptures.

Some writers indicate clearly that they regard a certain text as divinely inspired. In the Qumran commentary on Habakkuk the expositor says that God told Habakkuk to write the words (see 7.1-2). There are many other examples of this sort scattered throughout the second temple literature. To cite only one more case, Daniel 9:2 shows us Daniel pondering the word of the Lord to Jeremiah regarding the seventy years.

While we have references to categories of sacred books and clear indications that various writers thought books such as the law and the prophets were from God, we do not find a list of canonical books until the end of our period. Ben Sira knows large parts of the scriptures, as he shows in chapters 44–50 and uses the characters in them as examples, but he does not give us a list of books. It is safe to say that most of the books which were to become parts of the Hebrew Bible (= Protestant Old Testament) were regarded as authoritative throughout at least the latter part of the second temple, but it also seems likely that for some, such as the people from Qumran, books in addition to those were considered revealed. Examples are some of the Enoch literature and the *Book of Jubilees*. We do not know what factors may have led to the fixing of a canon of scripture for most Jews, but Josephus provides us with the earliest and most specific enumeration in *Against Apion* 1.37-43. There he says that the properly accredited books number twenty two: the five of Moses, the prophets in thirteen books, and four books of hymns and precepts. We may not be able to say exactly which books he put in each of the last two categories, but he does arrive at the traditional number of books in the Hebrew Bible.

Versions

One of the great contributions made by the Dead Sea Scrolls to our knowledge about biblical books is that they have documented the existence of divergent *Hebrew* texts of certain scriptural works. That is, there was not a single Hebrew text of each book of the Hebrew Bible/Old Testament; in some cases, such as the book of Jeremiah, there were Hebrew copies that diverged widely from each other. There was a shorter, probably more original version and one that was longer by about one-eighth and that had some material, such as the oracles against the nations, in a different place (in the shorter version they follow 25:19; in the longer one they are chaps. 46–51). This shorter version of Jeremiah had been known from the Greek translation of the book; now it can be seen that the Greek was not a free reworking of the one Hebrew original but was a faithful rendition of a Hebrew base text that diverged considerably from the one found in the traditional Hebrew Bible (called the Masoretic Text).

Not everyone in the second temple period read the biblical books in the same form. In the diaspora the Greek versions (revisions of the old Greek version were made as time passed) were read and studied, while in the land the Hebrew copies were used. We do know, however, that Greek copies were also available in the Judean wilderness, even at Qumran. The Samaritan community used one of the Hebrew versions of the Pentateuch and developed it further to meet their own needs. We have no evidence that anyone was concerned that the different copies failed to agree word-for-word, although from some of the Qumran commentaries it is apparent that the expositors were aware of variant readings. Rather than bemoaning these, they at times exploited them in their explanations.

Interpretation

Perhaps a way to close is by briefly reminding the reader that a widespread phenomenon in the second temple period was the interpretation and reinterpretation of older sacred texts. Many of the texts surveyed in the second section contain not only references to events and passages of the past, but creative reuses of them as writers applied the ancient scriptures to the concerns of their day. We have large-scale reworkings of older texts in 1–2 Chronicles, and a later book such as *Jubilees* does something formally similar for the books of Genesis and Exodus. Some of the prayers and speeches in our literature summarize events of the past. One thinks, for example, of Ezra's prayer in Nehemiah 9:6-37 or of Ben Sira's praise of the ancestors in chapters 44–50. In other cases specific parts of the scriptures may have served as the basis for further reflection. The Enoch literature shows repeatedly the authors' fascination with the story in Genesis 6:1-4. The Qumran commentaries supply instances of explicating entire texts to bring out their contemporary meaning. Other compositions from our pe-

riod center around a biblical character, interpreting, developing, and aug-
menting what was said about him or her. Examples include Aramaic Levi,
the Enoch texts, the *Testaments of the Twelve Patriarchs,* the Moses literature, and more. In still other types, the language of biblical poetry and
other passages is reformulated into new compositions, as in the Hodayot
or Thanksgiving Hymns from Qumran.

In all of these types and others as well, the scriptures served as the
starting point and inspiration for an enormous exegetical literature. It is
fair to say that the varied kinds of Judaism in the second temple period
were united around the sacred literature of the past and the ongoing attempt to apply and adapt it to contemporary concerns.

Bibliography

NOTE ON TRANSLATIONS

Translations of the following texts can be found in J. Charlesworth, *The Old Testament Pseudepigrapha*, 2 vols. (Garden City, NY: Doubleday, 1983-85):

Letter of Aristeas (vol. 2, pp. 7-34; trans. R. J. H. Shutt)
1 Enoch (vol. 1, pp. 13-89; trans. E. Isaac)
Testaments of the Twelve Patriarchs (vol. 1, pp. 782-828; trans. H. C. Kee)
Sibylline Oracles (vol. 1, pp. 327-472; trans. J. Collins)
Testament of Moses (vol. 1, pp. 927-34; trans. J. Priest)
Psalms of Solomon (vol. 2, pp. 651-70; trans. R. B. Wright)

Translations of the following texts are found in the New Revised Standard Version with Apocrypha:

1 Esdras
1, 2, and 3 Maccabees
Tobit
Judith
Susanna
the Greek Esther
the Wisdom of Ben Sira
Baruch
the Wisdom of Solomon
the Prayer of Manasseh

the Prayer of Azariah and the Song of the Three Young Men (or the Three
   Jews)
the Letter of Jeremiah
Bel and the Dragon

Quotations from the *Book of Jubilees* are taken from J. VanderKam, *The Book of
Jubilees,* 2 vols., Corpus Scriptorum Christianorum Orientalium 510-11,
Scriptores Aethiopici 87-88 (Louvain: Peeters, 1989).

Quotations of the Elephantine Papyri are taken from A. E. Cowley, *Aramaic
Papyri from the Fifth Century B.C.* (Oxford: Clarendon, 1923; repr.: Osnabrück:
Otto Zeller, 1967).

GENERAL WORKS

Freedman, D. N. *Anchor Bible Dictionary.* 6 volumes. Garden City, NY:
   Doubleday, 1992.
Grabbe, L. *Judaism from Cyrus to Hadrian,* volume 1: *The Persian and Greek
   Periods;* volume 2: *The Roman Period.* Minneapolis: Fortress Press, 1992.
Mulder, M. J., ed. *Miqra: Reading, Translation and Interpretation of the Hebrew
   Bible in Ancient Judaism and Early Christianity.* Assen/Maastricht: van
   Gorcum; Philadelphia: Fortress Press, 1988.
Safrai, S., and M. Stern, eds. *The Jewish People in the First Century: Historical
   Geography, Political History, Social, Cultural and Religious Life and Institu-
   tions.* 2 volumes. Assen: van Gorcum; Philadelphia: Fortress Press, 1974,
   1976.
Schürer, E. *The History of the Jewish People in the Age of Jesus Christ (175 B.C.–
   A.D. 135).* 3 volumes. Revised and edited by G. Vermes and F. Millar. Edin-
   burgh: T. & T. Clark, 1973-87.
Stone, M., ed. *Jewish Writings of the Second Temple Period: Apocrypha, Pseud-
   epigrapha, Qumran Sectarian Writings, Philo, Josephus.* Assen: van
   Gorcum; Philadelphia: Fortress Press, 1984.

WORKS ON JEWISH WRITINGS
OF THE SECOND TEMPLE PERIOD

Collins, John J. *Daniel*. Hermeneia. Minneapolis: Fortress, 1993.

————. *The Sibylline Oracles of Egyptian Judaism*. Society of Biblical Literature Dissertation Series 13. Missoula, MT: Scholars Press, 1974.

Cowley, A. E. *Aramaic Papyri from the Fifth Century B.C.* Oxford: Clarendon, 1923, reprinted· Osnabrück: Otto Zeller, 1967.

Endres, J. *Biblical Interpretation in the Book of Jubilees*. Catholic Biblical Quarterly Monograph Series 18. Washington, DC: Catholic Biblical Association of America, 1987.

Goldstein, Jonathan A. *I Maccabees*. Anchor Bible 41. Garden City, NY: Doubleday, 1976.

————. *II Maccabees*. Anchor Bible 41A. Garden City, NY: Doubleday, 1983.

Hadas, M. *Aristeas to Philocrates*. Dropsie College Edition, Jewish Apocryphal Literature. New York and London: Harper, 1951.

————. *The Third and Fourth Books of Maccabees*. Dropsie College Edition, Jewish Apocryphal Literature. New York and London: Harper, 1953.

Hollander, H. W., and M. de Jonge. *The Testaments of the Twelve Patriarchs: A Commentary*. Studia in Veteris Testamenti Pseudepigrapha 8. Leiden: Brill, 1985.

Kugler, Robert A. *From Patriarch to Priest: The Levi-Priestly Tradition from Aramaic Levi to Testament of Levi*. Society of Biblical Literature, Early Judaism and Its Literature 9. Atlanta, Scholars Press, 1996.

Milik, J. T. *The Books of Enoch: Aramaic Fragments of Qumrân Cave 4*. Oxford: Clarendon Press, 1976.

Moore, Carey A. *Daniel, Esther and Jeremiah: The Additions*. Anchor Bible 44. Garden City, NY: Doubleday, 1977.

————. *Judith*. Anchor Bible 40, Garden City, NY: Doubleday, 1985.

————. *Tobit*. Anchor Bible 40A. Garden City, NY: Doubleday, 1996.

Myers, Jacob M. *I and II Esdras: Introduction, Translation and Commentary*. Anchor Bible 42. Garden City, NY: Doubleday, 1974.

Porten, B. *The Elephantine Papyri in English: Three Millennia of Cross-Cultural Continuity and Change*. Documenta et Monumenta Orientis Antiqui 22. Leiden/New York/Cologne: Brill, 1996. [This volume has not only the Jewish Aramaic texts but all of the texts in several languages from Elephantine.]

Skehan, P., and A. Di Lella. *The Wisdom of Ben Sira*. Anchor Bible 39. Garden City, NY: Doubleday, 1987.

Stone, M. E., and J. C. Greenfield. "Aramaic Levi Document." In *Qumran Cave 4 XVII Parabiblical Texts, Part 3*, pp. 1-72. Discoveries in the Judaean Desert 22. Oxford: Clarendon, 1996.

Tiller, Patrick A. *A Commentary on the Animal Apocalypse of* I Enoch. Society of Biblical Literature, Early Judaism and Its Literature 4. Atlanta: Scholars Press, 1993.

VanderKam, J. *The Book of Jubilees.* 2 volumes. Corpus Scriptorum Christianorum Orientalium 510-11, Scriptores Aethiopici 87-88. Louvain: Peeters, 1989.

Winston, David. *The Wisdom of Solomon.* Anchor Bible 43. Garden City, NY: Doubleday, 1979.

WORKS ON QUMRAN AND THE DEAD SEA SCROLLS

Cook, E. M. *Solving the Mysteries of the Dead Sea Scrolls: New Light on the Bible.* Grand Rapids: Zondervan, 1994.

Cross, F. M. *The Ancient Library of Qumran.* 3rd edition. Minneapolis: Fortress Press, 1995.

de Vaux, R. *Archaeology and the Dead Sea Scrolls.* Revised edition. Oxford: Oxford University Press, 1973.

Fitzmyer, J. *Responses to 101 Questions on the Dead Sea Scrolls.* New York/ Mahwah, NJ: Paulist Press, 1992.

García Martínez, F. *The Dead Sea Scrolls Translated.* 2nd edition. Leiden/New York/Cologne: Brill; Grand Rapids: Eerdmans, 1996.

Schiffman, L. *Reclaiming the Dead Sea Scrolls: The History of Judaism, the Background of Christianity, the Lost Library of Qumran.* Philadelphia and Jerusalem: The Jewish Publication Society, 1994.

Stegemann, H. *The Library of Qumran: On the Essenes, Qumran, John the Baptist, and Jesus.* Grand Rapids: Eerdmans; Leiden/New York/Cologne: Brill, 1998.

VanderKam, J. *The Dead Sea Scrolls Today.* Grand Rapids: Eerdmans, 1994.

Vermes, G. *The Complete Dead Sea Scrolls in English.* New York/London: The Penguin Group, 1997.

Vermes, G., and M. D. Goodman, eds., *The Essenes According to the Classical Sources.* Sheffield: Sheffield Academic Press, 1989.

Wise, M., M. Abegg, and E. Cook. *The Dead Sea Scrolls: A New Translation.* San Francisco: HarperSanFrancisco, 1996.

WORKS ON MASADA

Masada: Final Reports. Jerusalem: Israel Exploration Society, 1989-99. [All of the texts and archeological evidence from Masada are published in this six-volume work.]

Yadin, Y. *Masada: Herod's Fortress and the Zealots' Last Stand.* New York: Random House, 1966.

Index